A GUIDE TO GOVERNING SCHOOLS

Peter Harding has substantial experience in the field of adult education and is currently tutor in education management at Bolton Institute of Higher Education. He is also Course Director for the Governors' Training Course provided by Bolton LEA.

A GUIDE TO GOVERNING SCHOOLS

PETER HARDING

Harper & Row, Publishers
London

Cambridge
Mexico City
New York
Philadelphia

San Francisco
São Paulo
Singapore
Sydney

Copyright © 1987 Peter Harding
All rights reserved

First published 1987

Harper & Row Ltd
28 Tavistock Street
London WC2E 7PN

No part of this book may be reproduced in any manner whatsoever without written permission except in the case of brief quotations embodied in critial articles or reviews.

British Library Cataloguing in Publication Data
Harding, Peter
  A guide to governing schools.
  1. School management and organization —— Great Britain
  2. School boards —— Great Britain
  I. Title
  379.1'531'0941   LB2901

ISBN 0-06-318379-X

Typeset by MFK Typesetting Ltd, Hitchin
Printed and bound by Butler & Tanner Ltd, Frome and London

To Helen

CONTENTS

Preface   xiii
Acknowledgements   xvii
About this book   xix

Part 1
INTRODUCTION

1 Being a school governor   3
    Origins of governing bodies; Why bother with governors?; Once a governor; A 'watching brief'; Learning the ropes; Finding out about the school; Reporting back and confidentiality; Publicity; In a nutshell; Self-test; Points to ponder; Governor's checklist; Further reading

Part 2
UNDERSTANDING THE EDUCATION SYSTEM

2 Central government of education   19
    Origins; The state system of education; A 'partnership'; Secretary of State for Education and Science; Department of Education and Science; HM Inspectors of Schools; How education policy is made; The education lobby; In

a nutshell; Self-test; Points to ponder; Governor's checklist; Further reading

3   Local government of education   35
    Origins; Duties and powers of LEAs; The 'partnership'; Education committees; Chief Education Officer; Education departments; Access to information; In a nutshell; Self-test; Points to ponder; Governor's checklist; Further reading

4   The schools   49
    Origins; Contemporary landmarks; Compulsory education; Classification of schools; Headteachers and schools; Parents and schools; Aims and objectives; Primary schools; Middle schools; Secondary schools; Sixth forms and tertiary colleges; Nursery schools; Special education; In a nutshell; Self-test; Points to ponder; Governor's checklist; Further reading

5   The governors   69
    Individuality of schools; Composition of governing bodies; Changes since the Education Act, 1980; Parent governors; LEA governors; Toe the party line?; Teacher governors; Headteacher as governor; Eligibility for chairman; Co-opted or community governors; Disqualification; In a nutshell; Self-test; Points to ponder; Governor's checklist; Further reading

Part 3
GOVERNING IN CONTEXT

6   Powers and functions   85
    Power-sharing; School governors as part of the 'education constitution'; Collective powers of

governors; Hitting the headlines; Uncertainty;
Instrument and Articles of Government; Powers
and functions of governing bodies; In a nutshell;
Self-test; Points to ponder; Governor's checklist;
Further reading

7   Finance   96
    The national dimension; The local dimension;
    Where the money comes from; Expenditure
    controls; Local government estimates; Finance
    committee; Timescale; Where the money goes;
    Capitation; Per capita allowance; School
    estimates; Headteachers and finance; Governors
    as a pressure group; In a nutshell; Self-test; Points
    to ponder; Governor's checklist; Further reading

8   School premises   112
    Accommodation subcommittee; Location;
    Grounds and environment; Buildings; Specialist
    accommodation; General facilities; Furniture,
    fixtures and fittings; Equipment; Heating, lighting
    and ventilation; Safety; Security; Vandalism;
    Open access; Falling rolls; In a nutshell; Self-test;
    Points to ponder; Governor's checklist; Further
    reading

9   Conduct and discipline   134
    Whose responsiblity?; Legal guidelines; Towards
    a concensus; Authority of the headteacher;
    Conduct of pupils; Causes of indiscipline; Types
    of misconduct; Governors' disciplinary
    committee; School rules; Factors influencing the
    application of disciplinary measures; Forms of
    punishment; Staff discipline; In a nutshell; Self-
    test; Points to ponder; Governor's checklist;
    Further reading

10 The curriculum   152
    Who decides the curriculum?; Change; The Great
    Debate; The primary curriculum; The secondary
    curriculum; Finding out about the curriculum;
    Teaching methods; Assessment and examinations;
    Reviewing the curriculum; In a nutshell; Self-test;
    Points to ponder; Governor's checklist; Further
    reading

11 Staffing schools   168
    Appointment of headteacher; Appointment of
    assistant teachers; What can governors do?; The
    role of the LEA; Distribution of staff;
    Qualifications; Application forms; In a nutshell;
    Self-test; Points to ponder; Governor's checklist;
    Further reading

Part 4
GOVERNING IN ACTION

12 Interviewing   189
    About interviews; Interview arrangements;
    Undercurrents at interviews; Guidelines for
    effective interviewing; Interview checklists;
    Making an effective contribution; Interview
    structure; Asking questions; Reaching a decision;
    In a nutshell; Self-test; Points to ponder;
    Governor's checklist; Further reading

13 Understanding meetings   202
    The nature of meetings; Frequency of topics;
    Setting the agenda; Extra meetings;
    Subcommittees; Possible proceedings; Minutes;
    Glossary of meeting terminology; In a nutshell;
    Self-test; Points to ponder; Governor's checklist;
    Further reading

14	Participating at meetings	218

Functions of meetings; Headteacher's report; A governor's role at meetings; At the meeting; Asking questions; Influencing events; Arguing a case; Making decisions; Making notes; Preparing and writing a report; Between meetings; In a nutshell; Self-test; Points to ponder; Governor's checklist; Further reading

15	Managing governors' meetings	232

Chairman of the board of governors; The appointment of chairman; Role of the chairman; Preparing the agenda; At the meeting; Taking a vote; Running the meeting; Closing a meeting; Following the meeting; Criteria for effective meetings; The clerk to the governing body; Advantages of LEA clerks; The clerk's role; In a nutshell; Self-test; Points to ponder; Governor's checklist; Further reading

16	Future trends	245

Government of education; The implications of more central control; Influence of agencies; And the DES?; Difficulties at local level; School finance; Schools as 'cost centres'; Schools and the community; Curriculum; Teachers; INSET; Training for governors

Postscript: The 1986 Education Act

17	Resources for information	256

Using a library; Official documents; Books; Organizations and associations; Journals and papers; Indexes/abstracts/bibliographies/reference books; Training packages; Addresses

Glossary of educational terms	270
Abbreviations and acronyms	277

Appendix: Governor's reference list 283
Index 287

PREFACE

In writing this book my aim is to provide a text for new and practising school governors – whether representing county or voluntary schools – one which you will find easy to use and which will help you to become more effective in your roles.

No one book can provide all the answers but I hope that I shall at least identify and address most of the questions which governors ask and point you in the right direction to find the answers. A significant amount of the content has been based on the kinds of concerns and demands expressed by new and experienced governors on training courses, and it is hoped that it will provide a practical flavour. Having said that, an attempt is made to envisage what the 'ideal' governing body could be, what it could be expected to achieve and how it might establish effective relationships with the local education authority, headteachers and parents. This, it is hoped, will lead towards the formulation of an overall 'mission' for governing bodies.

For governing bodies to become effective, however, much depends on a number of critical factors. These may be summed up, by and large, as the general attitudes displayed towards them, particularly by individual local education authorities, headteachers and teachers. Also, parent governors especially are likely to be confronted for some time to come by opposition from the more permanent LEA governors, who have by tradition represented local politics on governing bodies. The 'new', i.e. post-1980, governing bodies are going to have to fight hard to earn the respect of the professionals.

Whatever the barriers encountered by governors, it remains my fundamental belief that their effectiveness will be enhanced considerably by being well-informed. Indeed, the central message of this book is simply that the more informed governors are then the more likely it is that they will be able to operate effectively their part of the education partnership. To become well-informed requries a certain amount of preparation, initially in respect of the components of the role, i.e. powers and functions, followed by an appreciation of what governors can actually do, e.g. at meetings and interviews. There then remains the question of keeping up to date.

Keeping up to date with any subject is problematic, but writing this book has made me doubly aware of just how fast (or in some cases, how slow) things change and how difficult it is to be totally accurate and up to the minute. Virtually every day I read something in the press which could have implications for school governors. Although the new Education Act (1986) has been passed, even then, how long will it be before it all becomes law? Some parts may be implemented relatively quickly, while others may take years. In any event, how much more important information awaits governors just around the corner? So the best I can hope to achieve is accuracy at the time of writing.

Governing schools is a complex business and more than ever before is the lay person to have his say. Any 'say' will carry that much more weight when it is backed with knowledge and understanding of the issues involved and an awareness of the 'rules of the game' – hence the need to 'train' school governors, which, hopefully, will soon become a reality for governors everywhere.

In my experience of running training programmes for my local education authority (LEA), governors have a high level of commitment to their task and are eager to learn. But they need and want to learn quickly and this is more easily said than done. Being a school governor is an added role and, irrespective to how interested you are, there is a limit to the time you can devote to learning about education matters and generally building the sort of confidence you need to make an effective contribution as a governor for your school. Nevertheless, once you have the essential 'bones' you can soon begin to add the 'flesh' and bring the whole thing alive.

Knowing where to begin is a problem for any student and it is that much more acute when at first sight there does not seem to be very much information available. If you are fortunate, your local education authority will have produced its own governors' handbook to help you get started. However, there is a growing stock of material available for schools governors published by a wide variety of individuals and organizations.

My own experiences have made me very aware of the difficulties of finding one's way through the maze of education literature. As a trainer of governors and tutor in education, my work is totally with adults and, whether governors or teachers, they all experience some difficulty in getting to grips with the nature of the education system and how its related parts interact in order to produce the 'partnership', the basis on which the system operates. Consequently, to help reduce any difficulties, I have endeavoured to provide an easily digested guidebook which will serve to inform and support your work as a school governor.

Ultimately, however, much depends on your willingness to devote time and trouble to the role. Time in particular should be used to best effect. This means the systematic development of efficient study methods or fact-finding exercises, both of which can be improved greatly by following a few basic principles. As a school governor you will almost certainly have to develop new or neglected skills and throughout the book I have ventured to offer some guidance and advice.

Pitching any textbook to suit a wide audience is a difficult task in that every reader has slightly different needs. Therefore, the information provided is aimed at being straightforward and easy to understand for the new or inexperienced governor who may not possess much in the way of background information, but at the same time serves as consolidation and re-affirmation for the governor with more experience.

It is my avid hope that this book will open new doors and raise the level of awareness of governors in terms of the opportunities they have to work effectively on behalf of their individual schools. Information and knowledge is the key to effectiveness and, therefore, is worth pursuing in some depth.

There seems little doubt that the role of governors and their importance in policy-making at the level of the school seems set to grow at a time of increasing demands for public participation and accountability in respect of all educational institutions. Thus the potential contribution you can make for the future development of education in general and for pupils in particular is considerable.

Peter Harding

ACKNOWLEDGEMENTS

The author and publishers wish to acknowledge the following for permission to reproduce material: the Association of County Councils; the Chartered Institute of Public Finance and Accountancy; the Department of Education and Science (Architects and Building Branch); the Controller of HMSO; the National Confederation of Parent–Teachers' Associations.

Any book benefits from comments made by others during the preparation stages and my grateful thanks are extended to Brian Atkinson, Assistant Director of Education, Bolton LEA, for his painstaking reading of the draft. A word too for those members of the Bolton and District Governors Forum – Heather, Derek, John and Roger – who also took the time and trouble to read during the draft stages.

Finally, gratitude to my wife, Helen, who has worked patiently on the book since its inception and has provided not only the skills needed to produce the final copy, but a great deal of inspiration without which the task would have been even more formidable.

Peter Harding

ABOUT THIS BOOK

This book has been written with individual governors in mind – particularly those recently appointed who are seeking helpful guidelines to enable them to make an early and effective contribution. However, the book can be used equally well to support a governors' training course and should also prove useful to more experienced practitioners as a reference text. There is a lot to learn, and while much will be acquired by experience, a little advance knowledge is always worthwhile.

Although the book has been written in four parts, with careful consideration given to the content and structure of each, chapters are free-standing and may be read in any order, according to the particular needs and interests of the individual reader or in keeping with the order devised for specific training programmes. In any event, cross-referencing is provided throughout as appropriate.

Part 1 offers an introduction to being an effective school governor. Part 2 provides an overall administrative perspective, dealing in turn with the central and local government of education with schools, and should be viewed as the essential framework within which school governors operate. The powers and functions of governors are introduced in Part 3 and substantiated by considering in detail five central issues which are of direct concern to governing bodies as they attempt to exercise influence on the policy-making options available to them. Finally, Part 4 takes as its focus 'governors in action'. It concentrates on two important and specific governors' activities, namely those at interviews and at meetings, while addressing two fundamental considerations: (1) what governors actually do, and; (2) how they can do it more effectively.

Throughout the book a standard format has been employed, as follows. '*In a nutshell*' provides a brief summary of the main points covered in each chapter and will be particularly useful where a reader wishes to dip into the text at random. '*Self-test*' poses six straightforward factual questions all of which have been discussed and answered in the chapter and will be useful where a reader wants to check either his existing knowledge prior to reading the chapter or assess his recall and understanding of newly acquired information on completion of the reading. Rather than use the questions just as a memory test, it can be useful to consider the questions first and look out for the answers during reading.

'*Points to ponder*' are designed to take the reader a little further, to provide the basis for more detailed consideration of topics and issues, to promote discussion with other governors, to arouse interest, to enhance awareness and, above all, to act as a catalyst for further interest and involvement. In a sense there are no right or wrong answers to the types of questions raised. It is the quality of the arguments used for or against particular courses of action, or suggested improvements to be made to existing situations, which is significant. In the end, quality of argument rests not so much on emotion and beliefs but rather on the skilful application of substantial, accurate and relevant evidence. It is hoped that governors who use the book will cultivate and use their analytical and critical skills when helping to formulate policies and make decisions for the benefit of their schools. The topics included will be especially useful as the basis for discussion where the text is used as a course book in conjunction with a governors' training course.

'*Governor's checklist*' is a series of questions of a general nature presented at the end of each chapter. A governor can use the list to check against his own situation, for example, in terms of 'what *my* local education authority does or doesn't do', or 'what happens at *my* school', or 'what *my* headteacher does', and so on. Asking questions of one's own situation can also be a useful means of highlighting strengths and weaknesses or errors and omissions, and prompting you to seek additional help or information as required.

'*Governor's questions*', together with suggested answers, are interspersed throughout the book. It is felt that this approach, while adding a different dimension to the standard textbook format, will also provide additional information on topical items and refer to those questions which are asked regularly by newly appointed governors. The answers given are not meant to be prescriptive since some of the questions could be answered in different ways. The questions may also provide further discussion topics for group work.

In providing guidelines for using this book, it would be remiss not to refer especially to Chapter 17, Resources for Information, which has been compiled to enable the governor to make his own way through the maze of information sources which exists. Some of these sources are referred to in the main text but for ease and speed of location, readers are provided with all essential information in one reference chapter. This contains details of all the principal Acts of Parliament of direct relevance to school governors, as well as circulars and government reports. Information relating to agencies and organizations publishing relevant material is also included, plus a selection of textbooks which provide useful reading in addition to that included at the end of each chapter.

Throughout the book every effort has been made to ease the burden of the reader. Wherever possible, checklists have been used to summarize main points, and tables and figures have been incorporated to provide more graphic presentations of what can sometimes be complex data.

A glossary of educational terms and a list of abbreviations and acronyms have been included at the end of the book for quick reference.

The pronouns 'he', 'his' and 'him' are used in this text purely for the purpose of fluency in writing. This is no way intended to imply that the female equivalents could not be substituted equally throughout.

PART 1
INTRODUCTION

What does it take to be an effective school governor? Part 1 explains about being a governor, what governors actually do, and how they learn the ropes, gain expertise and find out about the school. Finally, it sets out the school governor's role in reporting back governors' meetings to interested parties and making a positive contribution to the life of the school.

1
BEING A SCHOOL GOVERNOR

ORIGINS OF GOVERNING BODIES

School governors are an essential element of the education system in England and Wales, being a part of a tradition of local control, influence and involvement in the affairs and activities of individual schools. The origins of governors go back at least to medieval times when the endowed schools and grammar schools were provided by religious institutions or guilds – the early craft associations.

WHY BOTHER WITH GOVERNORS?

To be a school governor is to fulfil a public duty or service and is part of the tradition of British public administration. Few would dispute the need for ordinary members of the public to participate in, for example, jury service. Schools also exist to provide a service to the community and are paid for out of public funds, so it is reasonable to expect that those having responsibility for the education and development of children, i.e. teachers, should be held accountable to representatives of that community. This helps ensure that schools provide an education which parents and society in general view as being relevant to the needs of children, as well as reflecting what is considered to be necessary if they are to make their way effectively in the outside world.

PUBLIC INVOLVEMENT

Governors provide an element of public involvement in the running of schools. On the one hand, they are able to bring into the school wide experience of the outside world, as well as providing an independent view on important issues. On the other hand, they provide a visible form of accountability for the headteacher, teachers and ancillary staff, and a mediating influence when disputes arise.

But what difference would it make if schools did not have governors? Without governors, accountability would pass directly to the local education authority (LEA). Thus all administrative and educational matters would be dealt with direct, between the school and the authority. In effect this would exclude public involvement and the opportunity for parents and members of the community to exercise influence in schools would be lost.

ONCE A GOVERNOR

Just what are governors supposed to do? There is no easy answer, despite the fact that there are literally thousands of governing bodies scattered across something like 32,000 schools in England and Wales involving approximately a quarter of a million governors (Scotland and Northern Ireland have their own education systems).

People from all walks of life, who reflect all manner of opinions and values and represent a broad range of political opinion, become school governors. Whatever their background or political beliefs, all governors have a keen interest in education and, in particular, the school(s) with which they are connected. However, even though there are so many governors around, one could be forgiven for thinking that the job is rather ill-defined and perhaps even obscure. General information and public awareness of what governors actually do is scarce, except on those occasions when they become involved in an issue which hits local or national headlines. However, even then detailed information is limited.

WHAT GOVERNORS DO

It sounds trite to suggest that being a governor is important, even though it is. However, what governors can decide and how much power they have depends on a particular situation, who is involved, the preceding chain of events, the nature and quality of the information governors have at their disposal and the particular context or set of circumstances. In other words, the decisions that governors are often called upon to make and the conclusions they are likely to reach are like those of life itself: full of problems and usually far from easy to resolve. The best that governors can do is bring a quality of judgement into school decision-making, which is based upon experience of life, an understanding of education in general and of the issues confronting the school in particular.

Most governors enjoy their role, but it is important to realize at the outset that, to be effective, it is likely to be time-consuming and often difficult. For example, coming to terms with the job will require an appreciation and understanding of the education system (see Part 2, p. 19). This in itself can be formidable since the system is complex and made more so by the use of a special language, jargon and a mass of abbreviations. To help overcome this problem, a glossary of terms and a list of abbreviations are provided at the end of the book.

Nonetheless, it is reasonable to expect that school governors will have a fairly detailed understanding of the education service and some knowledge of the current issues related to it. To be effective as a governor is to be able to talk confidently about education on equal terms with the experts, e.g. education officers, headteachers and teachers.

Not that governors are expected to have expert knowledge on education. However, if they are to play an important part in the decision-making policies of schools, then it follows that they need to know something about the system and the way in which it works, as well as the problems affecting their schools.

BEING INVOLVED

Being a school governor means two things for the individual concerned. First, it means working as a member of a governing body for the best interests of the school in all its aspects. Second, it means representing others, namely those who either appointed or elected the governor. Both of these mean getting involved in the life of the school by, for example: attending and contributing to governors' meetings; attending as many school functions and events as possible; getting to know and keeping well-informed about the school; establishing a point of view about school problems and policies; speaking at meetings; putting forward proposals; listening to others; applying knowledge and experience for the benefit of the school; knowing the rules of the game; identifying specific local issues and problems and relating them to the school's aims and objectives; keeping the curriculum under review; monitoring the conduct and discipline of the school; reporting back to constituents; and finding out about education.

A 'WATCHING BRIEF'

It is the governing body as a whole which has a 'watching brief' over several important aspects of the school. Consequently, it is required to: exercise influence over the general nature and direction of the school curriculum; help determine the overall aims and objectives of the school; act as an independent committee to help decide school policies; represent the interests of parents; represent the interests of the local community; interpret, on behalf of the school, the implications of LEA policies and plans; interpret, on behalf of the school, the implications of central government policies and initiatives; provide a means for parents, teachers and members of local political party associations to work together in the best interests of the school; ensure that children are educated according to the wishes of their parents; provide a forum for school decision-making; provide an effective means of accountability; support the headteacher and his staff in their best endeavours for and on behalf of the school; exert pressure and influence on the LEA by lobbying for adequate resources to help preserve and enhance the work of the school; and help schools reach their own decisions independent of the LEA.

This list goes a little beyond the precise legal requirements. For details of the powers and functions of governing bodies, see Part 3.

LEARNING THE ROPES

With constructive preparation, the individual governor's awareness and appreciation of educational issues can be increased immensely. This can be achieved efficiently with systematic planning, thereby saving time and effort – an important consideration given the busy lives most individuals lead. Confidence is the essential key to making a worthwhile contribution as a governor, the basis of which is being well-informed. After all, no one wants to look foolish by speaking out at a formal meeting without first knowing the facts. This applies equally to both educational issues and to procedures to be followed at governors' meetings. Therefore, confidence-building is a priority.

STEPS IN CONFIDENCE-BUILDING

The key to confidence is information. Being well-informed enhances morale and improves the prospect of making an effective contribution. The kind of information a governor will find indispensible includes that involving:

1. The school in all its aspects, including its aims and objectives, the nature and scope of the curriculum and the quality of work achieved
2. Conduct and discipline at the school, expected standards of behaviour, rules and possible sanctions

3. The context and setting of the school, the community it seeks to serve and local economic and demographic trends
4. Allocation of financial resources
5. Number of registered pupils attending the school
6. Number of teachers employed at the school
7. The pupil–teacher ratio
8. Detailed knowledge about the school buildings, facilities and equipment
9. The way the school is organized
10. The selection, interviewing and appointments procedures
11. Staff development needs for teachers
12. The provision made for special education
13. Ways of enhancing home–school links
14. The administrative system of education, how it works at national and local levels
15. General legal provisions relating to education
16. Specific legal provisions in respect of the appointment of school governors, their powers and responsibilities
17. Conduct and procedures of governors' meetings and how to make the most of them
18. Current educational issues affecting the life and work of the school.

The list does not include everything. Nonetheless, it represents a starting point. It can be added to or broken down into more specific subsections by the individual governor or by groups of governors. Information on each of the topics in the list is provided in this book and, if required, further details may be obtained by following up leads given in Chapter 17, 'Resources for Information'.

GAINING EXPERTISE

It pays to keep an eye on the national and local press in order to pick up information about education policy or issues affecting individual schools, and to keep a scrap book of cuttings on items which are of particular interest. This will become an extremely useful collection and have the advantage of being topical and up to date. A systematic approach is the best way of making sure that nothing is missed. Setting aside the same evening every week to read the papers and take the necessary clippings will help maintain the file in good order. Table 1.1 provides a list of examples of contemporary issues in education.

While all governors take a broad interest in educational matters, it is likely that on an individual basis they will want to develop special interests. It makes a great deal of sense to concentrate on a few issues or topics which have instant

Table 1.1: Contemporary issues in education

Falling school rolls
Marketing the school
Levels of spending on education
Standards in education
Curriculum content, with particular reference to 'relevance'
New secondary education examinations (the GCSE)
Computer literacy
Value for money (Audit Commission)
Future of middle schools
Future of sixth form and tertiary colleges
Pay and promotion prospects for teachers
Conditions of service for teachers
Teacher appraisal
Future of the Burnham Committee
Influence of governing bodies
Shortage of specialist teachers
Improving pastoral care
The nature/format of the school year
Accountability
Central government control versus local autonomy

appeal. One useful approach is for governors of a particular school to agree among themselves their topics of interest, so that they can then focus on a few areas with the intention of becoming 'experts'.

For example, two governors could agree to concentrate their fact-finding on separate issues. One might wish to look at finance, the appointment of teaching staff and conduct and discipline at the school. Another may be more interested in the curriculum, in improving home–school links and the state of the school buildings. A division of labour can be useful, especially when there are so many issues to deal with; in any case there is nothing to prevent a governor keeping up to date generally.

To direct effort into a few carefully defined topics pays dividends. It quickly helps to establish detailed information on specific educational matters, for example, on the role of the LEA, or current problems facing the school or national trends. Once having collected sufficient information, repertoires can be expanded to take in other topics.

FINDING OUT ABOUT THE SCHOOL

An immediate task is to find out as much as possible about the school. Collecting information is not, however, a once-and-for-all task, partly because things change, sometimes quite rapidly, and partly because in-depth information may be needed at a later stage on a particular aspect of the school.

Two lists are presented below: *first-order* information is of the type likely to be needed by the new governor to gain a quick impression of the school by becoming armed with basic facts (a pro-forma 'governor's reference list' for noting basic information is provided as Appendix I). *Second-order* information is the kind of in-depth detail needed to discuss issues and make decisions on behalf of the school.

FIRST-ORDER INFORMATION

The basic facts are: full name, address and telephone number of the school; name, address and telephone number of the headteacher; name, address and telephone number of the caretaker; name, address and telephone number of the LEA; names of people at the LEA with specific responsibilities; the school calendar, showing holidays and timetabled annual events; number of registered pupils on the school roll; number of vacancies, if any; school admissions policy; age range of pupils; the basis on which pupils are allocated to groups or classes; transfer arrangements to and from the school; composition of teaching staff, together with their names; whether any part-time teachers are employed at the school on a regular basis; delegation of specific duties to named teachers; dates, venues and times of governors' meetings; name of the clerk to the governing body and where he may be contacted; name, address and telephone number of the chairman of the governing body; names, addresses and telephone numbers of other governors; which governors represent which groups; general condition of the school buildings; transport arrangements to and from school; lunch-time arrangements and facilities for pupils; extra-curricular activities, clubs and societies provided for pupils; impressions of standard or quality of work attained – over a period of time and with the guidance of experts such as teachers; examination results; general reputation of the school from the point of view of parents and members of the local community; educational visits and school trips; school rules and regulations; arrangements made for pastoral care; arrangements for special education; and quality of home–school links.

SECOND-ORDER INFORMATION

This type of information includes: aims and objectives of the school, and how these are determined, reviewed and revised; class sizes, that is, the pupil–teacher ratio; shortages of materials or equipment; pupil conduct and behaviour at the school and the kinds of sanctions and procedures used to maintain discipline; the school curriculum, how it is kept under review and modified as appropriate; the quality of the relationship between the school and the parents and the ways in which it may be improved; liaison between the school and the local community, including industry and commerce; procedures used to evaluate the success of the school; the kinds of changes currently affecting the school and their likely implications for the future; ways in which the school is responding to change and innovation; the organizational structure of the school and delegation of responsibilities; specialist accommodation, for example, workshops, laboratories and so on; organization of the school day, allocation of teaching staff, accommodation, specialist facilities and timetabling; level of resource allocation by the LEA, particularly the per capita allowance; alternative ways of raising money; the overall 'atmosphere' of the school, for example, is it friendly and purposeful or threatening and dull?

QUICK SOURCES OF INFORMATION

Although Chapter 17 provides a range of useful sources of information, it can be useful to have quick access to fairly routine data. The following sources are usually available:

the school prospectus
the school staff handbook
Instrument and Articles of Government
local authority handbook
LEA policy statements in respect of, for example, equal opportunities
LEA support services, for example, education, social or welfare service, educational psychological services and so on
Department of Education and Science (DES) reports and other official documents on education, usually obtainable in public reference libraries
the headteacher
copies of previous headteacher's reports
copies of previous agendas and minutes (a friendly governor may oblige)
members of the teaching staff
the school secretary
the caretaker
the chairman of governors
other governors
the clerk to the governors
the parent–teachers' association (PTA)
parents
visiting the school

sitting in on classes (by arrangement)
attending staff meetings (by negotiation).

Some negotiation will clearly be necessary in respect of the last three items, and local practice varies in terms of what is acceptable.

VISITING THE SCHOOL

The most obvious way of collecting information is by visiting the school. The headteacher will invite governors, old and new, to visit from time to time, sometimes for a whole day. It is much more valuable to make such a visit when the school is in action. It may even be possible to sit in on a class in order to sample the atmosphere and get the feel of the place.

Careful preparation before the visit will help ensure that maximum benefit is obtained. This means devising a checklist of items (the contents of this book should help here) to make sure nothing important is missed. Questions should also be framed in advance and written down.

The list of items to be looked for and the questions which might be asked can be endless, and therefore it is necessary to apply some limitations in order to keep things in perspective as well as to make the task more manageable.

Step one

A sense of relevance may be maintained by considering what it might be useful for governors to know with direct reference to their powers and functions. This would restrict the initial fact-finding mission to the following: the organization and management of the school; finance and resources; school premises; conduct and discipline; curriculum; and staffing the school.

Step two

Each of the above topics can be broken down into several subheadings, and under each one a series of questions may be generated. For example, under 'organization and management of the school', the following subheadings could be used: aims and objectives of the school; standards; organization of pupils into groups/classes; timetabling and the school day; management of pastoral care; and delegation of duties. The same procedure may be used with each of the items listed under step one.

Step three

The number of subheadings in step two may be extended, but care must be taken not to overlap into the other topics in the original list. Once the subheadings have been decided, several questions may be raised under each one, as the following examples illustrate.

Aims and objectives of the school
1. Does the school have clearly stated aims and objectives?
2. Where are the aims and objectives published?
3. How are they kept under review?

Standards
1. What criteria are used to evaluate or assess pupil standards?
2. Are teachers' standards evaluated, for example, by an appraisal scheme?
3. How do the standards of the school compare with similar schools, both nationally and locally?

Organization of pupils
1. What arrangements are made for the transfer of pupils to or from the school?
2. What methods are used to allocate pupils into manageable groups, for example, classes, sets, forms?
3. Is level of attainment used to place pupils into groups?

Timetabling and the school day
1. What are the opening and closing times of the school?
2. Do you have access to school timetables?
3. How many hours per week are spent on, say, mathematics or English, by particular groups of pupils?

Management of pastoral care
1. Who is in charge of pastoral care?
2. What kind of services or support facilities are available?
3. How are external support services used, for example, education welfare?

Delegation of duties
1. Does the school have more than one deputy head?
2. What are the specific duties of the deputy heads?
3. Who is in charge of, for example, academic affairs, or external relations, or the library or PE?

The number of questions which may be asked under each subheading may be expanded. Further ideas may be obtained by looking under the relevant chapters in this book. The most important thing is to prepare in advance.

REPORTING BACK AND CONFIDENTIALITY

The role of governors also includes providing feedback about governors' meetings to other interested parties, such as political parties, parents or teachers.

Governors have an obligation to keep their 'constituents' informed, otherwise there would seem to be little point nominating or electing them in the first place. Reporting back can be a sensitive business. This issue is particularly important when preparing the agenda for the meeting of the governing body, and even more so when deciding the nature and contents of the minutes of the meeting. Being too open can compromise confidentiality; being too close can lead to suspicion and to accusations of secrecy.

It is difficult to decide what governors should reveal, but the following points help provide a basis:
1. Confidentiality must be maintained in relation to all papers marked 'confidential' and discussed at the meeting
2. Any discussion relating to an individual pupil and/or his or her parents must be kept confidential
3. Any discussion relating to named members of staff, particularly in respect of disciplinary matters, must be kept confidential
4. If there is any doubt about whether a topic is for the eyes and ears of governors only, then it should be kept confidential.

Governors tend to develop a sixth sense about what may or may not be a sensitive issue, and so the above points should be taken only as a general guide. To be an effective governor depends, to some extent, on how far others can rely on the discretion of individuals. Usually, the more successfully one establishes a reputation for keeping quiet when necessary, the more one is told.

Governor's question: I have been a school governor for quite a while now, but I still find it difficult to find out what other people expect of me – especially parents. In addition to this, there remains the problem of publicity, i.e. letting parents know just who the governors are. The headteacher and LEA have not been particularly helpful, hence this request for some advice. Can you help?
Answer: Whether a parent, teacher or LEA governor, the job involves representing the views of others, while taking care to retain one's individuality. Finding out what others expect is seldom easy or straightforward, and in any event, their views may conflict. Some ways and means of finding out the views of others, and making it known who the governors are, include: making sure that as many people as possible are aware of who the school governors are, for example, through letters to your local newspaper, or a PTA newsletter or political party leaflets; publicising when and where you can be contacted on school matters, e.g. by holding 'surgeries' at set times; attending meetings of the PTA; attending as many of the school's functions as possible; and collecting opinions of others informally, e.g. at the school gates.

PUBLICITY

Some schools have introduced a governors' noticeboard on which are displayed photographs of individual governors and items of general interest. The board is placed where it may be seen easily by parents and other visitors to the school.

In any event, securing publicity is a relatively easy task in an age of free local newspapers. It may be possible, for example, to persuade a local newspaper to publish information about the work of governing bodies, or for governors to write contributions themselves, either of which would serve to bring them to the attention of the public.

IN A NUTSHELL

Being an effective school governor is dependent largely on having detailed information about education in general and about the school in particular. The more informed governors are, the more likely it is that they will be able to make a positive contribution to the life and well-being of the school. It is a good idea, given the substantial nature of the task, to agree with fellow governors the areas on which to concentrate on finding out about. The job also involves promoting a point of view, taking account of the views of others, attending meetings, knowing when to keep quiet and what to report back to constituents. It is also important to help publicise the work of governors in order to increase public awareness of what they do and the kind of help they may be able to provide.

SELF-TEST

1. Why are there school governors?
2. Name three activities which governors undertake.
3. Suggest three quick sources of information which might be useful to a new governor.
4. Suggest six facts about the school which would be useful for a governor to know.
5. What does a governor need above all else if he is to be effective?
6. Suggest four factors a governor should take into account when reporting back to constituents.

POINTS TO PONDER

1. Identify possible obstacles when attempting to find out about the school.

2. With reference to the items listed under step one (p. 11), what subheadings might be applied? Formulate the kind of questions which might be applied in respect of each subheading you have listed.
3. Argue a case for governors to be able to attend, as observers, staff or departmental meetings at the school.
4. Discuss possible reasons which might be given to prevent this and suggest how they may be opposed.
5. How far should a governor go, and what approaches can be made, to find out the views of his constituents?
6. Discuss ways in which parent governors might increase their influence on governing bodies.
7. What are the possible advantages and disadvantages of governors concentrating on a limited number of topics?
8. What procedures should governors, schools and LEAs use to increase public awareness about governing bodies?

GOVERNOR'S CHECKLIST

1. Why be a school governor?
2. Are you expected to represent other interests at governors' meetings and how do you know what they want?
3. Does your school have any particular problems?
4. Does your LEA run courses for governors?
5. Does your LEA publish a handbook for governors?
6. Do you have a copy of the school prospectus?
7. Do you have your own copy of the *Articles and Instruments of Government*?
8. Does the headteacher encourage governors to visit the school regularly, including classroom observation and attendance at staff meetings as observers?
9. Does the school produce a staff handbook?
10. What can you achieve as a school governor?

FURTHER READING

Taylor Report (1977) *A New Partnership for Our Schools*, HMSO, London.
White Paper, Cmnd. 9469 (1985) *Better Schools*, HMSO, London. (See especially Chapt. 9.)

PART 2

UNDERSTANDING THE EDUCATION SYSTEM

Our goal was a school with enough independence to ensure its responsive and distinctive character, taking its place in an efficient local administration of an effective national service.

(Taylor Report, 1977, p. x)

The intention of Part 2 is to provide an overview of the education system in England and Wales. Although governors will find that they are confronted with a number of different problems relating to their schools, a general understanding of the total system will help to show how some of the problems arose in the first place. More significantly perhaps, awareness of who does what in the system, and when and where, may prove crucial in arriving at possible solutions.

Thus Part 2 is a general map of the educational terrain taken from the air. An aerial view makes the jungle of education look more manageable, gives it more shape and reduces its density when contrasted with the view of the man on the ground, who frequently cannot see the wood for the trees.

2
CENTRAL GOVERNMENT OF EDUCATION

ORIGINS

Education has not always been controlled by central government. Until the second half of the nineteenth century it was provided by a variety of religious denominations. Despite the fact that the Industrial Revolution had begun a century before, it was not until the Great Exhibition of 1851 that the demand for systematic provision began to gather momentum. This was due to the emergence of competition in the manufacture of goods by some European countries and the United States of America, and the resultant need for a better educated workforce.

Education in Britain lagged behind that of its main industrial competitors because of the persistent policy of *laissez-faire* (non-interference by government), an uncoordinated system of local government and a lack of any central authority. Heightened interest eventually led to the establishment in 1853 of the forerunner of the current Department of Education and Science (DES).

Central government control increased steadily towards the end of the nineteenth century and in the first three decades of the twentieth century, with successive reports and Acts of Parliament, culminating in the Education Act 1944, the principal basis for education legislation in England and Wales.

THE STATE SYSTEM OF EDUCATION

The state system of education in England and Wales is controlled by Parliament. In effect, the Secretary of State undertakes this responsibility and is answerable directly to Parliament for the general conduct of the education system. The Secretary of State works with and through the Department of Education and Science (DES), which is staffed by permanent civil servants and inspectors; it is the central government department with responsibility for determining and monitoring education policy across the system as a whole. Both the Secretary of State and the DES must work within a framework of legislation for education as set out in a number of education Acts and statutory instruments.

Education policy-making is not the exclusive preserve of the Secretary of State and the DES, since other central government departments also have an interest. However, they remain extremely influential and have a clear responsibility to provide a lead and initiate policy, while having a duty to listen to the views expressed by a wide variety of other national organizations, which are best described as the 'education lobby' (see Figure 2.2, p. 32).

CENTRAL GOVERNMENT CONTROLS

Although the Secretary of State and the DES undertake responsibility for the development of a national policy for education, they are constrained by the framework of government and by other central government departments. In addition, they must work closely with the local education authorities (LEAs), both singly and with their national associations.

The issue of education has, in the past, seldom received much attention by the Cabinet and the Prime Minister. However, a combination of factors, including control over public expenditure, long-term and high levels of unemployment and standards of education, has brought educational issues and concerns increasingly to the forefront in recent years and this is a trend which is likely to continue in the future.

The policies of the Secretary of State and the DES are influenced greatly by the Treasury, which has a central role in determining the amount of money to be spent on the education service nationally, as well as the level of grants to be awarded to LEAs. Consequently, the level of resources allocated to education reflects the priorities of the government of the day.

Other central government departments which are involved closely with local authorities, operating across the entire range of local services, are the Department of the Environment and the Department of Employment. In addition, two important national agencies – the Audit Commission and the Manpower Services Commission (MSC) – have considerable impact on the work of LEAs.

The Audit Commission is an independent body, operating in the same way a firm of private auditors would in industry and commerce. The commission conducts fact-finding exercises centred on obtaining 'value for money' in both schools and colleges of further and higher education, produces reports and makes recommendations incorporating suggestions aimed at cost savings.

The MSC has major responsibility for enhancing the provision of vocational education in schools and colleges as well as influencing decisions affecting the utilization of manpower. It is not an examining body nor does it provide courses of its own. Rather, it encourages the development of new and innovative approaches to training within schools, colleges, industry, local authorities and voluntary organizations. It has a very large staff scattered across the country, e.g. in Job Centres and skills centres and has significant financial resources at its disposal to facilitate its various activities. Examples of courses which operate under its aegis include the Youth Training Scheme (YTS) and the Training and Vocational Education Initiative (TVEI).

The system of central government control is shown in Figure 2.1.

A PARTNERSHIP

The education system in England and Wales is often referred to as a partnership because responsibilities for the provision of education are shared between central and local government. Central government has powers and responsibilities for the total provision of the education service, for determining national policies and for planning the direction of the system as a whole. On the other hand, local government is at the delivery end and has the statutory duty to make provision, i.e. to provide the schools and colleges within which education is to take place. The school governing body can also be regarded as a part of the partnership since it too has statutory obligations and duties.

The administration of education is made more complex for the Secretary of State and the DES by the fact that they can act only through intermediaries, i.e. the LEAs. Therefore, whatever directives they issue, they have to rely to a considerable extent on other organizations to implement them. This factor often frustrates a Secretary of State and the DES, since central government often lacks direct powers of control over what happens in a particular LEA.

POWER-SHARING IN EDUCATION

As a direct result of the partnership arrangement, there is a system of power-sharing between central and local government which means that neither has absolute control over education. This is what is meant by a decentralised system, i.e. one where responsibilities are delegated away from central to local

Figure 2.1: Central government control of education

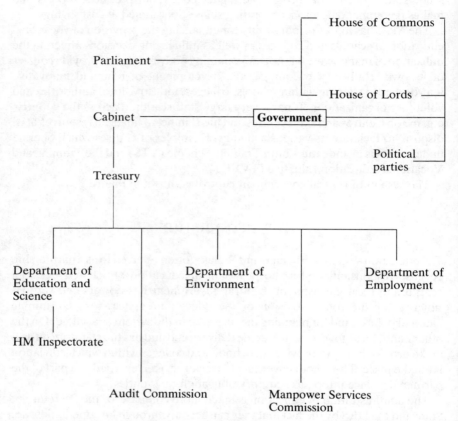

government. For example, the school curriculum is under the direction of LEAs and not the DES, although, of course, the latter may attempt to influence it.

Central government does, however, have direct control over a number of important areas in education, including: the amount of money to be spent on education; teachers' pay and salary structure; pre-service teacher training, including the type of training and the quota allowed; in-service teacher training; the nature and purpose of education support grants; the school-leaving age; levels of student grants; new school or college buildings; the secondary examination system; and inspection of schools and colleges. Chapter 3 gives further examples of central government involvement in education.

WHO DECIDES?

There is, however, no neat division of authority and responsibility between central and local government, and despite the fact that central government has the kind of powers listed above, there is still room for LEA autonomy in decision-making. For example, while central government grants may be awarded to LEAs, there is no guarantee that they will be spent in the ways in which the Secretary of State or the DES would prefer. Consequently, decentralization continues to exist. This is something of a tradition in the system of central and local government, but is increasingly under threat, as shown in Chapter 3.

On the LEA side, many authorities may be willing to improve their pupil–teacher ratios but often lack sufficient resources from central government to do so. Also, while it is the LEAs which employ the teachers, they do not determine the salary structure, even though they exert considerable influence and pressure to bring about improvements. For example, by acting collectively through the Council of Local Education Authorities (CLEA), the LEAs can themselves negotiate directly with the teacher unions. However, the teachers' salary bill cannot be met by the LEAs alone and so they have to rely on contributions from central government.

Similarly, the LEAs have a duty to provide school buildings, but they must have permission from the DES before they can go ahead and develop a new school or build an extension to an existing one. There is, therefore, some confusion in terms of who has the authority to decide what in education.

SECRETARY OF STATE FOR EDUCATION AND SCIENCE

The Secretary of State, known as the Minister of Education until 1964, is the political head of the DES and is appointed by the Prime Minister of the day. Table 2.1 lists the Secretaries of State since 1964. The post is a senior government job and has Cabinet status. There are also two or three other political appointments at the DES, known as Parliamentary Secretaries or Ministers of State, there usually being one for schools and one for higher education.

Since these jobs are subject to political changes there can be a high turnover of appointments, due, for example, to Cabinet re-shuffles by the Prime Minister or to changes brought about by general elections. The job has often been somewhat transient in nature in the past (see Table 2.1), making it difficult for Secretaries of State to bring policies to fruition while still in office.

Although the formal duties and powers look formidable, they often turn out

Table 2.1: Secretaries of State since 1964

Rt Hon. Quintin Hogg (later Lord Hailsham)	1 April 1964 to 16 October 1964
Rt Hon. Michael Stewart	19 October 1964 to 23 January 1965
Rt Hon. Anthony Crosland	24 January 1965 to 30 August 1967
Rt Hon. Patrick (later Lord) Gordon-Walker	31 August 1967 to 5 April 1968
Rt Hon. Edward Short (later Lord Glenamara)	8 April 1968 to 19 June 1970
Rt Hon. Margaret Thatcher	20 June 1970 to 4 March 1974
Rt Hon. Reginald Prentice	5 March 1974 to 10 June 1975
Rt Hon. Frederick W. Mulley	11 June 1975 to 10 September 1976
Rt Hon. Shirley Williams	11 September 1976 to 5 May 1979
Rt Hon. Mark Carlisle	6 May 1979 to 14 September 1981
Rt Hon. Sir Keith Joseph	15 September 1981 to 21 May 1986
Rt Hon. Kenneth Baker	22 May 1986

to be surprisingly weak, particularly in terms of 'directing' LEAs. The following extract taken from a leader article in the *Guardian* suggested:

> The Secretary of State for Education and Science is by no means as powerful a minister as he appears to be. He proposes, but the education authorities dispose. He can set up enquiries, he can wheedle money out of the Treasury, he can make as many elegant speeches as he has time to compose. But he has relatively little control over the way that the authorities, much less the teachers themselves, actually behave.
>
> (*Guardian*, July 1986)

As with many senior government appointments, it is not necessary to be an expert to be appointed. Once in office, however, most Secretaries of State do become very knowledgeable about educational issues. Nonetheless, their essential role is to give political leadership to the national system of education, reflecting the ideas, values and beliefs of the party in government while taking into account the professional advice provided by DES senior civil servants and the inspectorate.

POWERS, DUTIES AND RESPONSIBILITIES

The formal, i.e. legal powers of the Secretary of State are provided in the Education Act (1944):

> It shall be lawful for Her Majesty to appoint a Secretary of State, whose duty it shall be to promote the education of the people of England and Wales and the progressive

development of institutions devoted to that purpose, and to secure the effective execution by local authorities under his control and direction, of the national policy for providing a varied and comprehensive educational service in every area.

(Section 1)

Secretaries of State also have the power of final decision when it comes to resolving disputes which may arise. For example, under Section 68 the Secretary of State is empowered to decide where an LEA is acting unreasonably and to hear complaints by the public in respect of LEA decisions. Under Section 99 the Secretary of State has powers to direct LEAs and governors in the event of a complaint or where they may be in breach of their statutory duties. Although having significant and powerful functions, Secretaries of State must work within the legislative framework of education, which is based largely on the Education Act (1944) with its subsequent amendments. Failure to do so is to act *ultra vires*, that is, beyond the terms of reference as determined by legislation.

The main powers, duties and responsibilities of the Secretary of State for Education and Science may be summarized as follows:
1. To be accountable, to Parliament, for the direction and control of the education system in England and Wales (including the universities)
2. To represent education in the Cabinet
3. To compete with other high-spending central government departments for resources from the Treasury
4. To establish, as required, major new policies and directions for the education system
5. To work within the parameters of the legislative framework of education when exercising the powers and functions of office, e.g. when directing a local education authority to fulfil its statutory obligations
6. To sanction or veto local authority proposals, e.g. to extend a school
7. To influence the development of the education system consistent with the overall policies and beliefs of the government
8. To represent the DES and its policies in the national media
9. To actively seek the views of other nationally important organizations, and to listen to the education lobby before introducing significant policy changes in education.

CHANGING ROLE

The nature and role of the Secretary of State, like everything else, is subject to change. For example, among the most important proposals in the Education Bill (1986, clause 46) is that to abolish the need (under section 5 of the Education Act 1944) for the Secretary of State to make an annual report to

Parliament, 'giving an account of the exercise and performance of the powers and duties conferred upon him'.

The same Bill also proposes (clause 45) that the need (under section 4 of the Education Act 1944) for the Secretary of State to appoint two central advisory councils, one for England and one for Wales, should be discontinued. This particular requirement had led to the publication of major reports on education, e.g. the Newsom Report, *Half our Future* (1963) and the Plowden Report, *Children and their Primary Schools* (1967).

This does not necessarily mean that there will no longer be any further committees of enquiry but it does remove an important provision of the 1944 Act.

DEPARTMENT OF EDUCATION AND SCIENCE

The DES, previously known as the Ministry of Education, has a staff of around 2,400 and is a relatively small government department when compared with, for example, the Department of Health and Social Security. This is due largely to the fact that the DES has no executive functions and has no schools or colleges of its own to run. Much of the department's work is concerned with planning and monitoring the national system of education and with the publication and distribution of reports, circulars and memoranda to the LEAs in an attempt to control and co-ordinate their activities.

The DES has no regional structure as such and operates mainly from Elizabeth House in London. It does, however, have 'territorial officers' who, while based in London, are responsible for a regional group of LEAs. There is also a large DES office in Darlington which deals with statistics and teachers' pensions, as well as regional offices in some major towns and cities, although these are mainly for HMI purposes.

The department is divided into a number of branches; for schools, for further and higher education and for science. In addition, there are a number of specialist branches which deal with, for example, finance, school or college buildings and legal matters. The main functions and responsibilities of the DES, and the Welsh Office, include: the supply and training of teachers; curriculum initiatives, e.g., Certificate of Pre-Vocational Education (CPVE), sometimes referred to as the 17+, and the General Certificate in Secondary Education (GCSE); the teachers' superannuation scheme; commissioning major reports, e.g. Bullock Report, *A Language for Life* (1975) and the Cockroft Report, *Mathematics Counts* (1982); the funding of research initiatives by universities and the National Foundation for Educational Research (NFER) on, for example, school curricula or educational standards; establishment of the Assessment and Performance Unit (APU); the setting of the level of the rate support grant (RSG) to LEAs; the approval of building works for all LEA schools and colleges; and the control of capital expenditure for individual LEAs.

D E S MANDARINS

Senior civil servants, often known as 'mandarins' (from the Chinese word for counsellor), exercise considerable influence over the education system. At the head of the DES is a permanent secretary whose responsibility it is to keep the political head, i.e. the Secretary of State, well-informed and to offer advice as necessary. Nonetheless, it is the political leader of the DES who is responsible to Parliament for the development of national policies for education.

However, where policy for education is constrained by overall government policies, e.g. controls of public expenditure, then collective responsibility applies. This means that the Cabinet as a whole is responsible rather than any individual member. This is a longstanding tradition of British government originating out of the need to present a united front.

It remains the duty of the Secretary of State to initiate policies designed to bring about improvements to the national system of state education, and for the DES through its Inspectorate to ensure that they are implemented within each of the LEAs.

H M INSPECTORS OF SCHOOLS (HMIs)

A significant problem confronting the DES is that it not only has it to deal with 104 LEAs, but also with literally thousands of individual educational institutions. The development of a direct connection between the DES and individual schools has been provided since 1839 by Her Majesty's Inspectors, often referred to as 'the eyes and ears of the DES'. Originally, they were set up to monitor the spending of government money awarded to voluntary schools by the Privy Council.

The work of present-day HMIs has its statutory basis written into section 77 of the Education Act 1944, which requires the Secretary of State 'to cause inspections to be made of every educational establishment at such intervals as appear to him to be appropriate . . .' (section 7(2)). This includes primary and secondary schools (both maintained and independent), and all colleges of further education and public sector higher education, e.g. teacher training colleges, institutes of higher education and polytechnics (universities are not subject to inspection by HMI).

HMIs are usually appointed from senior staff of schools and colleges who have sufficient experience and appropriate qualifications. All HMIs are expected to have a broad knowledge of the education system as well as having in-depth expertise in a specialist area. The work they actually do may be summarized as: conducting frequent general inspections of schools and or colleges; assessing standards and advising the Secretary of State on performance of the system nationally; investigating current provision, either generally or in specific subject areas, either on a regional or a national basis; writing reports on inspections and on specific areas of investigation; identifying and making known 'good' practice; liaising with all levels of staff within all kinds of educational organizations; helping determine national policies for the further development of the national education service; organizing conferences for teachers with the intention of introducing new teaching skills or improving existing ones; attending conferences organized by other educational bodies; speaking at conferences on educational issues; and preparing papers for publication.

HMI REPORTS

Since January 1983, HMI reports have been made publicly available, and are obtainable direct from the DES. Before then, the reports had limited circulation only, e.g. to the LEA, governing body and headteacher concerned. Reports may be based on a general inspection of the school or college or on a specialist section or department as part of a national investigation. A fairly recent development has been the introduction of plans to conduct different kinds of inspections which include the total provision of education within a single LEA. Formal inspections of schools and colleges are intended to continue at about the rate of 260 each year. An annual survey of education expenditure is also produced.

Whatever the nature of the report, the very process helps to build up a picture of the general condition of the education system. Consequently, HMI reports of different kinds often form the basis of new policy initiatives within the DES. An example would be identifying deficiencies in certain specialist areas, e.g. computer technology, and linking them with the necessity to provide sufficient and good quality teacher training. Once such problems are identified, possible remedies can be formulated which will eventually be put to the Secretary of State for approval.

HOW EDUCATION POLICY IS MADE

The DES is involved in different levels of policy-making. Some are fairly routine, such as new rules or procedures, new school buildings or new levels of student grants. By comparison, other decisions may be fairly major, e.g. the raising of the school leaving age or the setting of new levels of teachers' pay. Whatever the case, the Secretary of State and the DES make their intentions known through the publication of a large number of official documents which are distributed to individual LEAs.

In effect, many of the documents will simply be a revision of existing policies, e.g. changes in schemes for teacher training or procedures to be adopted in respect of school meals or school closures.

EDUCATION REPORTS

The publication of reports on important aspects of the provision of education is something of an established tradition in education policy-making, an early example being the *Report of the Parliamentary Committee* (1816). The decision by the Secretary of State to set up a 'report of enquiry' is influenced by a number of pressures and interests prevalent at the time.

The chairman and members of each enquiry committee is appointed by the Secretary of State and the subsequent report is usually associated with the surname of the chairman of the committee. A report usually takes several years to complete, and can involve considerable research. On its completion, the Secretary of State will receive the recommendations of the report, which will almost certainly be adopted as government policy.

However, this does not mean that all, or any, of the report's recommendations will actually be implemented: this will depend on the priorities of the government of the day. For example, the Taylor Report (1977), *A New Partnership for our Schools*, contained a number of recommendations, of which only a few have been implemented ten years later. A change of government may sometimes be the reason why a particular report fails to be implemented.

OTHER DOCUMENTS

Several other official documents are used to advise LEAs on DES policy. However, there is little or no obvious relationship between the importance of the issue and the status of the policy document used. For example, both an 'administrative memorandum' and a 'circular' have a similar advisory status rather than the force of law. They are used typically to provide LEAs with information and advice which they are 'requested to accept and apply'.

Circulars are not directives but nonetheless have been used to secure major policy changes in the past, largely as a matter of political expediency. For example, the Labour Secretary of State, Anthony Crosland, used Circular 10/65 to 'request' LEAs to submit their plans to him for the introduction of comprehensive schools. On the subsequent return of a Conservative government, in 1970, the then Secretary of State, Margaret Thatcher, also used a Circular (10/70) to cancel Circular 10/65.

Where a circular deals with policies which require the use of additional resources, LEAs operate under the assumption that if they go ahead and implement, the additional resources needed will be made available.

GREEN PAPERS AND WHITE PAPERS

Green Papers are consultative documents issued when the Secretary of State and the DES consider the issue significant enough to sound out the opinion and reaction of a wide variety of different organizations and agencies in response to proposals for a significant change of policy. Following careful consideration of any advice received, the DES will then publish further proposals, usually in the form of a White Paper, the status of which is to set out the government's policy intentions for the future.

Not all White Paper proposals become part of education law, since they may be overtaken by events, e.g. a change of government or of financial circumstances which affect the government's priorities. In any case, legislation may not have been the intention behind a White Paper, but if appropriate and considered to be of sufficient priority, then the policies may be incorporated within an Education Bill, which is the first step in the formal development of a new Education Act.

For example, many of the ideas presented in the White Paper *Better Schools* (1985) were incorporated in the Education Bill (1986), which was subjected to numerous debates, changes and amendments as it progressed through three readings in both the House of Commons and the House of Lords.

ACTS OF PARLIAMENT AND STATUTORY INSTRUMENTS

Once an Education Bill has been read and passed, it becomes an Act of Parliament after it has received royal assent, which is something of a formality. The Act becomes part of government legislation to be implemented by all those affected by it.

Implementation of the requirements of any new Act vary from being immediate, as in the case of the Local Government (Access to Information) Act (1986), to being delayed for a number of years, as was the case with the Education Act (1980), aspects of which were only enforceable from September 1985. Indeed, it is the Statutory Instruments (SI), sometimes referred to as Regulations, which provide detailed procedures for implementing Acts of Parliament.

THE EDUCATION LOBBY

It is the duty of the Secretary of State for Education to take full account of the views of other organizations and individuals when determining education policy. This clearly means those organizations and agencies within and outside Parliament which make up what might be described as the education lobby. The organizations and agencies involved vary in terms of their particular interest and the extent of their formal involvement and influence, but their one common concern is in some aspect of the national provision of the education service. Figure 2.2 illustrates the nature and scope of the education lobby.

IN A NUTSHELL

Control of the education system is diffuse, with the power being shared between central and local government. The most influential figure is that of the Secretary of State who, along with his department, the DES, determines national policy for education through the preparation, publication and circulation of a variety of official documents to LEAs.

Additional influences also help shape the provision of education, including other government departments and agencies, the LEAs, special interest groups, voluntary organizations and religious denominations, which together constitute the education lobby and help to influence the final outcome of education policy-making.

SELF-TEST

1. Who appoints the Secretary of State for Education and Science?
2. Apart from the DES, which other government departments have an important influence on the education system?

3. Which Education Act provides the main basis for education law in England and Wales?
4. What is the difference between an 'administrative memorandum' and 'circular'?
5. What is the difference between a Green Paper and a White Paper?
6. Name three important functions of HM Inspectorate.

POINTS TO PONDER

1. In what ways is the education system likely to be affected by a change of government?
2. What are the main benefits for education to be derived from the publication of 'reports of enquiry'? Analyse a selection of existing reports (see Chapter

Figure 2.2: The education lobby

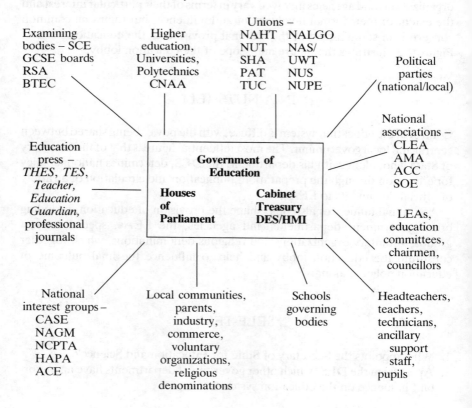

17) and consider new areas which might merit future investigation.
3. Identify the factors which tend to prevent the Secretary of State from exercising direct control of education.
4. What do you consider to be the main arguments for and against increased centralization of control over education? How might governors be affected by such a trend?
5. One of the principal roles of the HM Inspectorate is to conduct inspections of individual schools. What sort of things do you think they will be looking for? What effect is an inspection likely to have on the school or the authority? How might governors be involved?
6. Select three pressure groups included in Figure 2.2. How do they operate and exert pressure on education policy-making?

GOVERNOR'S CHECKLIST

1. Has education become a central political issue in British politics?
2. Which other central government departments in addition to the DES have a say in educational provision in your area?
3. Are you aware of the present government's financial policies for education?
4. What have been the direct consequences for: (a) your LEA, and (b) your school of government policies on education?
5. Do you consider that education policy, insofar as it affects your school, was determined by the Secretary of State for Education and Science or another central government minister?
6. Has your school been the subject of an HMI inspection within, say, the last five years?
7. What were the results of the inspection?
8. Are you familiar with recent DES publications on education in general?
9. Are you familiar with recent DES policy in respect of school governing bodies?
10. Is there any evidence to show that the education lobby is active in your area?

FURTHER READING

DES and Welsh Office (1983) *The Work of HM Inspectorate in England and Wales*, HMSO, London (free).
DES and Welsh Office (1985) *The Educational System of England and Wales*, HMSO, London (free).

Maclure, S. (ed.) (1986) *Educational Documents in England and Wales: 1816 to the Present Day*, Methuen, London.

Pile, Sir W. (1979) *The Department of Education and Science*, Allen & Unwin, Hemel Hempstead.

Prestel (around 250 pages of information about education prepared by the DES and Welsh Office, commencing on page 50043).

3
LOCAL GOVERNMENT OF EDUCATION

ORIGINS

The development of local government has a history of its own and significant changes in the system have often affected the way in which local control over education has been exercised. For example, the Local Government Act (1888) created the multi-purpose county boroughs and county councils, which together with borough, urban and rural district councils were eventually to undertake the main responsibility for providing local education in accordance with the provisions of the Education Act (1902). More recently, the Local Government Act (1972) reduced the number of local authorities, and as a result the number of LEAs fell from 150 to 104. The local Government (Access to Information) Act (1986) provides yet another example of the impact legislation *outside* the education system itself can have on the work of LEAs.

LOCAL GOVERNMENT ACT (1972)

The main effect of this Act in respect of education was that it reduced the number of LEAs and reorganized the system of local government generally. The boroughs, county boroughs and county councils, as well as rural and urban districts, were abolished. They have been replaced by: 39 non-metropolitan counties; 8 enlarged Welsh counties; 36 metropolitan boroughs or districts; 20 London boroughs; and one inner London education authority (ILEA).

DUTIES AND POWERS OF LEAs

The main statutory obligations of LEAs to provide education is set out in the

Education Act (1944), along with a number of amendments and new requirements made under successive education Acts. The Education Act (1944) states:

> It shall be the duty of every local education authority to secure that there shall be available for their area sufficient schools:
> (a) for providing primary education, that is to say, full-time education suitable to the requirements of junior pupils; and
> (b) for providing secondary education, that is to say, full-time education suitable to the requirements of senior pupils, other than such full-time education as may be provided for senior pupils in pursuance of a scheme made under the provisions of this Act relating to further education; and the schools available for an area shall not be deemed to be sufficient unless they are sufficient in number, character, and equipment to afford for all pupils opportunities for education offering such variety of instruction and training as may be desirable in view of their different ages, abilities and aptitudes, and of the different periods for which they may be expected to remain at school, including practical instruction and training appropriate to their respective needs.
>
> (Section 8(1))

Given that the work of LEAs is concerned with all aspects of the local provision of education, additional references to their duties and responsibilities will be made, as required, in appropriate chapters. Chapter 7 provides detailed information on the LEAs and finance.

DUTIES

Among the statutory duties of LEAs are:
1. To make available sufficient schools in their areas, in terms of numbers, character and equipment, as set out in the Education Act (1944), section 8
2. To provide a broad curriculum appropriate to the ages of the pupils
3. To comply with safety requirements and standards as set out in the Education (School Premises) Regulations (1981), Statutory Instrument No. 909
4. To provide education free of charge, Education Act (1944), section 61
5. To make special provision for the education of pupils with special needs, Education Act (1944), section 8.2 and, under the Education Act (1981), to make provision, where appropriate, for children with special needs to be educated in 'ordinary' schools
6. Make provision of adequate facilities for further education, Education Act (1944), section 41
7. To comply with legislation in respect of parental rights as set out in the Education Acts of 1944 and 1980
8. To make provision for the establishment of school governing bodies and the making of articles and instrument of government as set out in the Education Act (1980)

9. To provide details for parents of the LEA's admissions policies as required by the Education (School Information) Regulations (1981), Statutory Instrument No. 630
10. To secure for primary, secondary and further education adequate facilities for recreation and social and physical training, as set out in the Education Act (1944), section 53, and as further specified in Statutory Instrument No. 909
11. To appoint an education committee and a Chief Education Officer
12. To provide, as necessary, transport for pupils or students to and from school as set out in the Education Act (1944), section 55
13. To make provision for medical and dental checkups as required under the National Health Service Reorganization Act (1973), section 3
14. To make mandatory awards, e.g. student grants.

POWERS

Among the powers of LEAs are the following:
1. Closure of schools under the terms and conditions set out in the Education Act (1980)
2. Establishment of new schools
3. Compulsory purchase of land in pursuit of statutory obligations
4. Control of the appointment, allocation and dismissal of teachers
5. Control of secular instruction, i.e. control of the school curriculum, usually delegated to governing bodies
6. Provision, or not, of school meals and/or milk
7. Inspection of individual schools within the LEA's area
8. Discretionary awards
9. Provision, at the discretion of the LEA, of nursery schools
10. Assist parents to buy school uniforms and other clothing necessary for their children's educational activities.

While most of the duties and powers of LEAs have their roots in legislation, this does not itself guarantee the level or standard of service they acutally provide.

OTHER LEGISLATION AFFECTING LEAs

It is the responsibility of the Chief Education Officer (CEO) and other senior officials in the authority's education department to ensure that LEAs comply with all relevant legislation which affects their work. This includes all aspects of education law as well as other important legal requirements. For example,

LEAs must conform with the following legislation: Health and Safety at Work Act (1974); Sex Discrimination Act (1975); Race Relations Act (1976); Employment and Training Act (1983); and Local Government Access to Information Act (1986).

THE 'PARTNERSHIP'

As indicated in Chapter 2, there is no neat division of powers between central and local government, even though LEAs are required to work within a national framework, as determined under a variety of Education Acts and other official documents. What happens is that individual LEAs interpret regulations and advice according to their own individual circumstances or idiosyncrasies. This is, perhaps, somewhat inevitable given the extent of the differences between the LEAs. For example, many of the counties are largely rural, covering huge areas of land but are sparsely populated. Metropolitan boroughs, by comparison, cover relatively small territories but are densely populated.

Although there *is* a national system for education, LEAs have developed a tradition of autonomy in terms of its implementation, some barely complying with legislation, while others anticipate future developments and establish their own policies. For example, an LEA may determine to go ahead with its own system of teacher appraisal or decide to set up its own training courses for school governors. Others will wait until they are required to do so under new education legislation.

LEA APPLICATION OF NATIONAL POLICIES

LEAs have a tradition of considerable freedom over the ways in which they organize the provision of education within their areas. Although the broad requirement in terms of when compulsory education starts and when it finishes has to be observed by the LEAs, how it is organized in between is largely a matter for LEA discretion. Similarly, although the level of teachers' pay is determined by the Burnham Committee at national level, LEAs can influence its impact by virtue of their powers to determine school size, which is the basis for the provision of promoted posts. For example, the LEA can decide how many teachers to employ, and at what level or grade, in each of its schools. This has the effect of determining the class size, and the pupil–teacher ratio (PTR), which varies significantly from one LEA to another. Chapter 11 provides details on the staffing of a school.

Among the other decisions LEAs are able to make are: the level of per capita spending (see Table 3.1); the kind of schemes they wish to operate in terms of pupil transfers to and from schools; their own post-16+ arrangements, e.g. whether to make provision in sixth forms or tertiary colleges; how much to spend on schoolbooks; and how much to spend on school maintenance.

Table 3.1: Differences between LEA per capita spending (based on figures released by the Chartered Institute of Public Finance and Accountancy)

Education statistics (1984–85)	Primary cost per pupil		Secondary cost per pupil
	£		£
Highest: ILEA	1,298	ILEA	2,022
Lowest: W. Sussex	664	Kirklees	982

CHANGES IN THE 'PARTNERSHIP'

A report published by the Association of County Councils (1986), *The Way Ahead – Education*, suggests that changes are taking place in the relationship between the 'partners' and as a result, the tradition of non-interference by central government is giving way to continuous intervention. The report states:

> From approximately the mid-1970s, central government has increasingly sought to direct the activities of LEAs in matters of detail. Even while the subgroup (writing the report) has been meeting, central government has taken several further initiatives, including proposals to:
> – introduce a system of teacher appraisal, probably with some direct funding;
> – provide a significant specific grant to fund the in-service training of teachers, thus altering the balance of power between LEAs and school governing bodies;
> – extend the Youth Training Scheme (YTS) and provide a major new specific grant scheme for in-service training of teachers working on the Technological and Vocational Education Initiative (TVEI);
> – study the number and deployment of teachers employed by LEAs;
> – develop the nature of economic and science teaching in schools;
> – develop a policy for homework;
> – establish, through the Manpower Services Commission (MSC), a group to harmonize vocational examination qualifications;
> – give central government a higher profile in the nature and balance of the curriculum.
>
> (*The Way Ahead*, pp. 6–7)

Nonetheless, despite such trends, LEAs continue to have considerable discretion in a wide variety of decision-making areas affecting education.

HOW LEAs WORK

Local authorities are multi-purpose organizations having to provide a wide range of local services, from refuse collection to parks and cemeteries. Each local authority has to determine its own policies and establish its priorities in respect of individual services, and then provide the resources, equipment and personnel to carry out the activities needed. All local government policies are determined by a series of specialist committees, comprising locally elected councillors, who work in partnership with senior local government officials. Each committee has specific statutory powers to enable it to direct the particular service concerned.

EDUCATION COMMITTEES

It is the full county or borough council which is the education authority, but in effect it establishes an education committee to undertake the work and keep it informed. In fact, each local authority is legally required to appoint an education committee to undertake responsibility for the provision of education within its area.

The frequency of meetings (for both the full education committee and its subcommittees) will usually work on the basis of the council's cycle of committees, which is published well in advance. This is an essential requirement since councillors often work across several committees. Additional meetings to deal with any urgent business will be convened as required. The council's diary of meetings will be systematic, with meetings held according to the cycle; there will be a number of subcommittees, as shown in Figure 3.1, due to the sheer volume of business to be conducted.

The size of education committees varies enormously, which means that the larger ones can become more like the House of Commons 'bear garden' than an executive decision-making body. Hence the need for subcommittees.

The composition of the education committee requires Secretary of State approval, but will in any event be based on the balance of party political power within the authority. This will be reflected in the ruling party being able to appoint the chairman and vice-chairman.

CHAIRMAN OF THE EDUCATION COMMITTEE

The chairman of the education committee will be a councillor representing the ruling party within the local authority. The quality of the chairman can indeed

Figure 3.1: A committee structure

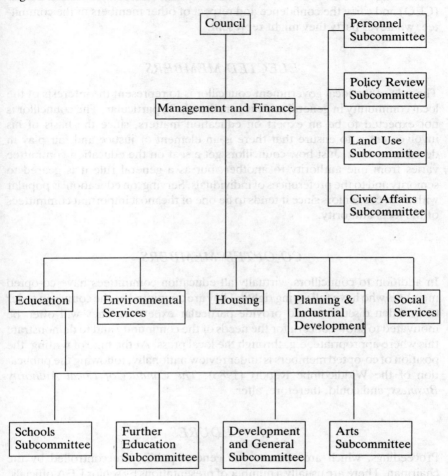

make or break the effectiveness of the education committee, the chair being the focal point of everyone's attention.

The chairman, who represents a political appointment, has a responsibility not only to his own party, but to the full committee as well as to members of the community at large, particularly parents and pupils. The work of chairman is not confined to running the meeting but carries with it the expectation that he will be working 'behind the scenes', on behalf of the committee. Consequently, an effective chairman has to be able to give sufficient time to what is a very demanding job. He needs to work successfully with the Chief Education Officer (CEO) and carry the confidence and respect of other members of the committee, whatever party they might represent.

ELECTED MEMBERS

The role of the local government councillor is to represent the interests of the local community in general and his constituents in particular. The councillor is not expected to be an expert on education matters, since the basis of his involvement is to ensure that there is an element of justice and fair play in decision-making. Just how councillors get a seat on the education committee varies from one authority to another, but as a general rule it is geared to seniority and to the preferences of individuals. Serving 'on education' is popular with most councillors since it tends to be one of the most important committees of the local authority.

CO-OPTED MEMBERS

In addition to councillors, virtually all education committees have co-opted members who have full voting rights. They are appointed by the council in order to broaden discussion and provide particular expertise. They will often be motivated to show concern for the needs of the community and to demonstrate this where appropriate, e.g. through the local press. At the time of writing, the position of co-opted members is under review nationally, following the publication of the Widdicombe Report (1986), *The Conduct of Local Authority Business*, and could, therefore, alter.

PROCEDURES

Proceedings, which are open to the general public, are controlled by the chairman. There are usually a number of presentations by senior LEA officials, whose job is to provide information and advice, to respond to questions and sometimes be cross-examined. The CEO will usually speak on major policies and interpret these for committee members. It is, however, the members of the education committee who have the final say by putting matters to the vote, which usually but not always, reflects party lines. Councillors who are members of a political party will often meet before the meeting to decide their point of view and the way they intend to vote on issues considered to be of local significance.

SUBCOMMITTEES

The main education committee tends to be a large and often unwieldy body, often making it difficult to debate issues in depth in the time available. Subcommittees, for example, schools or further education subcommittees, go some way to resolving this problem in that they are smaller and able to concentrate on fewer but more specific issues before making recommendations to the full education committee.

For subcommittees to be effective, it is necessary that they determine their priorities in terms of agenda items and concentrate on these instead of attempting to cover too much. The degree of involvement of subcommittees makes them the key decision-making units of the LEAs. It is the extent of the agenda, i.e. the amount of work to be done, which underwrites the necessity to establish subcommittees to deal with a specific range of topics and perhaps certain routine topics, providing that the full council permits such delegation. In any event, full control over every single issue which arises is an impossibilty, even for subcommittees. This means that the LEA officers exercise growing control through delegation derived on the basis of sheer expediency.

Members of the public are now able to attend meetings of subcommittees as well as education committee meetings as observers (see 'Access to information', p. 44).

CHIEF EDUCATION OFFICER (CEO)

The appointment of a Chief Education Officer, alternatively known in some LEAs as the director of education, is particularly important since, unlike the elected members who come and go, the position is permanent. The CEO occupies a unique position for setting LEA policy, since he can exert considerable influence over the education committee and subcommittee network, simply by the quality of advice he provides.

In some respects the capacity of local councillors to be effective decision-makers is dependent largely on the number of realistic choices they are given by the CEO and his senior officers. The CEO usually works closely with the chairman of the education committee, both formally and informally, by providing advice and information to be used as the basis for policy-decisions. He is assisted by a number of senior colleagues usually designated as deputy or assistant.

CONFLICTING DEMANDS

To fulfil the duties of the CEO can be extremely difficult, due to the often conflicting tensions generated between the demands of central and local government. For example, the LEA may receive directives from the DES to save money on a particular element of the education service, while the education committee may want to spend more on the same service. Whatever balancing act the CEO is expected to achieve, his main concern will be to ensure as far as possible that the LEA complies with, and applies as necessary, all relevant legislation, while at the same time taking full acount of the local situation.

EDUCATION DEPARTMENTS

The local education office is the nerve centre of educational administration. It is here that overall direction of the LEA schools and colleges is exercised through the varied activities of education officers, advisers and specialists of different kinds. The education office co-ordinates the work of schools and endeavours to ensure that they receive the support of specialist services as required and that they reflect, or implement if necessary, the policies determined by the education committee.

Many LEAs publish a directory of the services available to support education within their areas and, increasingly, education enquiry offices are being set up to act as an initial point of contact to help parents and other interest parties.

A selection of the range of services typically provided by LEAs is shown in Table 3.2, although it needs to be recognized that these are subject to change as a result of government policies or simply because certain services are regarded as being either necessary or desirable according to local circumstances.

ACCESS TO INFORMATION

Since the Local Government (Access to Information) Act (1986) came into force on 1 April 1986, the public has a right to attend as observers meetings of the full education committee and those of subcommittees as well. Information about when meetings are to take place can be obtained from the Education Enquiry Office at City or County Hall. Under the new Act, local authorities are required to: permit members of the public to attend its committee and subcommittee meetings; allow public access to information relevant to the meeting, e.g. to the agenda, minutes, reports and papers; give an explanation when asking observers to leave the meeting and later provide them with a summary; make available records such as agendas, minutes and reports for six years; make available internal, i.e. departmental documents, for four years; provide the

Table 3.2: LEA support services

- Adult education centres
- Advisory services for specific subjects, e.g. English, maths, *or* aspects of education service, e.g. primary, secondary and further
- Careers office
- Community services
- Education social work service
- Education welfare services
- Industrial language training unit
- Information technology (IT) centre
- INSET
- Language support services
- Nursery schools
- Outdoor pursuits
- Peripatetic teaching services
- Reading centres
- School meals and kitchen services
- School psychological services
- Special schools
- Special units
- Sports centres
- Swimming pools
- Teachers' centre
- Teaching staff/personnel section
- Training workshops
- Youth clubs
- Youth and community services and centres

names and addresses of all local councillors, plus details of the committees on which they serve; make known the identity of individual officers, giving details of the particular issues with which they deal and of their duties generally; and give specific reasons, admissible under the Act, for refusing access to information requested.

While the new arrangements appear to open up public access to information it is difficult to predict what will happen in reality since many of the proposals are not yet part of the traditional way of doing things. One of the advantages of the subcommittee system (for the members) was precisely that they worked in private, enabling them to get down to business. Admittance of the public as observers, while doing away with accusations of 'secrecy', will undoubtedly influence the nature of the conduct of meetings as well as perhaps affect the contents of an agenda. Nonetheless, the Act does open up the prospect of the electorate obtaining much more local information on education. Local authorities must comply with the Act or else run the risk of being taken to court. The Act does not apply to meetings of governing bodies, although some LEAs nevertheless encourage members of the public, particularly parents, to attend as observers – a trend which is likely to continue.

IN A NUTSHELL

The statutory responsibility for the provision of education, i.e. the schools and the colleges, belongs to the LEAs. They are delegated a number of duties and functions, principally under the Education Act (1944), along with successive education legislation.

There remains, however, something of a tradition of local autonomy among the LEAs, due perhaps to the differences between them in terms of their political complexions, geographical locations and their unique problems and priorities. All of these lead to local interpretations being placed on central govenment directives and advice. But this tradition is coming under increasing threat as central government gradually extends its influence and controls, for example, over the level of resource allocation.

Education committees comprise elected and co-opted members, who combine with education officials to determine local education policy through a committee structure, under the direction of the chairman and the CEO, who in turn exercise considerable influence over LEA policy-making. Recent legislation has brought about increased public access to LEA activities, including attendance as observers at its subcommittees and access to a variety of official documents.

SELF-TEST

1. Identify three statutory duties of LEAs.

2. Other than the schools, what other services may an LEA provide?
3. Suggest three reasons why the traditional freedom of LEAs might be under threat by the DES;
4. List the various factors which tend to make LEAs different from each other;
5. List the advantages of education subcommittees;
6. Under which Act are members of the public allowed to attend as observers education committees and subcommittees?

POINTS TO PONDER

1. 'Party politics should be kept out of education.' Discuss this view in the light of local political influence in your LEA.
2. Who has more power or influence, the chairman of the education committee or the Chief Education Officer?
3. Who *should* have most power and influence?
4. Decide what you think would be the essential characteristics of a 'good' LEA.
5. Consider whether you think LEAs are entitled to their freedom when making decisions about local education.
6. What possible advantages and disadvantages do you see developing as a result of the Local Government (Access to Information) Act (1986)? Think about the likely effects of the Act on both the general public and the LEA.

GOVERNOR'S CHECKLIST

1. Does your LEA have a clear policy for the education of the under-fives?
2. How does your LEA compare with others in terms of PTRs?
3. Does your LEA help to keep its governors well-informed about contemporary educational problems and policies, e.g. by sending them copies of reports, circulars and so on?
4. What provision does your LEA make for the 16 to 19-year-old age group?
5. What does your LEA do to ensure that the curriculum in its schools is kept under review and revised as necessary?
6. Would you describe your LEA as a 'good' employer?
7. How effective are the local political parties in developing effective education policy?
8. Is information and advice readily available from your LEA office?

9. Has your LEA publicised the availability of documentary information and public access to its education subcommittees?
10. Are you satisfied with the level and scope of educational support services provided by your LEA? Are there any serious omissions in this respect?
11. Has your LEA used its autonomy in education policy-making to good or poor effect?
12. Are governors' meetings open to members of the public as observers?

FURTHER READING

Audit Commission, Local Government Training Board and Institute of Local Government Studies (1985) *Good Management in Local Government: Successful Practice and Action*, Audit Commission.
Bush, T. and Kogan, M. (1982) *Directors of Education*, Allen & Unwin, London.
Cooke, G. and Gosden, P. (1986) *Education Committees*, Longman, London.
Widdicombe Report (1986) *The Conduct of Local Authority Business*, Department of the Environment, HMSO, London.

4
THE SCHOOLS

ORIGINS

The very first schools offering elementary education 'for the masses' were provided largely free of charge by a variety of religious denominations or philanthropists. Education, or what counted for it, was a means of exerting social control over the working classes. Schools concentrated on 'religious instruction'. In those provided and controlled by the Church of England, for example, children had to learn to recite the catechism by rote. It ws not until religious instruction finally gave way to secular instruction, mainly through the teaching of the 3Rs, that the foundations of the schools of today were actually laid.

The change was brought about by increasing involvement by both central and local government. The system of 'all through elementary schools', whether provided by local authorities or by religious denominations, had become obsolete towards the end of the First World War. The need for two separate schools for primary and secondary education, with transfer between the two at about the age of eleven, gained in popularity. The Labour Government (1924) had adopted the slogan 'Secondary Education for All' and the Hadow Report (1926) formulated proposals for these to be either grammar or secondary modern. Secondary modern schools were different in that they catered for shorter and more limited courses than the grammar school, but the emphasis in both was placed firmly on meeting the needs of children entering adolescence. The school leaving age was to remain at fourteen years as established by the Education Act (1918). This pattern of schooling was to have long-lasting effects on the education system up to the present day.

CONTEMPORARY LANDMARKS

Just as the end of the First World War culminated with the passing of a major piece of legislation, the Education Act (1918), so too did the Second World War. The Education Act (1944) still remains the cornerstone of legislation for education in England and Wales, although several amendments have been made with the passing of a number of education Acts since.

Post-war policy for secondary education has been determined largely by Circular 10/65, introduced by the Labour Government. This 'requested' that LEAs draw up plans for the introduction of comprehensive schools which in effect heralded the end of grammar schools and selection at eleven. Although a circular does not carry the force of law, most LEAs did in fact comply with the request, and continued to do so even after the return of a Conservative Government and the issue of Circular 10/70 which countermanded 10/65.

COMPULSORY EDUCATION

The Education Act (1944) states:

> It shall be the duty of the parent of every child of compulsory school age to cause him to receive efficient full-time education suitable to his age, ability and aptitude, and to any special educational needs he may have either by regular attendance at school or otherwise.
>
> (Section 36)

It is often wrongly assumed that sending children to school between the ages of five and sixteen is compulsory; in fact it is education which is compulsory, not school attendance. In practice, however, for the majority of parents, fulfilment of their obligations means to send their child to school.

The law sets out the precise details relating to compulsory education. It begins at the start of the term following a child's fifth birthday and ends when the child reaches sixteen years. Pupils may leave school at the end of the spring term it their sixteenth birthday falls on any day from 1 September to 31 January. For those having their sixteenth birthday on any day from 1 February to 31 August, pupils may leave any time after the Friday before the last Monday in May, which is usually the Spring Bank Holiday.

CLASSIFICATION OF SCHOOLS

As a result of the haphazard provision of education by both religious denominations and LEAs, ownership and control is still today subject to the origins of individual schools. Details of the various powers of religious denominations and LEAs are contained in each school's Articles and Instruments of Government. Schools are classified broadly on the basis of whether or not they are wholly or partially under LEA control, as shown in Figure 4.1.

Figure 4.1: Control and costs* of schools

Maintained schools:

County schools	Primary	Wholly provided and maintained by LEA
	Secondary	

Voluntary schools (primary and secondary)

Controlled	All costs borne by LEA (majority of governors nominated by LEA – one fifth appointed by voluntary body)
Special agreement	Shared costs and control between voluntary body and LEA (majority of governors appointed by voluntary body)
Aided	Shared costs and control between voluntary body, Secretary of State and LEA (majority of governors appointed by voluntary body)

* 'Costs' refer to buildings and repairs only and does not include such items as staffing and capitation. Where a school is in receipt of an 85 per cent grant from the DES (section 15(3), Education Act 1944), it refers to building/repair costs only.

HEADTEACHERS AND SCHOOLS

The headteacher is the manager of the school and has responsibility for its day-to-day affairs. A main characteristic of the job of headteacher is that it is concerned largely with the management of people, i.e. teachers, parents and pupils. The headteacher as a manager does not have extensive controls at his disposal since in many ways he is a 'site manager' working within a framework set out by the LEA. Unlike his industrial or commercial counterpart, the headteacher cannot hire and fire staff. Nor does he usually have an extensive budget to control, since there is no earned income to be managed. A further difficulty is that it is difficult to evaluate the quality of the final outcome, i.e. the end product.

HEADTEACHERS AS MANAGERS

Despite the limitations mentioned above, the headteacher plays a critical role in the life of the school. Indeed, the quality and effectiveness of the school depend largely on the style of leadership provided by the headteacher. Headteachers can, to some extent, choose their style of leadership, i.e. the way in which they decide to manage the school.

The main leadership styles are: *bureaucratic*, e.g. where the headteacher uses his authority simply because of his position rather than because it makes sense; *autocratic*, e.g. where the headteacher's opinion is law and where there is total failure to seek or listen to different points of view; *consultative*, e.g. where the headteacher sounds out the opinions of the staff before coming to a final decision; and *democratic*, e.g. where the headteacher invites wide participation in decision-making from the teaching staff.

Any headteacher will be influenced, of course, by the situation prevailing at a particular time when deciding the type of leadership style to be adopted. For example, it may be highly appropriate for him to adopt an autocratic style of leadership where a disciplinary problem arises, or where a member of staff is being particularly obstructive or stubborn. However, it may make sound sense to favour a participative approach where, for example, staff contributions may be varied and helpful. There is no best style: individuals will opt for a style with which they feel comfortable and adapt it as different circumstances demand.

PARENTS AND SCHOOLS

The education of children is a joint enterprise between parents and schools and so there is a need for schools to promote their activities in order to establish and sustain parental interest. It is generally accepted that such interest is at its highest in the case of primary school children, although in the case of older pupils it increases when they approach school-leaving age.

Where parental support is already strong it is likely to be sustained and even increased; where it is weak it is likely to remain so unless the reasons can be identified and overcome. There are a number of possible barriers to establishing effective links between home and school: among them are the following examples of views expressed by parents: schools only contact parents when they want something, e.g. sponsored swimming or car boot sales; insufficient time is allowed at parents' meetings for parents to discuss their child's progress with the teacher; it is often difficult to make a private appointment to see the headteacher or a particular teacher; the PTA is often seen by outsiders as a small unrepresentative clique; communication with parents of ethnic minority children is frequently difficult and sometimes non-existent; awareness of the existence of a school governing body is very low, and as a result the identities of parent representatives is frequently unknown.

ENCOURAGING PARENTAL INTEREST

There are no easy remedies. Parents often remain critical about the school and uninvolved simply because they feel apprehensive about the teachers or about the headteacher, and not necessarily for any particular reason. It is part of the job of a headteacher, and of teaching staff generally, to generate and sustain parental interest in the work of the school; this means making an effort to overcome some of the barriers already described.

While all school situations are unique, there are nonetheless a number of things which can be done to improve matters, including: the creation, publication and distribution of an attractive and informative school prospectus which should be translated into different languages as required (see Table 4.1); the establishment of precise procedures to be followed by those wishing to make private appointments with either the headteacher or a member of the teaching staff; the publication of a diary of events for the school year, to include details of parents' evenings, open days, sports days and other events; the prominent display of the names of parent governors and (with their permission) where they may be contacted; the formulation of a school development plan for parental involvement; the provision of opportunities for regular discussion on a variety of topics between teachers and parents; and the identification of skills needed to liaise with parents and the community, and to facilitate staff training as necessary.

AIMS AND OBJECTIVES

Schools, like any other organization, need to establish aims and objectives. They provide a sense of direction and a measure against which to evaluate success and effectiveness, while identifying any significant shortcomings or weaknesses.

It is not impossible for central government or LEAs to prescribe what the aims and objectives of individual schools should be, but the task is best undertaken by those people directly involved with the school. This fact was recognized in the Taylor Report (1977), which had this to say on setting the aims of a school:

> It is not for us to draw up model aims since this might limit the initiative of governors. It might be useful, however, if local education authorities were to draw the attention of governing bodies to some general statements such as the one quoted in 6.16. This would at least provide a starting point for discussion on the particular aims of the school concerned. The head and his colleagues might then be invited to submit a first draft of the school's aims for the governing body's consideration. The procedures adopted and the time spent on them will probably vary from area to area and school

to school and the only specific recommendation we would make is that in setting the school's aims, the governing bodies should give consideration to constructive suggestions made by any individuals or organizations with a concern for the school's welfare.

(Para. 6.25)

Table 4.1: Checklist for a school prospectus

1. Full details of the school's name, address and telephone number
2. A map of the location
3. School hours
4. The school year – term times, holidays, calendar of events (parents' evenings, sports days, etc)
5. Name of headteacher
6. Full teaching staff list, indicating subject specialisms and/or special responsibilities
7. Names and positions of non-teaching staff
8. A plan of the layout of the school and its facilities
9. Admissions policy
10. Details of year and class groupings
11. Aims and objectives of the school
12. The curriculum
13. Examination record
14. Examination entry procedures
15. Pastoral care
16. Extra-curricular activities, e.g. societies and clubs
17. School rules and regulations, e.g. uniform, lunchtime arrangements, absence, security of personal property
18. Conduct and discipline procedures
19. Home–school links
20. Homework
21. Biographies of former pupils
22. Ways in which parents might help the school

There is, therefore, ample justification for governors to involve themselves in the formulation of the school's aims and objectives. Indeed, by virtue of their broad and often substantial experience, governors can provide sound advice and insight into the kinds of procedure that should be adopted in developing aims.

The DES document *Getting Ready for Work* (1976) provided an illustration as to the nature of aims which might be applied to schools. Paragraph 6.16, which is referred to in the extract from the Taylor Report quoted above, runs as follows:

1. to enable children to acquire the basic skills of numeracy and to stimulate their curiosity and imagination

2. to enable them to acquire the basic knowledge, practice in skills and in reasoning to equip them to enter a world of work which is becoming increasingly sophisticated in its processes and techniques, which is competitive, and which is likely to demand the ability to adapt oneself to learn new processes from time to time.
3. to leave children at the end of their period of compulsory schooling with an appetite for acquiring further knowledge, experience and skills at different periods in later life; and able to benefit from additional education to a variety of levels
4. to prepare them to live and work with others in adult life; and to develop attitudes enabling them to be responsible members of the community.
5. to help them develop aesthetic sensitivity and appreciation, and skills and interests for leisure time
6. to mitigate the educational disadvantages that many children suffer through poor home conditions, limited ability or serious physical or mental handicap.

(*Getting Ready for Work*, DES, 1976)

These aims can be applied with varying degrees of emphasis to either primary or secondary schools and they provide an illustration of the character of the school as well as a sense of direction for all those involved with it. Further examples of aims and more detailed objectives are provided in Tables 4.2 and 4.3 below.

PRIMARY SCHOOLS

Attendance at primary schools begins at the age of five and usually ends at eleven, unless the LEA has adopted the policy of providing middle schools (see below). Primary education is provided on a locality basis in order, wherever possible, to be within easy reach of home for young children. The primary school is often divided into two sections – infant and junior. The usual arrangement is to allocate pupils to a class according to age. With a few exceptions this class will be under the control of the same class teacher throughout the school year. Where numbers are small, different age groups may be in the same class. Where a particular teaching specialism is required, e.g. in music or craft and design, this may be provided by a specialist teacher on the staff of the school or by a peripatetic teacher.

Primary schools are organized in different ways depending on the policies of the LEA, the preferences of the headteacher and the size of the school. Additionally, the school may be 'open plan' or it may operate on more than one site, so affecting the way in which it is organized and managed. A specimen organization chart for a primary school is provided in Figure 4.2. However, staff may be deployed and responsibilties allocated in different ways. For example, in a very small school there may be no deputy head or, where there is one, he

Figure 4.2: Organization chart for a primary school

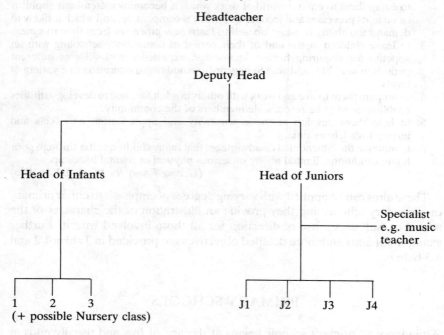

may be responsible for infants only, while the J4 teacher may also be the specialist music teacher, being replaced by a part-time teacher as required.

AIMS AND OBJECTIVES OF A PRIMARY SCHOOL

Table 4.2 lists 'statements of aims' which are general statements of intent providing a broad indication of the direction in which a primary school may wish to proceed. The 'general objectives' indicated refine the aims by suggesting ways in which they may be implemented. In practice, objectives will also be refined, this time by the teacher in the classroom, when they are translated into action statements which can be checked and modified as required.

An example of the process of establishing aims and objectives would be to say that one of the aims of the school is 'to provide education'. Translated into general objectives this would include a reference to reading, e.g. 'to teach children to read'; at the operational level the teacher would devise a scheme of work to achieve this objective.

Table 4.2: Aims and objectives of a primary school

Statement of aims	General objectives
1. To provide a pleasant and secure environment within which children may learn	(a) To provide adequate and safe accommodation, facilities and equipment (b) To ensure a sufficient level of heating, lighting and ventilation (c) To supply a suitable level of adult care and supervision during the school day
2. To encourage children to develop a sense of responsibility through co-operation with others	(a) To devise situations whereby children may work together in groups (b) To offer the opportunity for collective expression via dance, drama and music (c) To foster an understanding of the idea of 'team spirit'
3. To help develop a caring attitude to others and respect for their property and belongings	(a) To provide opportunities within the context of the day-to-day activities of the school for the development of caring attitudes and mutual consideration (b) To provide a framework of rules which form the basis for the promotion of self-discipline (c) To stimulate interest and involvement in the general appearance and care of the classroom
4. To develop each child's intellectual potential with particular reference to skills in reading, writing and arithmetic	(a) To develop reading ability via the provision of up-to-date and stimulating books and the encouragement of the parental involvement (b) To provide opportunity for systematic progression in achieving competence in both the mechanical and creative skills of writing (c) To provide each child with a recognized programme of mathematics to ensure that he attains a level of numeracy appropriate to his age
5. To help facilitate the maximum physical development of each child	(a) To provide a well-regulated, consistent and varied programme of physical recreation appropriate for the age group concerned (b) To ensure the provision of up-to-date facilities and equipment, which is used under supervision and properly maintained

Table 4.2 – *continued*

Statement of aims	General objectives
	(c) To foster interest in the importance of personal hygiene and awareness of healthy eating habits
6. To enhance children's awareness and appreciation of music, literature and art	(a) To provide opportunities to play a musical instrument (b) To incorporate poetry, plays and classical literature in the curriculum (c) To provide facilities for expression through art as well as an appreciation of artistic forms
7. To develop fluency in skills of expression, both oral and written	(a) To develop listening skills as a critical element in the understanding and assimilation of information (b) To encourage the development of communication skills through the formulation of coherent description, directions and instructions, these being either spoken or written (c) To provide opportunities to demonstrate and apply skills of communication (whether written or oral), both within the school and beyond
8. To provide children with an awareness of their environment and ways in which to appreciate it and relate to it	(a) To foster an awareness of the physical characteristics of the locality and its historical development (b) To reflect local culture by establishing two-way links with members of the local community (c) To develop an awareness and understanding of the social and economic setting within which the pupils live
9. To help children fulfil their moral and spiritual needs	(a) To develop the ability of children to distinguish between right and wrong (b) To foster an appreciation of the need to observe acceptable codes of behaviour (c) To provide religious and moral education
10. To encourage children to be independent and self-reliant	(a) To encourage children to take responsibility for aspects of their own learning

Table 4.2 – *continued*

Statement of aims	General objectives
	(b) To develop the capacity within each child to work on his own initiative
	(c) To build confidence by providing situations which require making judgements and reaching decisions

MIDDLE SCHOOLS

Some LEAs have introduced middle schools for children aged between eight, nine or ten, and twelve, thirteen or fourteen. The rationale for providing middle schools is that they allow for the earlier transition of pupils from the informal teaching of primary schools to the rather more formal arrangements of secondary schools.

SECONDARY SCHOOLS

Secondary education begins at the age of eleven and may end at sixteen. Secondary schools are large institutions because they are based on districts and have a number of 'feeder' primary schools.

Since comprehensive reorganization took place from 1965 onwards, most LEAs provide comprehensive, all-ability secondary schools in preference to a selection system. While many pupils leave school at sixteen, some schools provide education up to the age of eighteen or nineteen. More usually, however, the LEA makes alternative provision either at sixth form or tertiary colleges (see below).

The organization chart of a comprehensive school is complex due to the range of courses and subjects provided. Adolescents need different kinds of intellectual, physical and emotional support as they progress through their most formative years. To meet these needs the organization of the school provides academic and pastoral services, as shown in Figure 4.3.

AIMS AND OBJECTIVES OF A SECONDARY SCHOOL

Just as primary schools need to specify aims and objectives, so too do secondary institutions. Once again, aims reflect overall intentions while objectives attempt to break these down into more specific parts which are then translated by the

Figure 4.3: Organization of a secondary school

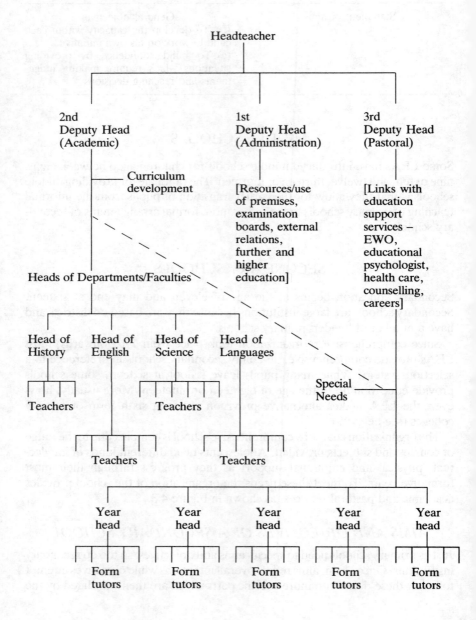

teachers who devise appropriate teaching strategies to cater for the curricular needs of their pupils. Table 4.3 provides suggested aims and objectives for a secondary school.

Table 4.3: Aims and objectives

Statement of aims	General objectives
1. To provide a balanced curriculum for all pupils up to the age of 16 on the lines indicated by the DES	(a) To present a programme of study which ensures the provision of core subjects (b) To reflect the age, degree of maturity and preferences of pupils (c) To ensure that pupils acquire a coherent portfolio of subjects to facilitate future progression beyond school
2. To raise the educational attainment of all pupils	(a) To establish systematic procedures to monitor the progress of pupils (b) To evaluate achievement levels at regular intervals (c) To review curriculum content as a result of monitoring and evaluation, and modify as necessary
3. To provide equal opportunities for all children in order that they may develop a feeling of self-worth, confidence and general well-being	(a) To recognize and make provision for different needs and abilities through the internal management of the school and the content and nature of the curriculum (b) To allow for the fact that individuals fulfil themselves in different ways (c) To promote and foster feelings of well-being on the part of individual pupils by giving them responsibilities in the day-to-day running of the school
4. To respond effectively to demands for change of the school curriculum to ensure continued relevance of all courses	(a) To liaise closely with external agencies and organizations (b) To recognize the social, economic and political context within which education takes place, and incorporate appropriate aspects in the curriculum (c) To continually modify and update all aspects of the school curriculum
5. To offer a sufficiently wide range of courses to enable the pupil to extend his talents	(a) To ensure the availability of a good selection of subjects from which to make a choice

Table 4.3 – *continued*

Statement of aims	General objectives
	(b) To provide the necessary resources to help pupils give expression to their strengths and achieve optimum standards (c) To promote versatility across a wide range of interests and expertise
6. To integrate the school with the local community	(a) To establish a network of contacts with local employers (b) To involve the local community in the activities of the school (c) To make available school premises/facilities for community use outside normal school hours
7. To provide teachers with opportunities for professional development and job satisfaction	(a) To ensure the provision of staff development on a regular basis through in-house programmes, short course attendance, secondment to industry or higher education (b) To develop administrative abilities through a sound process of delegation which takes account of the organizational structure of the school (c) To establish an effective system of communication and consultative procedures
8. To encourage parents to take an active and close interest in their children's education	(a) To provide a variety of opportunities for parents to become involved in the activities of the school (b) To establish an effective system of communication between school and home (c) To provide a facility for meetings between individual parents, the headteacher and the teachers
9. To stimulate interest in new and emerging technologies	(a) To provide the resources for 'hands-on' experience in the use of computers (b) To develop computer literacy (c) To enhance computer appreciation by demonstrating its application in industry and commerce
10. To help and advise each pupil to choose an appropriate career, vocational training or further/higher education	(a) To offer a sound careers and counselling service to help pupils select a career and plan their futures.

Table 4.3 – *continued*

Statement of aims	General objectives
	(b) To facilitate pupils in the transition from school to work
	(c) To enable pupils to compare and contrast different career paths available through further study at colleges of further/higher education, polytechnics or universities

SIXTH FORM AND TERTIARY COLLEGES

Until the 1980s sixth forms were largely the preserve of academic education for high achievers. Since then they have opened their doors to a wider range of pupils, and offer vocational courses as well as the traditional GCE 'O' and 'A' levels.

Sixth form colleges which provide full-time courses only were originally created as a cost-saving exercise in that several secondary schools could send their pupils there rather than satisfy the need themselves. Some LEAs have gone further than this by using a college of further education to supply all sixth form work, thereby converting them into what have become known as tertiary colleges which provide a mixture of full-time and part-time courses. The basis of such moves, in addition to cost-saving, is the changing nature of sixth form work due to large-scale youth unemployment.

Under the Education Act (1944), sections 8 and 144, there is a legal right to full-time education, whether in school or college, up to the age of 19 years. Legislation does not, however, include the right to choose between attending a school or college.

NURSERY SCHOOLS

There is no statutory obligation for the LEAs to make provision for nursery education, i.e. for children under five, although many do so. The Education Act (1980) made it clear that provision is discretionary, although where nursery schools are provided they cannot be closed without going through the procedures set out in section 12 of the Act. Nursery education often takes place in classes located within a primary school, under the direction of qualified nursery teachers and nursery nurses. Where there is no or insufficient LEA provision, there will usually be a number of playschools or groups set up by parents themselves.

SPECIAL EDUCATION

The Warnock Report (1978) represents a major policy document for the provision of special education. The report established a broader concept of special education that goes beyond listing categories of disabilities, to include any form of additional help which an individual might need from birth to maturity. Thus the emphasis was shifted from the nature of the handicap towards the educational needs of the child through one of three patterns of provision:
1. Full-time education in an ordinary class with any necessary help and support.
2. Education in an ordinary class with periods of withdrawal to a special class or unit or other supporting base.
3. Education in a special class or unit with periods of attendance at an ordinary class and full involvement in the general community life and extra-curricular activities of the ordinary school.

The precise arrangements adopted vary according to the needs of the individual child. In cases of severe handicap, i.e. where a child's special needs prohibit learning in an ordinary school and participation in the school community generally, education is provided in a special class or unit which is integrated with the main school. All of these recommendations take full account of the effect such integration may have on an individual school and the report indicates that successful integration, whatever the details of the scheme, can only be achieved where the nature and character of the school is maintained along with the interests of the children.

POST-1981

The Education Act (1981), which took effect from 1 April 1983, confirmed the Warnock approach in that pupils with special needs, i.e. those with 'learning difficulties', should be integrated, wherever practicable, into ordinary schools and colleges. The principle of integration is, however, subject to a number of problems. The assessment and diagnosis of special needs is the duty of the LEA, as are decisions about which school the child is to attend.

Where the LEA decides that special education of some kind is required, i.e. extra facilities in addition to those usually provided in schools, it must assess the child. This involves taking a wide range of professional advice and opinion, such as the educational, psychological and medical factors relating to the child concerned.

Actual provision of special education may take place in special schools or in special classes or units attached to ordinary primary or secondary schools. In certain circumstances, where special facilities are needed, the LEA may use a non-maintained special school, providing that it has been approved by the Secretary of State. Children with special needs may also begin their education earlier, from two years, either at the request of parents or with their consent, and have it extended to nineteen years if this is considered by the LEA to be necessary and desirable.

PARENTS AND SPECIAL EDUCATION

Parents always have an important part to play in the education of their children, but especially so where the child needs special education of some kind, i.e. where additional support is required. A number of procedures were laid down by the Education Act (1981) in an attempt to provide a joint endeavour by parents and LEAs to discover and understand the special educational needs of the individual child. However, the situation remains complex, with some LEAs going further than others to implement the spirit of the Act rather than merely fulfilling statutory obligations.

The main features are:
1. An assessment of the child's special educational needs is undertaken by the LEA to decide whether special education is needed.
2. A Statement of Special Educational Needs must be issued by the LEA where it has decided, following advice, that the child has special educational needs. Statements usually include: details of the LEA's assessment of the special educational needs of the child; and the special provision to be made for the purpose of meeting the needs identified.
3. Appeals can be made by parents against the statement made by the LEA following the assessment of their child.

GOVERNORS AND SPECIAL EDUCATION

Under the Education Act (1981) governors are required to use 'their best endeavours' on behalf of children with special educational needs. This involves checking to see, in the first instance, whether there are any pupils with special needs registered at the school and, if so, whether the additional facilities they require or need are, in fact, made available. It is also a good idea for governors to ask for regular reports to be presented at governors' meetings in order that they may be kept up-to-date.

Detailed information about a wide variety of special educational needs is produced by a number of different organizations.

IN A NUTSHELL

The schools of today are complex in that they serve a dual purpose: they provide education and pastoral care. Great interest is taken in the effectiveness of schools, as evidenced by the necessity under the Education Act (1980) to publish an individual school prospectus setting out, for example, the aims of the school, the nature and content of the curriculum and the admissions policy. While the headteacher is the formal legal executive of the school, he too is accountable, to the governing body, for the day-to-day management of the school and its organization. Together, they must shape the overall aims and objectives of the school. The increasing involvement of governing bodies exemplifies the trend towards accountability in education, particularly to the consumers, i.e. parents. This trend is also part of the move towards establishing new policies for special education.

SELF-TEST

1. Draw an organizational chart of your school.
2. What is the difference between a maintained county school and a voluntary aided school?
3. Who is responsible for providing nursery education?
4. What do you understand by the term 'compulsory education'?
5. Suggest three reasons why the organization chart of a secondary school is more complex than that of a primary school.
6. What services might you expect to find a secondary school offering as part of its pastoral care?

POINTS TO PONDER

1. What do you consider to be the main advantages and disadvantages of the system of one teacher per year group in a primary school, from the points of view of both pupil and teacher?
2. What do you consider to be the essential role of the secondary school – to teach or to provide pastoral care? Do you think there are any tensions between these two functions and what might be done to overcome them?
3. What are the likely problems to arise in the integration into ordinary schools of children with special needs?
4. How might these problems be overcome?

5. Using the appropriate sample of aims and objectives evaluate the aims and objectives of your school. To what extent are they relevant? Do they need to be revised? Are they being fulfilled?
6. What kind of management style does you headteacher use? Do you consider it appropriate for your school?

GOVERNOR'S CHECKLIST

1. Does your LEA make provision for nursery education? If so, do you know whether or not it is adequate?
2. Does your LEA make adequate arrangements for the education of children with special educational needs?
3. What provision does your school make for children with special educational needs?
4. Is the governing body kept well informed about children with special educational needs?
5. Does your school prospectus look attractive?
6. Does your school prospectus contain sufficient information to be of real value to pupils and parents?
7. What arrangements are made to ensure that all parents, local libraries and other interested parties receive copies of the school prospectus?
8. Are the names of governors included in the school prospectus?
9. Are genuine attempts made by the school to attract the interest and support of parents?
10. Does your LEA provide the sixteen to nineteen-year-old age group with sufficient education, either in sixth forms or tertiary or colleges of further education?

FURTHER READING

Adams, F. (ed.) (1986) *Special Education*, Councils and Education Press, London.
DES (1984) *Designing for Children with Special Educational Needs – Ordinary Schools*, Building Bulletin 61, HMSO, London.
DES (1984) *Access for Disabled People to Educational Buildings*, Design Note 18, HMSO, London.
Frith, D. (ed.) (1985) *School Management in Practice*, Longman, London.
NCC (1986) *The Missing Links between Home and School*, National Consumer Council, London.

Richards, C. (ed.) (1980) *Primary Education – Issues for the 80s*, A. & C. Black, London.
Taylor, F. (1986) *Parents' Rights in Education*, Longman, London.
Whitaker, P. (1983) *The Primary Head*, Heinemann Educational Books, London.
Woods, P. (1984) *Parents and Schools: A Report for Discussion on Liaison between Parents and Secondary Schools in Wales*, School Curriculum Development Committee, London.

5
THE GOVERNORS

INDIVIDUALITY OF SCHOOLS

One of the main reasons for having school governors is to ensure that each school develops its own individuality and is not viewed simply as a satellite of the LEA. Somehow, all schools are the same and yet they are also quite different. Governing bodies can help sustain the unique identity of a school by influencing its character and overall aims and objectives. This can be achieved through, for example, building firm links with members of the local community and through the development of a relevant curriculum, i.e. one which reflects the particular needs of pupils within the area.

Although schools can be put into broad categories, such as primary and secondary, or county or voluntary, this reveals nothing about individual character, tradition and location. The individuality of schools arises for a number of reasons, including: historical background and development; ownership, e.g. LEA, or voluntary aided or special agreement; type of school (primary, middle, secondary, special); traditions built up over the years; influence of the personalities of a nucleus of teaching staff; number of years in existence; overall size (number of registered pupils); age and quality of buildings; availability of adequate resources; extent and quality of the curriculum; local reputation; context, i.e. catchment area; level of parental support; and local politics.

NOT OPTIONAL EXTRAS

Governing bodies are not optional extras in the education system. Every school is required by the Education Act (1980) to have its own individual governing body, unless there are special circumstances. Legislation will not, of course, ensure that governing bodies will be effective. This depends on several things, including the support given to them by the LEA, through perhaps the setting-up of adequate and realistic training courses and the provision of useful information, co-operation by headteachers and their colleagues and the commitment of individual governors.

COMPOSITION OF GOVERNING BODIES

At the time of writing, the rules relating to the composition of governing bodies are detailed in the Education Act (1980), sections 1–5. The different categories of governors to be represented are as follows:
1. Two elected parent governors in county, voluntary controlled and special schools;
2. One elected parent in voluntary aided or special agreement schools, but in addition, one foundation governor must also be a parent of a registered pupil at the school;
3. One elected teacher in a school with fewer than three hundred pupils;
4. Two elected teachers if there are more than three hundred pupils;
5. The headteacher (if he so chooses) as *ex officio* member;
6. LEA representatives;
7. Foundation governors in aided or special agreement schools are to have a majority of two in the case of a body with eighteen or less members, and three in the case of larger bodies;
8. Foundation governors in controlled schools are to be at least one fifth of the total governing body.

There are regulations in the 1980 Act in terms of the size of governing bodies; consequently, the prescribed composition tends to be seen by many LEAs as a minimum rather than a maximum. Some LEAs, although not legally required to, encourage non-teaching staff to elect their own governors, while others have established pupil governors in their secondary schools. DES Circular 4/81 did, in fact, recommend that LEAs incorporate a much wider membership on their governing bodies in order to secure representation from local industry and commerce.

NEW PROPOSALS

Since the Education Act (1980) there have been a number of proposals directly concerning the membership and composition of governing bodies. The first significant step came with the publication of the consultative document *Parental Influence at School* (Green Paper, 1984). Among its main suggestions were that parents should be in a majority on all governing bodies, instead of LEA representatives. Ensuing discussion between interested parties and the DES eventually led to the withdrawal of such proposals; new recommendations were published in their place, this time in the form of a White Paper, *Better Schools* (1985, Chapt. 9). This time the proposal emphasized that

> no single interest will predominate. Neither the governors appointed by the LEA, nor those elected by the parents, nor those representing the teachers will have a majority.
>
> (para. 221 (1))

The proposed composition of governing bodies contained in this White Paper (see Table 5.1) was eventually carried forward in the Education Bill (1986), section 3, and subsequently retained in the Education (No. 2) Act (1986), despite criticism to the effect that teacher governors were under-represented and that pupil governors (over the age of sixteen) should be included.

Table 5.1: Example of proposed composition of governing bodies

Number of pupils	Parents	LEA	Head-teacher	Teachers	Co-opted or for controlled schools		Total
					F	C	
Less than 100	2	2	1	1	3		9
					2	1	
100–299	3	3	1	1	4		12
					3	1	
300–599	4	4	1	2	5		16
					4	1	
600 plus	5	5	1	2	6		19
					4	2	

Notes: F = Foundation governor; C = Co-opted governor. (Source: White Paper (1985) *Better Schools*, para. 221, put forward in the Education Bill, 1986).

CHANGES SINCE THE EDUCATION ACT (1980)

The effect of the Education Act (1980) was to bring about a number of far-reaching changes, including:
1. Abolition of the term 'school manager', previously applied in respect of primary schools, to be replaced by the common term 'school governor';
2. Introduction, in the case of primary schools, of 'governing bodies' and Articles and Instruments of Government;
3. Restriction of the grouping of schools, whereby one governing body, for example, an education committee, could represent several schools;
4. A requirement that every school, county and voluntary, have its own governing body;
5. Confirmation of the right of LEAs to appoint their own representatives on school governing bodies;
6. For the first time in the case of county and voluntary controlled schools, the election of at least two parents to serve on governing bodies;
7. In the case of voluntary aided and special agreement schools, one parent to be elected and one parent to be part of the foundation group;
8. For the first time, the election of teachers to serve on the governing bodies of their schools, one in the case of a school with less than three hundred registered pupils, two in every other case;
9. The right of parents to express a preference as to which school they wish to send their children and this wish to be accommodated by the LEAs and governing bodies unless special circumstances apply, for example, where to do so would lead to inefficiency or where it could be shown that it would not be in the best interests of the child;
10. The publication by the LEAs and the governing bodies of each school's admissions rules and procedures;
11. The establishment of an appeals procedure, including the constitution of an appeals committee, to deal with cases where parents are refused the school of their choice. (The LEA is responsible for setting up procedures in respect of county and controlled schools, whereas individual governing bodies have the responsibility in all other cases.)

EQUAL LEGITIMATE INTERESTS

Following the requirements of the Education Act (1980), the composition of governing bodies has been altered to ensure that quite different but equally legitimate interests might be represented. As a result, parents and teachers now have a legal entitlement to representation alongside the LEA governors, their maximum number being prescribed by law, under the Education (No. 2) Act (1986). Broadly interpreted, this means that the larger the school the more 'seats' there are available.

Whether a parent, teacher, LEA, co-opted or ancillary staff governor, it is often useful to find out more about the other governors in order to appreciate their particular interests and the nature of their involvement on school governing bodies.

PARENT GOVERNORS

Since September 1985, elected parent governors have become a statutory requirement in all county, voluntary controlled or aided and maintained special schools.

HOW TO BECOME A PARENT GOVERNOR

To become a parent governor, a parent must have a child who is a registered pupil at the school concerned. This is a minimum requirement which is specified in the Education Act (1980), reinforced in the White Paper *Better Schools* and contained in the Education Bill (1986).

Under current and anticipated legislation, parents wishing to serve as governors must be elected by their fellow parents. A vote will only be necessary where the number of parents wishing to serve exceeds the minimum seats available. The headteacher or the local education office will be able to deal with any questions concerning eligibility and election procedures.

Elections will be by secret ballot organized by the LEA. Only parents of registered pupils attending the school concerned are eligible to vote. There are as yet no standard rules on procedure. However, an example of best practice might be for parents to be nominated and seconded by fellow parents. Under the Statutory Instrument No. 809, a parent governor ceases to hold office when the child concerned is no longer a registered pupil at the school. The regulations state:

> If on the first day of any school year there is no longer a registered pupil at the school of whom a governor to whom this Regulation applies is the parent, he shall, on that day, cease to hold office as a governor.
>
> (para. 2)

However, following the Education (No. 2) Act (1986) new statutory instruments will be published to the effect that parent governors will serve for four years. Such changes will need to be incorporated into a school's new Instrument of Government.

Governor's question: **One of my fellow governors has told me, much to my surprise, that he is a governor of five schools within this LEA. Can this be right and is there no limit to the number of schools one can represent as a governor?**
Answer: **Under the Education (School Governing Bodies) Regulations (1981, Part II, para. 4) (also known as Statutory Instrument No. 809), an individual is restricted to serving on a maximum number of five governing bodies. In practice, this applies to LEA or co-opted members only. The basis for membership of other governors is, in the case of a parent, having a child who is a registered pupil at the school, and for a teacher, being a member of staff. Technically it is possible for someone to have five children, all registered at different schools, and to be a parent governor at all five. Alternatively, one could have four children registered at different schools and be a teacher at a fifth. However, such situations would be extremely unlikely.**

PARENTAL INFLUENCE

As consumers, it is vital that parents have an effective means of becoming involved in the school's policy-making. Parents have a significant stake in the well-being of the school and their wishes should be taken fully into account. Indeed, the Education Act (1944) made it plain that pupils are to be educated in accordance with the wishes of their parents.

The role of the parent governor is to represent the views of parents, particularly at formal meetings. They have exactly the same status as the other governors, including the right to stand for election as chairman and vice-chairman.

GETTING ELECTED

Experience suggests that it is inadvisable for a parent to wait to be approached to become a school governor. Find out in advance what the situation is, for there may even be a current vacancy. If no vacancies exist, the best time to make enquiries is in the summer term, since most governing bodies are newly constituted with effect from the beginning of September to coincide with the start of a new school year.

It is often a good idea to make informal soundings first, perhaps through discussion with an existing governor, the headteacher, one of the teachers, or with members of the parent–teachers' association (PTA), if there is one.

Indeed, the PTA in many schools gets involved in supporting would-be parent governors, so enlisting its backing may prove to be a vital first step.

Election procedure

Precisely how the election procedure is handled varies from one LEA to another. Some go to considerable trouble to publicise vacancies and election procedures, others do not. Ideally, it is a good idea to have a number of parents' meetings where they can listen to the candidates speak and then cast their votes by secret ballot. This kind of activity should take place on a specified evening during the week, with, perhaps, an additional meeting on a Saturday morning for those who cannot attend in the evening. Parents standing for election should prepare a brief statement: this will form the basis of their address should an election become necessary. The address should be brief and contain an outline of the parent's interest in the school.

FOLLOWING THE ELECTION

Once elected, the parent governor has a clear responsibility to find out the views of parents on a variety of issues affecting the school. Although there is a need to be aware of the views and opinions of others, it nonetheless remains important that the parent governor puts forward his own opinions and ideas. In any event, there will seldom be a consensus on educational issues.

The clear duty of the parent governor is to take account of the views held and stated by other parents when making his own contribution or exercising his own judgement.

LEA GOVERNORS

LEA governors are appointed by the major local political parties which operate within the LEA. This arrangement is part of a tradition which was based originally on local government councillors having representation on all governing bodies. The effect of this was that many councillors were governors of several schools within a single local authority (sometimes in excess of twenty). However, under Statutory Instrument 809 the maximum number of schools which may be represented is five.

Increasing pressures on councillors to attend more and more committees brought about a situation where it became necessary to reduce their involvement on governing bodies, although a great many councillors still do manage to keep up their work as governors.

When this is simply no longer possible, political nominees are chosen to represent the LEA on governing bodies. Those chosen as LEA representatives are usually members of one of the main local political parties, although this is often rather more informal than it sounds. The actual procedures used to choose the LEA representatives can be quite complex, especially now that every school is to have its own governing body.

The more LEA governors required, which may run into several hundred in a large LEA, the more stretched a local party political machinery becomes. This can lead to mistakes being made if sufficient care is not taken to check out carefully would-be governors. LEA representatives still hold the majority interest on school governing bodies. In effect, this has often meant that the chairman was automatically an LEA representative (often a local councillor, but not necessarily so).

Many LEAs continue to operate a special arrangement whereby the dominant local party receives backing (i.e. their nomination is unopposed) for the chairmanship of governing bodies, while the 'opposition' continues to provide the vice-chairman. If a change takes place as a result of local elections, then such an arrangement would simply be reversed.

However, since the Education Act (1980) came into force in 1985, securing the position of chairman has been rather less of a formality, there being genuine competition for the position between LEA representatives and elected parents. This trend is likely to increase in the future.

Governor's question: I have just completed my term of office as a parent governor. It seems a pity that the experience I have gained cannot be put to good use as a governor of another school. How can I get onto a governing body again – or even several? Could I become an LEA governor for instance?

Answer: Many parents presently active as governors are looking for ways to sustain or increase their involvement. It is a good idea to contact one of the main local political parties, preferably one for which you have a general sympathy. Enquire whether they have any vacant seats. There may be an interview – usually very straightforward – and a requirement to become a member of the party concerned.

TOE THE PARTY LINE?

As appointed rather than elected governors, LEA representatives often find it difficult to decide in whose interest they should operate, especially during formal meetings. The extent to which local parties put pressure on their governors to 'toe the party line' is a critical factor. Since local branches behave in different ways due to the characteristics of the local area, traditions and expectations, it is difficult to generalize about what actually takes place. Also, some issues are likely to be seen by individual party members as being more significant than others, just as some local parties may be seen to be more or less moderate depending on the individual's point of view.

Consequently, there may be a number of tensions involved in what amounts to being a 'political' nominee. On the other hand, it is fair to expect LEA governors to maintain close links with their supporting group.

TAKING A BALANCED VIEW

All governors, whatever the basis for their nomination or election, represent clearly defined interest groups, for example, parents, teachers or local political parties. However, this should not lead to a blind following of a party line, if there is one. This is especially the case where the individual concerned simply does not believe in the approach advocated by the local party, or other parents or teachers. In the case of the LEA governor, he should not oppose the 'other side' just because it *is* the 'other side'. No one party has a monopoly on good ideas and sensible policies. The views expressed in the *Handbook for Labour Governors* (1985 edition, published by the Socialist Educational Association) sums up the position of LEA governors:

> Do not be ashamed of being political; a local authority representative is a political appointment. But be warned, being political means arguing constructively for the ideas you wish to promote. It does not mean being blindly opposed to anything a Conservative may suggest or blindly supporting a Labour Council whatever it suggests or does. (p. 7)

Terms of office for LEA governors are provided in the Instruments of Government. Tenure will usually be for three or four years, with the possibility of being nominated again for a further term of office.

TEACHER GOVERNORS

While a number of LEAs have had teacher governors for some time, this became a statutory requirement under the Education Act (1980). To become a teacher governor is possible by election only, the procedures for which are as yet unstandardized. However, only teachers at the school concerned will be allowed to take part in the vote. Should a teacher be nominated unopposed, then there will be no need for a formal vote. Where there is to be a vote, it will take the form of a secret ballot. Many LEAs have developed a central system to co-ordinate elections, organize ballots and establish procedures.

PROFESSIONAL ADVICE

Teacher governors provide specialist and professional advice. They have the advantage of being able to bring day-to-day classroom problems to the attention of the governing body. As elected members representing their colleagues, consideration needs to be given to the nature of their role as governors. Is the teacher governor to be a delegate, i.e. simply to express the views of fellow teachers, or is he to be a representative and express general views, his own as well as those of his colleagues? The answer, perhaps lies in the value of the role of teacher governor, that is, its representational nature, which should allow for the expression of a wide variety of viewpoints rather than a narrowness of views.

Teacher governors, as major 'stakeholders' of the school, bring to governing bodies a number of positive advantages, including: a detailed working knowledge of the day-to-day life of the school; an awareness of the problems currently confronting the school; an understanding of pupil attitudes towards the school; a variety of professional opinions by representing teacher colleagues; a direct communication between the governing body and the teaching staff; professional advice when required, e.g. on curriculum issues or pastoral care procedures; information about the development needs of teaching staff.

The teacher governor has a responsibility to find out the views of the staffroom, especially if there are any controversial matters on the agenda, and to formulate an effective reporting-back system to keep everyone informed. This is of particular importance if teachers are to become familiar with the activities of the new governing bodies.

Reporting back to colleagues may sometimes be a sensitive issue, especially where discussion at the governors' meeting has included reference to either individual teachers or to pupils and their families. Colleagues, not unnaturally, are likely to want their representative on the governing body to elaborate on some of the bald statements made in the minutes. It is difficult to know where to draw the line. However, if teacher governors feel uncertain about the degree of confidentiality required in respect of certain items which are to appear in the minutes, they should seek the guidance of the chairman *before* the end of the meeting.

HEADTEACHER AS A GOVERNOR

The headteacher has the right to choose to be a governor or not, by virtue of his office; this is known as *ex officio* membership. Whether he chooses to be a governor or not, the headteacher has the right to attend any meeting of the governing body (Statutory Instrument No. 809, para. 9). In effect, many headteachers decide not to be a member of the governing body, preferring to attend as professional advisers without voting rights. Headteachers are, however, in a separate category from teachers and should not be regarded as being the same as teacher governors.

ELIGIBILITY FOR CHAIRMAN

Neither headteachers nor teachers nor any employees of the LEA *at the school in question* are eligible to become chairman or vice-chairman of governing bodies. Indeed, they are specifically excluded from holding this office according to Statutory Instrument No. 809, para. 8(5). Headteachers and teachers cease to be governors when they are no longer employed at the school.

CO-OPTED OR COMMUNITY GOVERNORS

Co-opted governors, sometimes known as community governors, are appointed by the full governing body, usually at its first meeting. It is the LEA which determines the procedures to be adopted. It is intended that co-opted members should bring to the governing body special knowledge or expertise which is especially relevant to the needs of the school. They have full membership rights and appointments may be for the duration of the new governing body or for a fixed period. Details of tenure and general terms of office are in the school's Instrument of Government.

ADVANTAGES OF CO-OPTED GOVERNORS

Co-opted governors are not intended to represent any specific interest group such as parents or teachers, and consequently do not have to sound out the opinions of others in order to reflect these at governors' meetings; nor do they need to provide feedback to any one group. On the other hand, co-opted governors, like all other members, should make it their business to find out about the school and any special interests or difficulties. The same principles of confidentiality apply.

New proposals for governing bodies underline the importance of co-opted members, as the following extract from the White Paper, *Better Schools*, illustrates:

The co-option of governors will serve to broaden the membership of governing bodies and will provide an additional opportunity, which the Government hopes will be used freely, to associate industry and commerce with the work of schools.

(para. 221(3))

DISQUALIFICATION

The rules relating to the disqualification of governors are contained in Statutory Instrument No. 809, The Education (School Governing Bodies) Regulations, 1981. Reasons for disqualification are: bankruptcy; criminal conviction, within five years of the appointment or election, without the option of a fine, and whether or not the sentence of imprisonment was suspended; failure to attend meetings of the governing body for a continuous period of twelve months.

IN A NUTSHELL

Significant changes in the composition of governing bodies for all schools have taken place since September 1985, when the requirements of the Education Act (1980) had to take effect. This meant the inclusion of parent and teacher governors in all governing bodies, and the requirement that the chairmen be elected rather than left to LEA nomination. All governors are to be of equal status. Governing bodies help ensure that the individuality of schools is maintained.

SELF-TEST

1. How many categories of governor are there?
2. What does *ex officio* mean?
3. Which governors are ineligible to stand for election as chairman?
4. Give three examples of the benefits of having parent governors.
5. Give three examples of the benefits of having teacher governors.
6. What are the main rules relating to disqualification of governors? Where are the rules stated?

POINTS TO PONDER

1. Suggest some of the reasons why parent governors are likely to feel at a disadvantage or less confident compared with some of the other governors. What steps might be taken to enhance their position?

2. What are the main advantages and disadvantages likely to accrue by having an LEA representative as chairman of the governing body?
3. What are the particular qualities to be looked for when considering the co-option of members to serve on your governing body?
4. What might be done to attract more parents to stand as candidates for election to your school's governing body?
5. Argue the case for and against the election of pupil governors at a secondary school.
6. How far should LEA governors be prepared to accept the direction of their political party when making decisions on important issues on a governing body?

GOVERNOR'S CHECKLIST

1. How are parents at your school informed of the need to appoint parent governors?
2. Does your LEA have procedures for the election of parent governors?
3. Does your headteacher organize the elections for parent governors?
4. Is the headteacher a member of the governing body?
5. What arrangements are made at your school for parent governor candidates to present an election address to other parents?
6. Do the local political parties put pressure on their nominated members of governing bodies to 'toe the party line'?
7. Are any of the LEA members on your governing body members of other governing bodies?
8. What are the criteria at your school for selecting co-opted governors?
9. Do the teacher governors provide sufficient 'inside information' to the governing body about pupils, curricula, staff morale and buildings?
10. Has the chairman formulated rules relating to what has to be regarded as confidential, with particular reference to teacher governors?

PART 3

GOVERNING IN CONTEXT

All the powers relevant to school government should be vested in the local education authority. There should be as much delegation of these powers by the LEA to the governing body as is compatible with the LEA's ultimate responsibility for the running of the schools in its area, and as much discretion in turn granted to the headteacher by the governing body as is compatible with the latter's responsibility for the success of the school in all its activities.

(Taylor Report, 1977, p. 111)

The powers and functions of governing bodies are at first sight extensive, covering the whole gamut of a school's activities. Governors must exercise their duties collectively, through collaboration with the headteacher and in the light of any recommendations made by the LEA. In short, the role is something of a balancing act between stamping a certain amount of individuality on school decision-making, and taking full account of the headteacher's role as manager and the ultimate responsibility of the LEA for schools in its area.

Part 3 includes a number of points of interest. Chapter 6 sets out the formal framework, and successive chapters concentrate on specific features such as finance, premises, conduct and discipline, the curriculum and staffing.

6
POWERS AND FUNCTIONS

POWER-SHARING

Power-sharing is a typical characteristic of British administration, with no one person or institution having overwhelming powers over others. Even the Secretary of State for Education and Science, while having powers (under the Education Act (1944), sections 68 and 99) invested in him through his office (rather than on a personal or individual basis), must work within the statutory framework of education law.

Power-sharing occurs because of the way in which central government has developed in not having written constitution, i.e. a formal declaration of State legislation regarding the rights of individuals under the law. The system of local government is a good example of power-sharing between many organizations and individuals. For example, local councillors, individually and through the committee network, and chief officers and their staffs respond to and interpret central government policy and its directives. Any judgements made have to be taken in the light of dependence on central government funding, while at the same time preserving local autonomy in decision-making.

Power-sharing weaves through the education system like a spider's web, with different institutions reflecting the interests of society as a whole on a wide range of issues (see Figure 6.1).

THE PARTICIPANTS

Who has power to do what depends largely on the nature of the situation. For example, central government, through the DES, has the power to determine

Figure 6.1: Power-sharing network of education

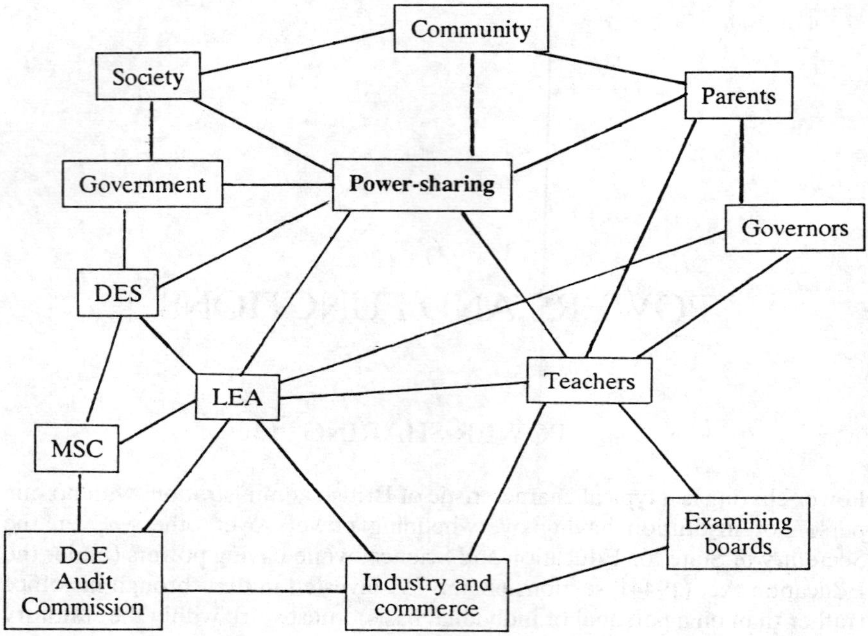

the framework and nature of the secondary school examinations system, as illustrated in the introduction of the General Certificate of Secondary Education (GCSE). LEAs have powers to determine the nature and scope of the secondary school curriculum for their own area, taking into account the individual or special circumstances of each school and its needs.

Parents too have a right, which may be interpreted as 'power', to send their children to schools of their choice. They can also combine to exert influence over the nature of the school curriculum, as illustrated in what has become known as the 'William Tyndale affair'. Briefly, this concerned an ILEA infant and primary school, William Tyndale, where the parents' expectations of what the school should be doing for the education of their children broke down. Parent power, expressed by withdrawing children and complaining to ILEA, led to an enquiry and to subsequent changes in the curriculum.

The complex process of power-sharing comprises a continuous cycle of events and decisions, with the final say being determined by the nature of the situation. As a result, it is seldom possible to arrive at definite conclusions over many educational issues, particularly over who is responsible for what and who

has the power to decide when problems arise. Indeed, it is precisely because the powers and controls over education are shared among different institutions and individuals that the following situations arise:
1. Lack of co-ordination and control over the total provision of the education service
2. Confusion as to the division of powers between central and local government
3. Uncertainty as to the nature, scope and content of the school's curriculum
4. Difficulties, at school level, in deciding overall aims and objectives in the interest of all pupils
5. Problems at national and school level of establishing criteria for quality in education and, subsequently, evaluating levels of performance
6. Obscurity of the precise powers of governing bodies.

SCHOOL GOVERNORS AS PART OF THE 'EDUCATION CONSTITUTION'

Governing bodies are a part of what might be described as the 'education constitution' of England and Wales. Their place is secured within the provisions of the Education Act (1944) and their increasing importance has been emphasized in several government policy documents since the mid-1970s, starting with the publication of the Taylor Report (1976) and leading up to the Education (No. 2) Act (1986).

DIRECT INVOLVEMENT

The main function of governing bodies is to make policy decisions and recommendations within the rules set out in their Articles of Government. The Articles determine the scope of the powers of governing bodies, while reinforcing the overall responsibility of the LEA to determine the character of its schools.

In reality, LEAs cannot give close attention to every one of their schools. Consequently, they delegate to governing bodies, which in turn are expected to work in partnership with the headteacher. Governing bodies, unlike officials at city or county hall, are on the spot and thus are in a position to take a special interest in the school. One of the essential roles of the governing body, then, is to determine the main lines of development of the school, while working within the parameters and guidelines set by the LEA, and through close collaboration with the headteacher.

LEGAL BASIS FOR GOVERNING BODIES

As formally constituted bodies, governors are empowered to take executive decisions which are legally binding, e.g. in relation to the admissions policy or disciplinary procedures, providing that they conform to the terms of reference as set out in their Articles of Government. This means that governing bodies have considerable potential to influence a range of activities within their schools, in that they do not simply offer advice and make recommendations, which may or may not be acceptable. Many of their decisions have the force of law behind them.

However, not all of the decisions governing bodies have to take fall within the statutory framework; when this is the case, they can only make suggestions and offer advice. Examples could include the question of raising additional school funds and whether to set up a working party on school buildings and facilities.

Whatever the nature of the decision-making undertaken by governing bodies, it must comply with the general directions of the LEA. It is important, however, that governing bodies maintain an independent view and do not simply act in a rubber-stamping capacity.

COLLECTIVE POWER OF GOVERNORS

It is important to recognize that the powers of governing bodies relate to the body as a whole and not to individual members, who have no powers of their own. It is the collectivity of governors, acting as a corporate group, which has the power of decision. Consequently, it is particularly important that individual governors should not make promises, e.g. to parents, about what they can or cannot do. On their own they can do very little, except perhaps bring issues to the attention of the governing body as a whole.

LIMITS TO POWER

Governors cannot do what they like. Unfortunately, the exact nature of their powers and functions is somewhat obscure. The Articles of Government are not definitive documents and as such are open to interpretation. Whatever attempts are made to modify the powers and functions of governing bodies in order to strengthen them, there is always bound to be an element of uncertainty about where powers begin and end.

Interpretation of any legislation is dependent largely on precedent set by case history. Even then, judgements are closely related to the unique set of circumstances surrounding the individual case. Consequently, what governors can or cannot do and the powers they have or do not have, depends on the individual situation.

HITTING THE HEADLINES

No reference to the powers of governing bodies would be complete without reference to the fact that, from time to time, the subject of governing bodies hits the headlines in the national press. Sometimes these will be of a general nature, e.g. when a new education Bill is heralded:

> Parents to get more powers in schools
> (*Daily Telegraph*, 21 February 1986)
>
> Government for schools
> (*The Times* editorial, 21 February 1986)
>
> Will more parents mean less politicking on school governing bodies?
> (Maureen O'Connor, *Education Guardian*, 4 March 1986)

At other times the focus may be concentrated on specific issues:

> Parents to meet over Honeyford
> (*Sunday Telegraph*, 22 September 1985)
>
> Parents halt Honeyford boycott for talks
> (*Guardian*, 24 September 1985)

This case centred on the headteacher of a primary school in Bradford. Mr Ray Honeyford had written an article which was alleged to have been racist, criticizing the LEA for its multiracial education policy. He was suspended by an education subcommittee vote with a majority of one. However, the school governors recommended his reinstatement, which is what happened following a decision by the High Court.

> Graffiti dispute threatens 250 schools
> (*The Times*, 12 October 1985)

This referred to what become known as the Poundswick case, a dispute which led to the walk-out of teachers at a comprehensive school in Manchester in the summer of 1985. Five boys were suspended by the headteacher. At a meeting of the governing body the governors backed the headmaster and decided to expel the boys. The boys were accused of daubing obscene slogans in letters one foot high across an array of panels and windows at the school. The LEA decided that the boys had to be reinstated, but the teachers, with the backing of the governing body, refused to teach them and went on strike. The action gained support from other teachers within the authority and a protracted dispute followed. This was a clear case of the LEA attempting to override the decision taken by the governing body. The dispute was finally settled when the boys in question reached school-leaving age.

Whatever the rights and wrongs of these two cases, the fact remains that the powers of governing bodies were tested, not so much by the outcome of each case, but simply because they were able to make a major impact on the local politics of education. Uncertainty remains both for governing bodies and for individual LEAs in terms of the extent of their own powers.

Governor's question: **I have not been a school governor for very long – in fact this is my first year as a parent governor at a county primary school. I have heard references made to the Instrument and Articles but, never having seen them, I wondered whether these were published for secondary schools only. If not, am I entitled to my own copies and where do I get them from?**
Answer: **No one can be expected to play an effective part as a school governor without knowing the framework within which decisions are to be made. Every school is required by law to have its own Instrument and Articles of Government, and governors are entitled to their own personal copies. Most LEAs send them direct to governors and if you have not received them shortly following election or appointment, it is likely to be an oversight rather than a deliberate omission. Contact the education enquiry desk at city or county hall.**

UNCERTAINTY

Although it can be frustrating for governors not to know precisely where they stand in relation to a particular issue, the same uncertainty affects everyone else involved. In many ways, flexibility is to be preferred to any 'straitjacket' arrangement imposed by central government, since not only are LEAs all different, but so too are the schools. Local circumstances vary considerably: nonetheless, there are a number of common powers and functions which are the responsibility of school governors everywhere, and which are embodied within the statutory framework of education.

RESPONSIBILITIES

If governing bodies have powers and functions, they also have responsibilities, and failure to fulfil them gives rise to dramatic media headlines such as, 'School governors threatened with jail'. Such situations arise from the good intentions of governing bodies to act in the best interests of the school, albeit outside their precise powers as stipulated in the Articles of Government.

This would be less significant if the governors were in harmony with the LEA. However, in cases where there are not, i.e. where the LEA places a different interpretation of what is or is not in the best interests of the school, then technically at least, governors *may*, by refusing to conform to LEA directives, be operating beyond their jurisdiction or failing to fulfil their responsibilities. For example, if governors refused to take part in the appointment procedures for a new headteacher, they would be in breach of their statutory duties and responsibilities. This would have the effect of preventing the LEA making an appointment, since an appointment cannot be made without governor participation under the Articles of Government. It is in this kind of situation where the LEA has to find a compromise or, if so inclined, put pressure on the governors, which may (but rarely does) result in the threat of legal action.

PROCEDURAL POWERS

This refers to the process of consultation which must take place between the principal parties having responsibilities for the day-to-day management, conduct and general well-being of the school, i.e. the LEA, the governors and the headteacher. The White Paper *Better Schools* (1985) indicated that the functions of those involved would be guided by two procedural powers:

1. Since the LEA, the governing body and the headteacher are each concerned with the affairs of the school, each needs to be informed about what the others are doing. The governing body will have a duty to supply the LEA with such reports relating to the discharge of its functions as the LEA may require; and the headteacher will be under a similar duty to supply reports to the governing body and the LEA.
2. In urgent matters arising from the day-to-day functioning of the school it will sometimes be necessary for the governing body to act quickly. In such cases, the chairman (elected annually by the governors) will be empowered to act on behalf of the whole governing body.

(para. 230)

INSTRUMENT AND ARTICLES OF GOVERNMENT

All organizations have committees. For example, a tennis club or a local branch of a national union must operate under the control of a management committee, which in turn must abide by the constitution of the club. A constitution simply refers to the rules and procedures governing the running of a business or club. For example, eligibility to stand for election or nomination to become a member of the committee or organization is determined by the rules. The rules referring to eligibility, tenure of office and disqualification of governors are known as the Instrument of Government.

The specific purpose of committees varies according to the aims and objectives of the organization, which also form a part of its constitution. Nonetheless, management committees will almost certainly be involved in deciding future policies of one kind or another or settling difficulties and conflicts as they arise from day-to-day. The scope of decision-making powers of governing bodies is contained in the Articles of Government. Therefore, in the case of governing bodies, the rules are known as the Instrument and Articles of Government. The details contained within each of these two documents are listed below.

Instrument of Government includes reference to: membership, giving details of, for example, the number of LEA, parent and teacher governors; terms of office, including tenure and procedures for filling casual vacancies should they arise mid-term; disqualification due to failure to attend or incapacity to fulfil duties due to physical or mental illness; resignations and 'removals' from office by the LEA; appointment of a clerk to the governors; convening of meetings, including period of notice, frequency, quorum, circulation of agendas; chairman, rules relating to eligibility and election procedures; termination and adjournment of meetings; right to attend meetings (e.g. the Director of Education or Chief Education Officer and members of the education committee); records of those present.

Articles of Government include reference to: conduct of the school; school funds; finance; school premises; appointment and dismissal of headteacher; appointment of assistant teachers; appointment and dismissal of non-teaching staff; designation of clerk to the governors; organization and curriculum; school holidays; admission of pupils; providing, with the headteacher, reports and returns as required to the LEA.

It is particularly important for governors to check carefully their Instrument and Articles of Government since they vary, sometimes quite considerably. However, all governing bodies have certain general powers and functions.

POWERS AND FUNCTIONS OF GOVERNING BODIES

The powers and functions of governing bodies may be summarized as follows:
1. To determine, with the headteacher, a statement of the school's curricular aims and objectives, and to review this from time to time

2. To provide the headteacher with guidance and support regarding the day-to-day operation and management of the school
3. To direct the headteacher to terminate any debarment of pupils according to the direction of the LEA
4. To call for reports from the headteacher regarding the day-to-day management of the school and the curriculum
5. To determine the school's curriculum, following consultation with the headteacher and in accordance with LEA policy
6. To determine the general conduct of the school, taking account of the aims and objectives, the aspirations of staff and pupils and the general discipline of the school
7. To be represented on the appointment panel of teaching staff and during the selection process
8. To be consulted regarding procedures leading towards the dismissal of a member of teaching staff, taking full account of the views of the LEA, while recognizing that the final responsibility is the LEA's.
9. To maintain close involvement in the appointment of non-teaching staff;
10. To oversee the allocation of finance in the school, and in consultation with the headteacher determine priorities within the framework established by the LEA
11. To ensure that the local community served by the school is offered reasonable opportunity to make use of school premises out of school hours (control of premises must, however, remain with the LEA for safety, security and upkeep)
12. To provide the LEA (under its direction) with details of admission procedures for the benefit of parents who, under the Education Act (1980), are entitled to express preferences.

IN A NUTSHELL

Power-sharing is a tradition in central and local government and governing bodies have a key part to play in terms of their involvement in education. While it is possible to produce a list of formal powers and functions of governing bodies, in reality this is far from precise. This is because the rules are written into legal documents which require interpretation as to exact meaning, and governors have to work through consultation with their LEAs and headteachers.

The links between the LEA and their governing bodies have undergone a fundamental change, with the introduction of elected parent and teacher governors which has weakened the hold of LEA representatives. This is likely to lead to more cases of conflict between LEAs and governing bodies in the future.

The formal legal documents relating to governing bodies are the Instrument and Articles of Government and The Education (School Governing Bodies) Regulations 1981 (Statutory Instrument 809).

SELF-TEST

1. What do you understand by the term 'power-sharing'?
2. How does power-sharing affect school decision-making?
3. What is the purpose of the Instrument of Government?
4. What is the purpose of the Articles of Government?
5. Identify six main powers and functions of governing bodies.
6. What two procedures are governing bodies recommended to follow in the White Paper *Better Schools* when fulfilling their responsibilities?

POINTS TO PONDER

1. Identify the ways in which you consider your governing body to be genuinely involved in power-sharing at your school.
2. What limitations are imposed on your governing body by its Articles of Government?
3. 'Everyone is agreed that the Articles of Government are obscure as far as rules go.' How far do you agree with this? Are there any advantages to be gained from this situation?
4. Suggest possible areas of conflict which are likely to arise between LEAs and their governing bodies. What steps might be taken to reduce such a possibility?
5. In a dispute, where does the main priority of a governing body lie?
6. In what circumstances would you anticipate or even expect your LEA to overturn a decision taken by your governing body?

GOVERNOR'S CHECKLIST

1. Does your governing body play an effective power-sharing role at your school?

2. Do you think that the work of your governing body is restricted, e.g. by the LEA, the headteacher or the Articles of Government?
3. Do you have your personal copy of the Instrument and Articles of Government?
4. Does your school attempt to involve the governing body in its day-to-day life?
5. How much discretion does your LEA allow your governing body to make decisions, say, about finance or school buildings and equipment?
6. To what extent does your governing body feel constrained or uncertain about the nature of its powers and functions as presented in the Articles of Government?
7. Does your governing body play an active part in determining and keeping under review the school's aims and objectives?
8. Does your governing body play an active part in determining and keeping under review the school's curriculum?
9. Are there situations at your school in which the extent of governors' powers and functions are questioned?
10. What initiatives does your LEA take to keep governing bodies well informed?

FURTHER READING

Administrative Memorandum (1945), *Model Instrument and Articles of Government*, A/M25/45, HMSO, London.
Instrument and Articles of your school.
The Education (School Governing Bodies) Regulations (1981), Statutory Instrument, No. 809, HMSO, London.

7
FINANCE

THE NATIONAL DIMENSION

The level of financial provision for state education is determined ultimately by the government of the day. The finance of education is of national interest, often featuring in current affairs programmes or stealing the headlines in the national press. The overall amount of central government money to be spent on education is negotiated each year by the Secretary of State for Education and Science and the Treasury. The discussions are set against the background of a general framework of government control over levels of public expenditure.

The Secretary of State for Education is one of several 'high-spending ministers' and must compete for financial resources with the others, e.g. Secretaries of State for Environment, Health and Defence.

THE LOCAL DIMENSION

LEAs also play a key part in making financial provisions for local education. Every authority has to identify its priorities when deciding how much money is needed to maintain services. Each will assess how it is to fulfil its statutory obligations within education and the other services under its control.

The level of financial support an individual school finally receives is determined by the LEA. Consequently, the total amount of money a school is allocated varies from one LEA to another, while the actual allowance placed at the disposal of the headteacher and the governing body is usually quite small. This is due largely to the fact that most of the money allocated to education by both central and local government is spent directly by the LEA on keeping the system going, for example, on staff wages and salaries, the maintenance of school buildings, and heating and lighting bills. Teachers' salaries alone account for between 60 and 70 per cent of the total of an individual school's running costs. All this means is that there is little freedom for headteachers and governors to manouevre when it comes to dealing with the school's finances.

WHERE THE MONEY COMES FROM

It must be recognized that education is but one service provided by local authorities. Each service is financed jointly, but not equally, by both central and local government. The total amount of money involved is considerable. For example, the government's 'planned level of net expenditure by English Local Authorities in 1985/86 is £24.4 billion, of which expenditure on the education service acccounts for some £11.5 billion, i.e. about 47 per cent of the total' (ACC Report, *Education, the Way Ahead*, 1986).

In the main, the education service is financed by: central government grants, especially the Rate Support Grant (RSG) – including the block grant element – and the Education Support Grant (ESG); local authority general rates; borrowing; government agencies, e.g. DES and MSC in support of specific projects; charges for services, e.g. fees, rents and loans; school funds – e.g. PTA activities.

GOVERNMENT GRANTS

The level of central government funding for education cannot be isolated from the general condition of the economy and the other services which both central and local governments have to provide. Therefore, in order to appreciate the way in which the education service is financed, it is necessary to look at *all* the activities of an entire local authority rather than confine discussion to a local *education* authority. Central government, under its public expenditure policy, decides the amount to be paid out to local authorities on an annual basis. The purpose of the money (grants) is to help local authorities provide a typical standard of service, taking account of its general circumstances and responsibilities. The main source of money paid to local authorities to support *all* its services is known as the Rate Support Grant (RSG), i.e. a block grant.

RATE SUPPORT GRANT (RSG)

The intention of the RSG is to make up the deficiency of a local authority's projected spending in the next financial year. The level of deficiency is the estimated difference between the costs of maintaining all services set against the level of income the local authority can realistically anticipate to collect through the local rates and charges. The level of the provision of services is not left to individual local authorities to decide, particularly when central government is anxious to set public spending limits. Consequently, central government formulates a level of provision for each authority in the light of its circumstances, using a mechanism known as grant related expenditure (GRE).

The calculations include the general characteristics of the authority, such as the number of old people, the size of the school population and levels of unemployment. This is an extremely contentious area and often leads to conflict between central and local governments, particularly where the political complexions are at variance.

Setting the level of RSG

Individual local authorities do not receive the same amount of RSG. The reason for this is that they are all different and, therefore, each has different needs. Calculation of the RSG for the individual local authority will be based in part on keeping the existing services going, either at the same level or reduced in some way (rarely increased), and on the basis of what is known as the 'needs' element. This refers to special categories of local authority need in relation to special circumstances, e.g. poor stock of houses, environmental decay and an inadequate level of social services provision.

Among the factors leading to differences between local authorities are the following: overall size – both geographical area covered and population; distribution of the population – e.g. widely spread (as in a predominantly rural area) or closely packed (as in a predominantly urban area); demographic trends – e.g. movement away from or to the area; size of school population, both now and in, say, five years' time; demand for and the quality of housing stock within the authority; industry and its growth or decline within the authority.

The nature and quality of such differences clearly help to underline the reasons for each authority being treated individually. The RSG is intended to provide an 'equalization' mechanism in order to achieve, as far as is practicable, even provision of services across the different authorities.

EDUCATION SUPPORT GRANTS (ESG)

In addition to the RSG element of financial support for education, central government makes available Educational Support Grants (ESGs). These are specific grants and can only be spent on special projects and activities as determined by the DES to 'support specific activities in the interest of Education in England and Wales'. Examples include: the curriculum in rural primary schools; science and technology in primary education; educational needs of those from ethnic minorities; training for school governors; teaching under-fives with special educational needs; action to combat drug abuse. Topics may be repeated from one year to the next or be replaced entirely by new projects.

Bidding for ESG

To obtain ESG money, which unlike the RSG is not automatic, the LEA has to submit a bid to the DES, which means that LEAs compete with each other. The total amount set aside for ESGs is not the same for each project area, and indeed they vary enormously. Announcements are made about the ESG topic areas in the national press, usually in early summer, results being announced in midwinter.

Governors need to watch out for such press announcements, both in relation to ESGs and generally, and where necessary, follow up what might appear to be any prospect of obtaining extra funds for their schools. A member of the education committee will usually have information about such matters.

Other main forms of financial support provided by the DES to LEAs are student grants and in-service education of teachers (INSET) (see p.180).

LOCAL GOVERNMENT RATES

Local authorities collect most of their own money through the general rating system, and although this is a somewhat antiquated system, it does have one enduring quality in that it is relatively easy and cheap to collect.

Rates are often the subject of intense political argument, especially when the local authority wants to spend more than central government wishes. After several conflicts, the government has introduced a number of controls over local authority expenditure, which include the level at which the rates can be set, i.e. 'rate capping', under the Rating Act (1984), aimed at 'high-spending authorities' and capital expenditure controls (see below).

The setting of local authority rates continues to be one of potential conflict between central and local government, particularly where the dominant political ideologies are different. However, the government is in the driving seat. It controls the level of grants to authorities and at the same time imposes ceilings on the amounts authorities are permitted to raise themselves through local rates. Should local councillors decide to spend beyond the limits set, then they face the prospect of being surcharged, i.e. of having to repay the money out of their own pockets.

EXPENDITURE CONTROLS

Having received government grants, local authorities cannot simply spend money on anything they like. There must be a statutory reason for any expenditure incurred, i.e. there must be a specific Act of Parliament which requires them to do so. Central government does, however, have powers to control the overall expenditure of authorities by virtue of the Local Government and Planning Act (1980), which enables central government to penalize those which exceed the expenditure allowance. An auditor is appointed to monitor local authority spending.

Nonetheless, once the local authority has received its grants allocation, and providing that it operates within the parameters set by central government, money can be spent on what the authority thinks fit, with little or no regard for what the allocation might have been intended for in the first place. Local authorities are able to do this by exercising 'virement', i.e. the right to switch spending under designated headings to others. There is ample evidence to show that LEAs make considerable use of their autonomy, e.g. the differences between LEA spending on books and capitation allowances.

Such local freedom is seen as a distinct advantage by local government but as a disadvantage by central government, which is keen to exert more precise control on levels of expenditure. The tensions between them are likely to remain as are the complexities inherent in the central–local funding of education, which, while adding to the confusion, also helps to sustain LEA autonomy.

In any event, to have an effective system of local government, i.e. one which is responsive to the needs of the electorate and works in the best interests of the authority as a whole, is perhaps incompatible with the pressure towards a more uniform service, i.e. one which simply implements policies dictated by central government. Also, there can be no guarantee that central controls will produce more efficient services, since uniform policies can be extremely wasteful when applied to areas and circumstances which are broadly different.

Governor's question: **I heard someone from the DES on the radio saying how much money was being spent on education. In fact he claimed it was an all-time record. Not long after this, I picked up my local newspaper to see the headline 'Council forced to reduce education spending due to government cuts'. I should be grateful, as a newly appointed school governor, if you could explain this apparent contradiction.**

Answer: **This is a difficult one. The main reasons for the differences between the two statements are that they are made by two quite separate and distinct authorities, one from central and the other from local government. However,** actual expenditure on education is not the same as the level of grants provided to be spent on education. From the point of view of central government, there is no doubt that the levels of their contribution to local government spending as a whole have gone up, and they may very well have reached an all-time high in terms of the money, as an element of the Rate Support Grant (RSG), handed to the LEAs.

However, the distribution of the RSG within the individual local authority is a matter for the Finance or Policy Review Committee (different terms are used by different authorities). They take the final decision as to how much each of their spending departments is to receive, including education. Such decisions will be taken in the light of expenditure controls and the amounts received in the form of grants and rates, and local spending on education may have to suffer further cuts as money is used for other services or simply to maintain the existing level of provision.

LOCAL GOVERNMENT ESTIMATES

To fulfil its statutory obligations to provide a range of services, the authority has to raise its own revenue, which is both a complex and time-consuming operation. For much of the year, local government officers collect data to estimate the finance required in order to maintain or enhance the level of services provided, including education.

Each spending committee prepares initial departmental estimates which are subsequently pruned following discussions between the chairman, members, the chief officer and his advisers. A re-submission follows, this eventually being passed on, along with all the other estimates prepared by other spending departments, to the finance committee.

On the basis of the estimates, the local authority can determine the level of general rates for the forthcoming financial year, having predicted the amount of RSG likely to be made available, plus revenue from fees, loans, charges and so on.

FINANCE COMMITTEE

The RSG, once received by the local authority, is distributed by the finance committee to the spending committees, though not necessarily according to the exact estimates made. The entitlement to switch expenditure from one heading to another, i.e. 'virement', is perfectly legal, providing certain rules are observed. Again, this may (in fact, it usually does) require further cuts in departmental budgets, as the finance committee attempts to arrive at an acceptable overall figure, i.e. one which does not increase the rate beyond central government allocations, observes the rules set about spending generally and meets, as far as possible, the spending needs of the authority.

TIMESCALE

While the procedures of local government finance are complex, they do run to a well established timescale, which is largely standard among local authorities. Once the whole process has been completed for one year, it starts again for the following financial year.

LEA governors will be able to advise other governors of when particular finance meetings take place, as well as when the education committees deal with the estimates. Such information is vitally important from the point of view of governors contemplating applying pressure within the LEA on behalf of their schools. A typical LEA calendar of events looks like this: September – annual reports, reviews prepared; October – policy review, including estimates of the likely school rolls for the next school year; November – review of the staffing situation; December – choice between policy options; January – costing policy proposals; February – modification of budget; March – level of general rates set.

WHERE THE MONEY GOES

Part of the problem confronting LEAs is that they are faced with having to maintain a service which already exists in the form of staff, buildings and equipment. Indeed, most of the money for education is spent on keeping the service going rather than on improving it. For example, an authority with, say, 300 primary schools and 48 comprehensive schools, automatically has the accompanying bills for salaries, heating, lighting and other expenses. These constant features are the 'givens' in the situation over which the LEA has little or no control. The age of school buildings, the number of staff employed and the size of the school population are all factors which have to be managed by the LEA.

Examples of where the money goes include: salaries for teaching staff, ancillary staff (e.g. technicians, caretakers, secretaries, cooks), city and county hall administrative staff (e.g. education officers), and specialist support staff (e.g. advisers, inspectors, education welfare officers, librarians, education psychologists); maintenance of buildings; and costs for transport, equipment and textbooks.

HOW IT IS USED

The main elements of education expenditure are as shown in Figure 7.1.

Figure 7.1: Education estimates 1983/84: England and Wales

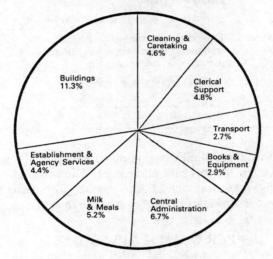

Teachers' salaries represent the remaining 57.4 per cent of the total.

(Source: Chartered Institute of Public Finance and Accountancy)

SCHOOL FINANCE

Schools have very little to spend in terms of ready cash, since the usual arrangement is for all purchases and orders to be paid direct by the education office. This applies also to the school's capitation allowance (see below). The LEA may also determine rules on how the allowance is to be spent, or the parameters within which it is to be used, or even where it has to be spent. A typical example of expenditure in a secondary school is shown in Table 7.1.

CAPITATION

This is the amount of money an LEA decides to spend on each of its pupils on a per capita basis during the financial year. The figure includes all the costs

Figure 7.1: Estimated school expenditure
Meanswell County Secondary School

Source	Purpose	Amount
LEA pays direct	Teachers', clerical and technicians' salaries, including superannuation and insurance	£ 1,029,000
LEA pays direct	Maintenance, including rates, gas, water, electricity, transport	189,000
LEA pays direct	Caretakers, cleaners, cooks, dinner ladies	94,000
Capitation allowance (LEA/school)	Equipment, textbooks and library, stationery, examination fees, printing costs, materials, educational visits	83,000
Non-capitation (LEA/school)	Telephones, postage, miscellaneous	9,000
	Total	£ 1,404,000

concerned in providing an individual pupil education, e.g. teaching and staff costs, maintenance, services and equipment. The amount of capitation in respect of pupils varies from one LEA to another, as indicated in Chapter 3, with the amount for secondary pupils being higher than that for primary pupils.

PER CAPITA ALLOWANCE

This is the amount allowed on a per capita (per head) basis for spending by the school, and is probably the most significant area of involvement for governors in terms of financial aspects. The amount allocated to an individual school depends on the level set by the LEA and then on how many registered pupils are in attendance. This will be an average figure, since the financial year does not neatly fit in with the school year. For example, if the per capita allowance for primary pupils is set by the LEA at £23, and there are 300 pupils in attendance, the total allowance would be £6,900, whereas the per capita allowance for each secondary pupil, set at £38, would realize a total of £57,000 in a school with 1,500 pupils.

SCHOOL ESTIMATES

All schools will have to prepare annual estimates for the next financial year, and these will usually be collated in the autumn, i.e. before the detailed spending plans of the LEA are known.

In the case of a primary school, much of the work involved will fall to the headteacher, who will usually consult with his colleagues about special items of equipment needed. For a secondary school, the procedure will inevitably be more complex, and require each of the heads of departments to submit their own departmental estimates to a deputy head, and ultimately to the headteacher, in order to arrive at a total figure for the school.

It should be possible for the headteacher to provide information regarding the school's finances for the next school year towards the end of May or early in June, since the LEA's capitation figures will have been published by then, plus the school's per capita allowance. It is also likely that a fairly reliable prediction can be made about the number of registered pupils who will be in attendance during the next school year.

Once the calculations have been made, the extent of any deficit between the estimates made and the actual amount to be made available to the school should be clear. It is at this point where the school's fund-raising activities assume importance.

CONSUMABLES AND CAPITAL EQUIPMENT

Capitation operates under two main headings – spending on consumables and spending on capital equipment, with a ceiling set by the LEA. These general headings are then broken down into coded subheadings in order to impose fairly detailed control of expenditure.

The LEA usually sets the framework within which money is to be spent, e.g. the percentage to be spent on consumables such as textbooks, stationery and all kinds of other materials, and a percentage to be spent on capital equipment items, e.g. a television set, a video or a computer. Major capital equipment items will be subject to central government spending limits, e.g. the purchase of land, buildings or heavy plant. LEAs, although setting down their headings. permit schools to exercise virement, i.e. they allow a certain amount of switching between headings. For example, if the school has a shortage of textbooks it may be allowed to use money allocated for furniture for this purpose.

The LEA may also determine *where* the money is to be spent, since it may have a contract with a purchasing agency such as a warehouse from which bulk purchases may be made on preferential terms negotiated by the LEA.

SCHOOL FUNDS

Most schools have their own private funds raised by the voluntary activities of interested and supportive groups such as the PTA or its equivalent. Fund-raising can be a very worthwhile activity and of enormous benefit to the individual school. However, privately raised funds, i.e. those outside the control of the LEA, should be used ideally to enhance the quality of provision of education rather than, as is increasingly becoming the case, to provide for the basic essentials.

After all, compulsory education is supposed to be provided free of charge; neither parents nor anyone else should be required to buy textbooks and materials. Surveys taken in recent years by the National Confederation of Parent–Teachers and by HMI have commented on the decline in expenditure by LEAs on such needs and hence the increasing reliance on outside support. Unfortunately, parental capacity to contribute varies tremendously from one area to another, with the effect that prosperous schools become even more prosperous while poorer schools become that much the poorer.

Fund-raising

Whatever the arguments for and against fund-raising, there is no doubt that it can greatly enhance the quality of many schools and their activities. It is also a distinct way in which many parents feel that they can contribute and become involved in the life of the school. Fund-raising initiatives do not belong to any particular group, but it is usually the PTA or the governing body which helps to get things started.

Funds are likely to come into the school from a variety of sources, including: voluntary and modest contributions from pupils; fund-raising activities by 'friends of the school', e.g. the PTA; school events (concerts, sports days); school trips (holidays, field studies, visits); school club fees; and a savings club.

However much comes into the 'school fund account', the headteacher and the governors should ensure that an independent annual audit of the accounts is made available for inspection each year. This makes it clear to all interested parties exactly where the money has been spent and helps build up the confidence of all concerned. Indeed, some Articles of Government make this a responsibility of the governing body.

Governor's question: **The textbooks, what few of them there are, at our primary school are a disgrace. Not only are there not enougth to go around, but they are dreadfully out of date and falling to bits. The headteacher and the teachers are very worried about the situation but quite simply do not have enough money to remedy things. The school is situated in an inner city area and there is little parental interest and support. The governors are very anxious to improve matters but need some suggestions on how to go about this effectively and achieve positive results.**

Answer: You raise an important issue. If things are as bad as you say, then the LEA is clearly in danger of failing to fulfil its statutory duties under the Education Act (1944), section 8(b), which states that 'it shall be the duty of every local education authority to secure ... for their area sufficient schools ... in number, character and equipment to afford all pupils opportunities for education'. Refer this kind of situation, initially perhaps, to the clerk to the governors with the intention of reporting to the Chief Education Officer and subsequently to the education subcommittee.

It is a good idea to collect evidence to support your case. List the books in question. Show how many there are as compared with the number of pupils, their condition (perhaps obtain some samples to emphasize this point) and when they were published. If nothing is done, the chairman of the governing body could try contacting a member of the education committee to exert influence on behalf of the school. If all else fails, suggest that the local press might be interested in running a feature on the item, complete with appropriate photographs.

HEADTEACHERS AND FINANCE

The headteacher determines a policy for spending the capitation allowance, following consultation with staff. Nonetheless, he must work within the rules for spending set down by the LEA, since it is ultimately responsible for the finance of the school, although it delegates the actual function to the headteacher and the governors.

Once he has received the school's allowance, the headteacher has to decide how to distribute it, especially in the case of a large school which will be made up of different departments with different spending needs. The headteacher will need to consider whether to give each department the same, or whether to provide more for some than others.

Care needs to be taken by governors not to come into conflict with the headteacher when helping to shape financial policies. Day-to-day management of the school remains the headteacher's responsibility. The idea of partnership should be fostered; the governors, having listened to advice and expressed their opinions, should then delegate school financial matters to the headteacher.

THE ROLE OF THE GOVERNORS

The headteacher has a duty to keep the governors informed about his spending plans. However, it is open to the governors to make suggestions. The involvement by governors in decision-making relating to the resource allocation in their schools provides an opportunity to express an independent view, which is an essential part of the consultative process between the governors and the headteacher.

The Articles of Government refer to the powers of governing bodies in relation to finance and this is the statutory basis for their involvement. For example, some Articles make provision for governors to provide estimates of the school's running costs for the next financial year (in reality, this would mean the headteacher and his staff); others invite governing bodies to make proposals for expenditure they would like to see incurred on behalf of the school. These special requests should be made at the appropriate time of the year (see 'Timescale', p. 102), i.e. before estimates are finalized.

GOVERNORS AS A PRESSURE GROUP

Governing bodies are sometimes required to exert pressure to secure more adequate resources on behalf of their schools. Many schools experience the same problem, i.e. shortage of money, which in turn brings about a shortage of resources, sometimes of serious proportions. Indeed, without parental support in terms of fund-raising activities, many schools would be facing extreme difficulties in providing an adequately resourced school. Failure by the school to renew outdated textbooks, to provide sufficient work materials or to become involved in curriculum development in response to rapid change is to fail to provide an adequate level of education.

One way in which governors can bring about influence to improve the level of financial provision for their schools is to operate as a pressure group. This is not to advocate a policy of agitation, but rather to underline the importance of being fully aware of the rules and procedures of local government committees and access to information.

Members of governing bodies have a much better chance of exerting influence where it matters if they know where and when to apply pressure. This in turn requires an appreciation of the way in which the system of education finance works – nationally, locally and within the individual school.

LOBBYING THE LEA

The message from the diary of events (see p. 102) is clear enough. Governors need to act between September and January before the estimates are finalized if they are to influence the policy-makers on the education committee on behalf of their school. The procedures adopted by individual authorities, though different in detail from each other, will be very much the same from one year to the next.

It should be fairly easy to obtain a list of all the relevant committee dates which will help decide when and where pressure should be exerted. A most effective way of lobbying is by direct contact with local councillors serving on the main education committee. The education enquiries office will provide the names of councillors who are members of this committee. Alternatively, the LEA representatives on the governing body can often help bring to the attention of local education committee members issues of importance about which they would otherwise remain unaware.

A further strategy is to enlist the support of other interested parties such as the teachers and the PTA, and combine to exert pressure on council members. In order to mount any sort of pressure of this kind, it is necessary to be in full possession of the necessary facts and to have these written down, preferably in the form of a report (see p. 227) for distribution to those concerned.

Voluntary schools

There are special responsibilities for governors of voluntary schools. In the main these concern general aspects of the school buildings and premises. Governors should make a point of establishing the precise nature of their liabilities as distinct from any which belong to the LEA. Specific attention should be given to the maintenance of properly audited accounts.

IN A NUTSHELL

The system of education finance in complex. Central government provides around 50 per cent of the money needed to finance state education, the rest being found by the LEAs through the rating system and other sources of income. Despite the imposition of controls by central government aimed at controlling high-spending authorities, the LEAs are still able to exercise some freedom on how they choose to spend their money.

This freedom extends to the levels at which LEAs set their capitation figures in respect of their schools. This ultimately determines the allowance given to the individual school and which the headteacher, after consultation with colleagues and the approval of his governing body, is able to spend.

The role governors can play is an important one, even though their involvement is somewhat limited. Perhaps their most important roles in respect of finance centre on overseeing how the resources are used, and whether this is to good effect, and to promote a case to the LEA for increases in the allocation to the school in the future.

SELF-TEST

1. Where does the money for education come from?
2. What kinds of controls are used by central government over levels of education spending?
3. What is the Education Support Grant?
4. What do you understand by the term 'per capita allowance'?
5. What is meant by the term 'virement', and how might it be applied by an LEA or a school?
6. What can governors do with direct reference to the finance of their school?

POINTS TO PONDER

1. How does the autonomy of your LEA in respect on education spending affect your school?
2. Does your LEA encourage governors to participate effectively in decisions taken at school level with reference to its finance? Do your Articles of Government strengthen the role of the governing body in this respect?
3. What action would you advise in cases where your school is seriously underfunded? What kinds of pressures might be exerted on the finance and education committees?
4. Are you aware of additional or alternative sources of funding which might be available for your school, e.g. ESGs, money from the MSC or EEC? Has your LEA investigated such possibilities?
5. Suppose a gap emerges between the level of expenditure included in the school's estimates and the actual capitation figure eventually given. What alternative courses of action are available to governors to rectify the situation, and which of these is likely to prove beneficial for your school?
6. What overall factors should determine the spending priorities at your school, e.g. between the relative merits of the spending needs of the art department as against those of the science department? How should these be decided and who should be involved?

GOVERNOR'S CHECKLIST

1. Is your LEA a high-spending authority?

2. Is the level of capitation used by your LEA adequate?
3. Does your school have a finance committee? If so, who are the members, how frequently does it meet and does it publish its proceedings?
4. Are governors in at the 'draft estimates' stage?
5. Are the spending plans related to the overall aims and objectives of the school?
6. Is the topic of school finance often or seldom discussed by the governing body?
7. Are members of the governing body aware of the calendar of events used by the local authority finance and education committees?
8. What lobbying techniques might be used to improve the level of your school's resources?
9. What system is used to assess whether school spending has been efficient and brought about improvements?
10. To what extent do your school's finances depend on parental support?
11. What procedures are used to monitor deficiencies in school spending levels?

FURTHER READING

Atkinson, G. B. J. (1983) *The Economics of Education*, Hodder & Stoughton, London.
Audit Commission (1986) *Towards Better Management of Secondary Education*, Department of the Environment, HMSO, London.
Educational Publishers' Council (various dates) *Schoolbook Spending (Series 2)*; and *Guide to Schoolbook Spending*, Educational Publishers' Council, London.
Hough, J. R. (1981) *A Study of School Costs*, NFER, Windsor.

# 8
SCHOOL PREMISES

First impressions can be lasting. How pleasant it is to go into a bright, welcoming, well-cared-for school with a business-like atmosphere, plenty of signs of activity and evidence of children's work and achievements displayed proudly on the walls and in display cabinets. Contrast this with entering a dull, dingy, neglected school with little or no sign of vitality, displaying hopelessness and despair at virtually every turn. Irrespective of how adept teachers might be at camouflaging deficiencies within a school, serious shortages of money will ultimately take their toll.

Many financial decisions taken about schools are concerned directly with buildings and equipment. Major building projects are tackled by the LEA and do not come out of school resources. On the other hand, minor items will usually fall within the responsibility of the individual school. The amount of money the headteacher receives from the LEA to spend on maintenance and the purchase of equipment is likely to be limited, and consequently there will be a need for him and the governors to determine the order of priorities.

Governors have a responsibility under their Articles and Instruments to keep their school premises under review. The *Model Articles of Government* state that 'the governors shall from time to time inspect, and keep the local education authority informed as to, the condition and state of repair of the school premises....'

However, governors should look at their own Articles which will provide an indication of their duties and responsibilities in this respect. Articles might well make reference to inspecting the use of buildings, reviewing equipment, furniture and appliances, and giving attention to aspects such as heating, lighting, ventilation, health and safety. In fact, responsibility could include anything to do with the management of premises and facilities and their general state of maintenance and repair. However, ultimate responsibility for the maintenance and use of school premises rests with the LEA.

ACCOMMODATION SUBCOMMITTEE

It is usual for a governing body to set up an accommodation subcommittee (or something similar) to undertake the duties involved. Where possible governors with particular expertise and interest, such as architects, builders, surveyors and cratfsmen, should be encouraged to serve on this subcommittee.

There are several distinct areas which are likely to be of direct concern to governors in relation to the condition and use of school premises: location; grounds and immediate environment; buildings; specialist accommodation; facilities; furniture, fixtures and fittings; equipment; heating, lighting and ventilation; safety; security; vandalism; open access; and community use.

LOCATION

Schools of all kinds are located in different and often starkly contrasting areas. The precise location of a school, particularly a primary one, is a major determinant of its pupils since proximity to home will be a prime consideration for parents of young children. Where a school is located has repercussions in all manner of ways, not least of which will be the condition and use of its premises.

For instance, a school situated adjacent to a busy roundabout and next to a factory manufacturing heavy industrial machinery will experience related problems such as noise, pollution, road safety, pupil access to local shops and transfer to playing fields. On the other hand, a school in a residential area within a leafy suburb will encounter fewer problems in relation to its location.

Location will have particular effects on the nature of maintenance problems and how frequently these occur. For instance, a busy city centre location will tend to produce more demands for external cleaning and paintwork, soundproofing, double glazing and enhanced security.

GROUNDS AND ENVIRONMENT

Dependent on location, schools may have either substantial grounds including playing fields or they may have no grounds at all, being accessed directly from the pavement in a town centre. Generally, the age of the school will be the determining factor; most post-war schools will tend to be set in their own grounds with playing fields and other facilities attached.

Schools having the advantage of a pleasant environment with their own playing fields have the added responsibility and expense of keeping these in good order; those without facilities incur the inconvenience, and sometimes expense, of having to transport groups of pupils to and from playing fields or other facilities elsewhere.

BUILDINGS

When reviewing actual buildings, several factors need to be taken into consideration. These will include: age; type, e.g. single building, split-site accommodation, clusters of building, single storey, several floors annex accommodation (Portacabins); fabric, i.e. traditional (e.g. brick or stone) or modern (e.g. pre-fabricated); state of repair (e.g. broken windows, leaking gutters, cracked walls); external decoration (e.g. flaking paint, dirty windows); internal decoration (e.g. drab, dirty paintwork, graffiti); layout (e.g. corridor classrooms, central hall or quadrangle, open or semi-open plan); space allocation; number of classrooms; size of classrooms; thickness of dividing walls; soundproofing; acoustics; insulation; condition of staircases; firedoors and emergency exits; and wiring.

The general state of buildings is an area which receives much attention and concern, not only from teachers and parents who are directly involved, but from official sources such as HMI reports and interested national agencies such as the National Confederation of Parent–Teachers Associations (NCPTA).

The following extract is based on selected quotes received in response to a questionnaire used as part of a survey and produced in the form of a report published by the NCPTA:

On deteriorating fabric:
'No one can remember when the school was decorated internally';
'Headteacher often paints walls to keep standards high';
'Windows are poor, plaster is poor, constant roof leaks. Condensation. Last painted internally/externally in 1843 (or so it seems)';
'Diabolical indoor toilets. In wet weather we need wellies to get into the toilets dry-footed';
'County Hall will supply paint for do-it-yourself decoration';
'Substandard wiring, leaking roofs, rotten window frames, peeling internal plaster, cracked and broken external rendering. School not re-decorated for very many years';

'Painting? What's painting';
'Recent re-wiring – if the school hadn't been so damp, you'd have had a fire!';
'Windows haven't been cleaned for six or seven years';
'The fabric of the building is in very poor condition with leaks, rising floors, crumbling plaster and inadequate heating'.
(*The State of Schools in England and Wales, Crumbling Schools – Fact or Fiction? Parental Funding – How much and for what?* NCPTA, October 1985)

To many people's surprise, despite the high level of public expenditure on state education, many children's first taste of school will be in a building constructed in the nineteenth century, with all its associated disadvantages (expensive to heat and maintain, often badly laid out, with perhaps one classroom leading off another, and virtually no staffroom accommodation).

LIAISON WITH THE HEADTEACHER

An accommodation subcommittee will need to work closely with the headteacher on matters affecting the condition of school grounds and buildings. The precise course of action they will need to take will depend on the urgency and nature of the problem.

Such issues are likely to be the subject of governors' reports which will be submitted to the education office for action. If this is not forthcoming, governors should submit further reports and, in addition perhaps, contact members of the education committee. This may indeed be a matter for the chairman of governors to pursue.

PREVENTION RATHER THAN CURE

Governors should not simply wait for problems to arise. Responding to a problem is all very well but it will be preferable to be alert to likely future difficulties and deficiencies before they occur so that requests can be lodged and bids drawn up well in advance, and certainly before matters reach crisis proportions.

SPECIALIST ACCOMMODATION

Virtually all school accommodation could be termed 'specialist' as the curriculum in both primary and secondary schools becomes increasingly diverse with the introduction of many new subject areas. In some respects the extent of accommodation determines the curriculum in that some things simply cannot operate without specialist facilities. However, this can be overstated and a balanced view needs to be taken, as illustrated by the following quote from a headteacher when considering the accommodation at his school:

> As one of the major resources available to the school, accommodation has to be given serious consideration when planning the curriculum. It is difficult to determine whether the buildings dictate the curriculum or vice versa. Besides, there is greater flexibility in staff than buildings.

Illustrations of the complexities of secondary school buildings, many of which operate on split sites and on several floors, are shown in Figures 8.1 and 8.2. A glance at the key plan shows just what small elements of the overall building two aspects (languages and mathematics) of the curriculum absorb in terms of accommodation, yet they both require specialist facilities. Also, the subject areas illustrated do not demand the highest quota of specialist provision when compared, for example, with science and technology subjects.

The range of typical specialist accommodation called for in schools will include: art rooms; computer centres; cookery rooms; craft rooms; demonstration areas; gymnasiums; language laboratories; libraries; music rooms; science laboratories; sports halls; and workshops.

Effective teaching of certain subjects is dependent, therefore, on access to specialist accommodation. Such areas also require separate consideration and treatment in that they may need special wiring, special layouts, strengthened floors, tiered seating arrangements, soundproofing, ventilation and humidity controls, acoustic properties, enhanced safety standards and the inclusion of special items such as kilns, climbing chimneys, carrels and projection cubicles.

For example, it would be unreasonable to locate a music room amidst normal classrooms unless proper attention was given to soundproofing and acoustics. Similarly, it would be inadvisable to locate expensive computer technology in a room which was unfit for the purpose.

GENERAL FACILITIES

The condition and adequacy of general facilities within a school will be determined largely by its age and whether or not it is purpose-built. Ideal school facilities should include: reception/enquiries; headteacher's room; meetings room; school secretary's office; general office; assembly hall with stage; caretaker(s) or janitor(s) room(s); staff common rooms and quiet rooms; senior pupils' common rooms and quiet rooms; staff toilets and washrooms; pupils'

School Premises 117

Figure 8.1: Secondary school accommodation – languages (second floor)

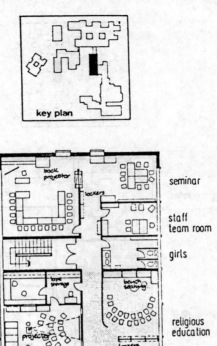

(Source: Design Note 6, DES Architects and Building Branch)

Figure 8.2: Secondary school accommodation – mathematics (third floor)

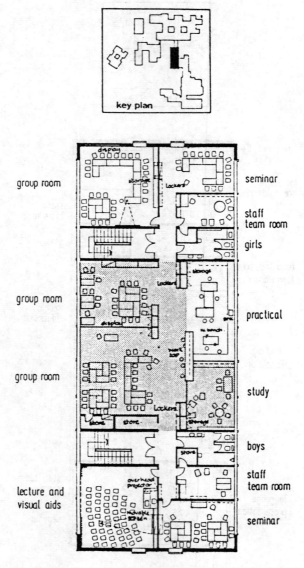

(Source: Design Note 6, DES Architects and Building Branch)

toilets and washrooms; cloakrooms and locker provision; changing rooms; shower facilities; medical rooms; sick room; rest room; dining hall; kitchens; family/community rooms; cleaners' room; technicians' room; storage rooms; flammable liquids and solvents store; boiler room; and public telephones. Additionally, all schools should provide facilities for the disabled, e.g. ramps and special toilets.

What constitutes essential facilities within a school will vary. Governors may use the list above as a basis for checking the range, condition and appropriateness of the facilities provided by their particular school, and note any shortcomings with a view to promoting action as necessary. There may even be scope for governors to recommend a change of use in respect of certain facilities. For example, where falling rolls have led to spare capacity in terms of classrooms, governors could suggest their conversion to extra library accommodation, quiet rooms or staffrooms. Such recommendations would commit relatively few resources and require little in terms of funding, but could greatly enhance the facilities of the school.

Governor's question: **Recently, a former member of the governing body of my school died and left a substantial bequest in her will for the improvement of accommodation and facilities within the school. I am a member of the working party formed to look into needs and recommend how the money might be spent. The school is badly equipped all round, so how do we prioritize?**
Answer: **Your school sounds to be in a fortunate position thanks to this bequest, although you do not indicate the precise figure. However, irrespective of the amount, it will make sense to ensure that you consult as many people as possible before reaching a decision. For example, you might approach the headteacher to conduct a survey among the staff in order to gather their views and suggestions. Also, dependent on current curriculum development within the school, there may be an area of special shortage. If the sum is a large one, it may be worthwhile investigating the particular interests of your benefactor. You may be able to harness these within your final project, which could be anything from a new resource centre of some kind to an improved section of the library. Where there is any suggestion which directly involves the refurbishing or extension of existing buildings, the LEA should be consulted since they may be in a position to make a contribution.**

FURNITURE, FIXTURES AND FITTINGS

This term is relatively self-explanatory, but in addition to essential items such as desks, chairs and storage cupboards, it would also include things like blackboards, whiteboards, noticeboards, wall planners, display cabinets, trolleys for moving equipment, blinds and blackout curtains. These items have a limited life-span and should not be viewed as once-and-for-all expenditure. Therefore, their condition needs to be reviewed continually and their replacement budgeted for accordingly.

EQUIPMENT

As an extension of furniture and fittings, schools will need to acquire items of equipment to support curriculum content, afford pupils the opportunity of essential 'hands on' experience and provide alternative teaching strategies and techniques.

The acquisition of equipment is a major resource problem for many schools simply because they find it difficult to fund the purchase of what are often very expensive items. This can lead to considerable reliance on parental support through fund-raising activities in order to purchase the kind of equipment needed. Thus a school in a poor neighbourhood is likely to experience greater difficulty in obtaining up-to-date equipment than one located in a middle-class area. What schools have in the way of specialist equipment varies markedly from one school to another. Whether a school is in the primary or secondary sector and the nature and scope of its curriculum will also have a bearing on the equipment it requires. However well equipped, schools are likely to require access to the following types of equipment: colour televisions; video recorders; video cameras; microcomputers; tape and cassette recorders; slide projectors; film projectors; typewriters; duplicating and photocopying machines; calculators; science equipment; workshop equipment (e.g. lathes, tools); domestic science equipment (e.g. cookers, fridges, washing machines, food mixers, sewing machines, irons); musical instruments; sports equipment; microfiche readers; and overhead projectors.

It is also important to note that many of these items require the support of a range of software and consumables, without which the equipment is rendered useless. Lack of sufficient materials is a problem which faces many schools.

HEATING, LIGHTING AND VENTILATION

The DES has made recommendations in respect of temperatures in schools in Statutory Instrument 909 (1981), which stipulates desirable temperatures in all areas of school activity (e.g. temperatures in classrooms should be 18°C where there is an average level of clothing and activity). It is interesting to note that this is slightly higher than the minimum temperature (16°C) deemed reasonable after the first hour of work in the Offices, Shops and Railway Premises Act 1963, which is still the only piece of general legislation which actually prescribes minimum accepted heating standards for workers generally. While this Act does not, however, stipulate a maximum temperature, the DES document does make a recommendation in respect of schools, and this is 27°C. Recommendations are all very well, but enforcing standards is a very different matter.

In terms of lighting, the School Buildings Regulations (1981) require that schools should comply with DES Design Note 17. Here the stipulation is that the main source of light should be daylight but that the lowest level of illumination on working surfaces should be at least 150 lux. Lighting requirements depend on many factors, ranging from the location and positioning of buildings and rooms within them, to the type of building, its layout, the number and size of its windows and the type of work being carried out. Lighting charges can be surprisingly high in many schools, even where the lighting use may be relatively modest, in that they do not benefit from off-peak tariffs.

Schools are also required to ensure that adequate ventilation is provided and maintained, and that there is a good circulation of fresh air.

SAFETY

Many of the concerns expressed by parents, teachers and governors over the condition of school premises and facilities relate to aspects of health and safety. Under the Health and Safety at Work, etc Act 1974, all people in the workplace, both employers and employees, have a duty to ensure, 'as far as is reasonably practicable', the health and safety of themselves and others in the workplace.

This piece of legislation is what is termed an 'enabling Act' in that it confers powers on organizations to produce regulations which must be implemented in the interests of health and safety. The Act itself, therefore, deals with generalities which need to be interpreted by different bodies according to their own needs and circumstances. However, where properly formulated they will carry the force of the law. The Act became law on 1 April 1985, and LEAs or governing bodies, as employers, will have prepared a statement of safety policy in respect of health and safety at work. This is likely to be a short statement of general intent and it will be issued to all employees, usually for insertion in some form of staff handbook.

Additionally, a specific statement of intent will be prepared by individual schools and these will be further broken down into Codes of Safe Working Practice, as appropriate. Such codes will be likely to make reference to: the school's organization structure in terms of responsibilities for safety (see Figure 8.3); the duties and responsibilities of key staff (see below); the duties of the safety officer, where applicable (see below); the duties of the safety committee, where there is one (see below); the appointment of safety representatives; the duties and responsibilities of staff and pupils generally; emergency procedures, e.g. lighting failure, gas leaks, explosions, bomb hoaxes; fire prevention and control; evacuation and fire drill procedures; accident procedures, including reporting mechanisms and location and completion of accident book; first aid, including location of first aid boxes and identification of qualified first aiders; general safety matters; identification of restricted areas, i.e. those which cannot be used in the absence of a member of staff; electrical safety aspects; the use of hazardous materials, machinery and equipment; supervision in science laboratories and other workshops; safety in physical education; safe layouts of workplaces; cleanliness and tidiness; hygiene; clothing.

DUTIES AND RESPONSIBILITIES OF THE HEADTEACHER

The duties and responsibilites of the headteacher in respect of health and safety in the school are likely to be along the following lines: to have overall responsibility for health, safety and welfare; to promote liaison with the LEA, other schools, the DES, HMI and local community safety experts and groups; to notify the LEA of any safety hazards or any requirements in the interests of health and safety; to activate initiatives to alleviate environmental hazards and dangers; to approve the cessation or modification of unsafe operations or equipment as deemed necessary; to ensure the adequate communication of safety information and instruction throughout the school; to include safety as an item in the headteacher's report to the governing body; to initiate school safety training programmes.

DUTIES AND RESPONSIBILITIES OF THE DEPUTY HEAD

These duties and responsibilities will vary from one school to another but could include the following: to act as chairman of the school safety subcommittee; to oversee the safety budget and authorize expenditure; to set up accident investigations, as necessary; to ensure staff training programmes are carried out; to organize and supervise emergency evacuation and fire drill procedures; to ensure that safety rules are published in the school prospectus; to arrange the

Figure 8.3: Secondary school safety organization and structure

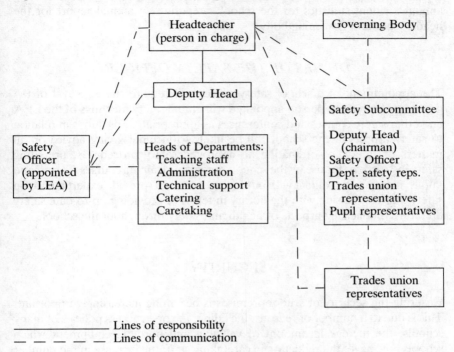

preparation of school safety reports for submission by the headteacher to the governing body.

DUTIES OF THE SAFETY SUBCOMMITTEE

Where a school has a safety subcommittee (see Figure 8.3), it will have specific terms of reference outlining its duties in terms of its work in the interests of health and safety in the school. These are likely to include: meeting at least once a term; recommending approved safety procedures throughout the school; considering new safety measures and advising the headteacher and governing body accordingly; disseminating health and safety information to staff and pupils; promoting the integration of health and safety matters within aspects of the school curriculum; considering reports of visits to the school by specialist safety officers, e.g. representatives of the Health and Safety Inspectorate, representatives of the fire service, and passing on information to the headteacher and governing body; keeping a register of any accidents and reviewing annual accident statistics for the school; preparing an annual report for the headteacher and governing body.

DUTIES OF THE SAFETY OFFICER

The appointment of a school safety officer will require the approval of the governing body. The person appointed will attend safety meetings of the LEA and other safety courses and conferences as appropriate. His duties in relation to safety aspects at the school will be likely to include: giving advice on all matters of safety; co-ordinating all approved safety procedures; preparing safety instructions for use by the school; organizing training courses for staff and pupils; maintaining contact with outside agencies who provide expert advice on safety matters; liaising with the library in terms of providing up-to-date safety literature; publicizing aspects of health and safety throughout the school.

SECURITY

Ensuring the security of school premises is becoming increasingly important. This is due to a number of reasons, including: the open access policies of many schools; the increasing amount of valuable and portable equipment which schools now have; the reduction in caretaking staff; the increase in the number of break-ins and attempted break-ins; the threat of vandalism; the legal need to safeguard personal information held, particularly on disk, about staff and pupils; increased insurance premiums.

The location and type of premises will greatly influence the extent to which security is a problem, isolated low-rise buildings being decidedly more vulnerable. Where security is a major issue, steps need to be taken by the school to minimize risk. Ideally, this should involve 'designing out' problems at the building or alteration stages, e.g. avoiding potential 'hiding places'. Other basic precautions will be to ensure that valuables are locked away and that access to keys is restricted. Staff will also be encouraged to be extra vigilant and to report anything of a suspicious nature to the headteacher.

Governors might suggest measures such as the installation of alarm systems, although consideration has to be given here to the need to name a contact in the event of the alarm going off. Another possibility is the organization of some form of voluntary patrol by parents, perhaps as an extension of a neighbourhood watch scheme. However, any such steps should be entered into with some caution and only after due consultation with the headteacher, the LEA and the police.

VANDALISM

The extent to which there is a need to combat vandalism depends on how serious it is, how sporadic and how systematic. Whatever steps are taken are likely to involve a wide range of services and individuals both in terms of general prevention and possible follow-up action. Several questions need to be asked when contemplating how vandalism might best be tackled.

At the level of the school, although the scope for action may be somewhat limited, the headteacher, his colleagues and the governing body can do much to positively influence the overall attitudes of pupils towards vandalism. There will, of course, be differences in perceptions between what is acceptable to young people compared with adults, just as there are different codes and standards of behaviour.

A school with a generally run-down appearance can degenerate even further. Schools, as public buildings, tend to produce negative attitudes among people which might be summed up as, 'The school doesn't belong to anyone and so it doesn't matter what happens to it'. Anonymity of buildings is an open invitation to vandals since not only does it appear 'not to matter' but 'no one really cares anyway'. Also, the chances of culprits being caught are somewhat remote.

Therefore, part of a positive response to reduce vandalism is to ensure that it is made apparent that school premises do belong to someone and that it does matter about their condition. Prompt repairs are also essential to add weight to this fact. Vandalism might be discouraged if the governors and the headteacher report cases in the school magazine or newsletter to create a general awareness among pupils and their parents about the costs involved in repairs.

If the culprits are caught they can be made to repair the damage themselves if this is feasible, although the most significant deterrent is to ask the parents to come to school, view the damage and discuss the problem.

In any event, the school should develop some sort of systematic strategy in order to minimize the likelihood of vandalism and this might include: formulation of a policy designed to encourage a positive attitude among pupils towards the general upkeep of the school premises; the involvement of parents and the community in the life of the school by opening up the buildings outside school hours; taking steps to keep the school in good repair; making sure that the locks, fences and other 'defences' are tough enough to discourage would-be invaders; introduction of regular patrols of buildings; installation of additional security lighting, alarms and detection systems; deciding the action to be taken against offenders when caught, e.g. whether to inform parents, the police or both.

OPEN ACCESS

While an open access policy can present problems in terms of security, it can bring an added dimension to the life of the school by bringing the accommodation and facilities to the attention of a wider range of people than would otherwise be possible. This can be a two-edged sword in that as well as promoting the modern, well-equipped school it can bring to public attention Dickensian conditions and poorly equipped ones.

Where a school has an 'open all hours' policy, deficiencies in provision will be much more likely to be observed and brought to the notice of those who are in a position to take some positive action.

FALLING ROLLS

With the prospect of falling school rolls continuing towards the end of this century, opportunities for the alternative use of school premises are potentially exciting and challenging.

Forecasts indicate that the overall school population is likely to fall from a peak of just under nine million in 1979 to around seven and a half million by 1990. Secondary schools in particular face a substantial decline in pupil population, from around four million in 1980 to somewhere in the order of two and three-quarter million by 1990.

Against this background, a number of questions might be asked about school closures and the alternative use of school premises, made possible by the spare capacity produced by falling rolls. Account must be taken, and certainly will be by the LEA, of the fact that inefficient use of space is an expensive business, since costs still have to be met in terms of rates, heating, lighting, general upkeep, maintenance and cleaning. In certain circumstances, e.g. where buildings are especially poor and beyond rescue, falling rolls present a golden opportunity to close them down altogether. However, different opportunities present themselves where this does not apply.

OPEN ALL HOURS

Perhaps the most dramatic use that can be made of school premises is to open them up for community use. After all, a school is one of the most valuable resources in any area and for it to remain closed for long periods tends to be somewhat wasteful. A number of LEAs actively encourage greater use of school premises by parents and members of the local community.

New schools are increasingly designed to incorporate community use (see Figure 8.4). This often involves members of the community representing different interest groups, e.g. societies, clubs and associations, in the design stage and possibly in partial funding. There is also some scope for integrating an existing school more fully with its local community. Ideally, it is preferable if a designated area can be put at the disposal of the community, thus protecting some of the essential day-to-day facilities of the school itself. Figure 8.4 shows how a junior school might provide a considerable area of space for shared use by the community, mainly after school hours and during the holiday periods. Some school community centres, instead of working to the usual school year, are open for seven days a week and for almost fifty-two weeks in the year. In short, the school becomes a local amenity, a family and community resource centre with all kinds of benefits being brought into the school.

In terms of financial benefit, any rent received for hiring purposes may be paid direct into the school fund. If warranted, part of the funds received could be used to appoint a part-time manager to help run the scheme, e.g. to take bookings, ensure that facilities are available when required and locked away safely when not in use. Alternatively, payment may be made in kind, e.g. by one of the user groups providing new stereo equipment, video or television.

If demand is sufficient, there may be a need to consider ways of improving facilities, perhaps by extending the school or by improving the quality of furnishings. Any scheme of this nature will need to be led by a committee of interested parties, including representatives of the governing body. The committee would draw up the rules and oversee the project. They would need to reach agreement with the LEA regarding the costs and how these are to be shared. Also, the LEA would continue to have overall responsibility for safety and caretaking facilities. Examples of the kinds of community activities which can take place at a community school include: nursery school/playgroup/crêche; adult education courses; private functions (e.g. fashion shows, wine tasting, bingo, parties, discos, social evenings of various kinds); concerts by different groups; sports activities by groups or individuals; PTA meetings and similar; lettings to a wide variety of groups and societies; exhibitions.

ALTERNATIVE USE OF SPACE

There are a number of possibilities worth considering in the event of falling rolls in terms of alternative use being made of any space available. For example,

128   A Guide to Governing Schools

Figure 8.4: Community use of a junior school

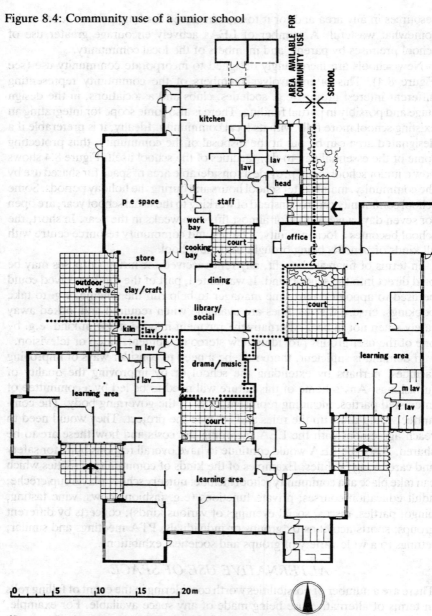

(Source: Design Note 6, DES Architects and Building Branch)

empty classrooms could be converted into staffrooms thereby improving the working conditions of teachers, or used to provide additional library facilities. Any spare capacity might lend itself to use by parents and teachers as informal meeting areas.

Sometimes, an opportunity might present itself where the interests of the staff can be harnessed directly to those of members of the local community. An example of a project which would improve facilities for staff, while making it available from time to time for community use, is shown in Figure 8.5 and described by the DES Architects and Building Group:

> The school staffroom has been converted by community funding to providing a lounge for use by staff, parents and other members of the community. The lounge area is comfortably furnished with easy chairs, low tables and a dartboard and bar billiards table. While staff noticeboards still occupy one wall of the lounge, the provision of curtains over these boards gives the opportunity to remove staff notices from public view quickly and easily.
>
> The old staff locker area has been converted to adjacent storage facilities. The coffee bar is available to staff and community during the day, while the lounge and licensed bar are used extensively in the evenings for parents, community and staff meetings, private parties and social gatherings of adult education students. On some other evenings the bar is open for casual visitors and the lounge then develops the atmosphere of a local social club.
>
> (DES Architects and Buildings Broadsheet No. 19, 1984)

The staff originally had their own individual staffroom accommodation based on their departments spread across the school. Such arrangements often lead to isolation between individual teachers, which is a common problem in a large secondary school. An ideal solution for increasing integration and ending such isolation appears to have been found in this example.

Governor's question: **I am a governor at a community school and part of our policy is to make the premises available for use at the request of a wider range of organizations and societies. We have just received a request to hold a one-day conference next Easter holidays from a political group which many members consider to hold extreme views. While this would bring considerable money into the school, some anxiety has been expressed by members of the community. There is even talk of demonstrations. What do you advise?**

Answer: **It depends what you mean by extreme. In any case, to obtain a balanced view, further soundings should be taken as to the general attitude of parents and others who regularly use the premises. Once this has been done the matter should be put before the governing body – you may need to call an extraordinary meeting to deal with this specific item – and a vote taken.**

When voting on a matter like this it will be necessary to consider the wider

implications, including any possible damage to the school on the day in question and the likelihood of subsequent withdrawal of regular support by community users – and not just personal preferences or emotional reactions.

Figure 8.5: Staff/community lounge

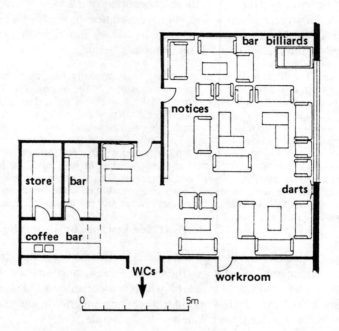

(Source: DES Architects and Building Broadsheet No. 19, 1984)

IN A NUTSHELL

Governors have certain powers under their Articles of Government to exercise oversight with reference to school premises and their use. Generally, this can be extended to include accommodation, facilities and equipment. The main area of direct concern for governors is likely to be that of maintenance and general upkeep. Some schools may very well decide to set up a subcommittee to deal with aspects of school premises and their maintenance, dependent upon particular circumstances. In any event, some kind of monitoring system needs to be set up if governors are going to fulfil their responsibility in a meaningful way. Any problems encountered should be dealt with quickly rather than left to deteriorate, and in cases of difficulty governors may need to lobby members of the education committee to get things done.

Checks should also be made with regard to the arrangements for security of the premises and all aspects of safety in the working environment. Reference to the conditions of premises, accommodation and facilities, and full details of safety policies applying to the school should appear in the headteacher's report. Governors should ensure that sufficient attention is given to these matters at meetings of the governing body.

In a time of falling rolls there may be an opportunity to consider alternative uses to which school premises might realistically be put, especially in terms of enhancing the role of the school in the community.

SELF-TEST

1. Which two aspects of school premises directly concern governors under the Articles of Government?
2. Suggest six types of specialist accommodation you would expect to find in either a primary or secondary school.
3. Which Act covers safety legislation in schools?
4. Suggest six areas which would be likely to be included in a Safety Code of Practice drawn up for a school.
5. Suggest three steps which could be taken to increase the security of school premises.
6. Give three advantages of extending the school's community role.

POINTS TO PONDER

1. Identify any serious shortages of specialist facilities which are detrimental to your school's activities in general and to the curriculum in particular. Devise a plan of campaign to bring about improvements, indicating the expert advice you would need, e.g. architects, space planners, the time-scale you would envisage to undertake the exercise and the means by which you would co-ordinate activities.
2. How might governors improve the standard and range of equipment in your school? What kind of help might be forthcoming from parents and the community? How might such equipment be kept secure?

3. What benefits are there for a school in the appointment of a safety officer and the establishment of a safety committee? How might governors be involved?
4. What recommendations would you make to your governing body when dealing with persistent vandalism in the school? In what circumstances would you support/not support police intervention?
5. To what extent, if any, is your school used as a community resource? Consider or suggest ways in which improvements could be made to existing provision.
6. What benefits are likely to accrue to a school which is integrated effectively into its community? Consider this with particular reference to enhancing school buildings and facilities.

GOVERNOR'S CHECKLIST

1. Does your school have a clear policy in relation to the general maintenance and upkeep of the school?
2. What reference is made in the Articles of Government to the role of your governing body in respect of premises?
3. Are regular inspections made of your school's premises in order to monitor its condition?
4. Is maintenance work carried out quickly by your LEA?
5. Is there a clear policy in terms of the treatment of culprits who have been engaged in acts of vandalism?
6. Does your school have a safety committee?
7. Are all members of staff – teaching and non-teaching – fully aware of the school's safety policy and of their duties and responsibilities?
8. Are regular fire drills carried out within the school?
9. Is security at the school sufficient, including the storage of expensive or dangerous items, e.g. chemicals?
10. Does your school have a policy aimed at increasing and maintaining community integration?
11. To what extent is any surplus accommodation likely to be available at your school in the near future, and what plans are there to make use of it?
12. Do matters regarding the school's premises and facilities, including condition, safety, security and use, feature regularly in your headteacher's report?

FURTHER READING

DES (1976) *School and Community (2) Provision for Joint Use in a Changing World*, Architects and Building Group, Design Note 14, HMSO, London.

DES (1981) *Opportunities for Improvement: NE Wiltshire, a Review of Secondary Education Facilities in the Light of Falling Rolls*, Architects and Building Group, Design Note 28, HMSO, London.

DES (1986) *Crime Prevention in Schools: building-related aspects*, Architects and Building Group, HMSO, London.

Education (School Premises) Regulations, SI 909 (1981).

Health and Safety at Work, etc. Act 1974.

Maclure, S. (1984) *Education Development and School Building: Aspects of Public Policy 1945–1973*, Longman, London.

9
CONDUCT AND DISCIPLINE

Schools reflect the values of the society and to operate effectively they need to have a sense of order. By their very nature children can be high-spirited and mischievous and sometimes it will be difficult to differentiate between high spirits and misconduct. However, such distinctions will be necessary for all schools in order that control may be exercised. Although primary schools will sometimes be required to deal with issues of conduct and discipline, the volume of serious cases is likely to increase in secondary schools.

WHOSE RESPONSIBILITY?

The sharing of problems between teaching staff and governors, relating to the conduct and discipline of the school, is described in the White Paper *Better Schools* (1985), which states:

> The Government believes that the conduct and discipline of the pupils should be primarily a matter for the school, on the basis that operational and day-to-day issues are managed by the headteacher and his staff, but that ultimate responsibility, at the level of the school rests with the governing body.
>
> (para. 234)

However, the Green Paper *Parental Influence at School* (1984), draws attention to the fact that the LEA has an interest in and a responsibility for conduct and discipline in its schools:

> As discipline is an aspect of standards, the LEA too has an interest in this area so that it can discharge its duties relating to the provision of efficient education. In the Government's view this interest does not warrant LEAs having unspecified and

broad powers to override governing bodies and headteachers in matters of discipline; but it does mean, for instance, that in the last resort LEAs should be able to step in to prevent the collapse of order in a school.

(para. 52)

Conduct and discipline are not, therefore, the responsibility of any one individual or group. The partnership principle is once more applied as the basis for dealing with conduct and discipline problems. The levels and intensity of involvement by the interested parties, i.e. headteacher, teachers, parents, governors and the LEA, will be determined by the nature and seriousness of the issue in question.

LEGAL GUIDELINES

The law in relation to school conduct and discipline is imprecise, subject to change and provides only general guidelines. Nonetheless, it is possible to set out the general conditions within which any rules relating to the maintenance of conduct and discipline must apply:

1. The LEA is ultimately the body responsible for maintaining the conduct and discipline of its schools
2. Under a school's Articles of Government the headteacher has the authority to make and uphold the school rules
3. Parents have no automatic right to be consulted before a suspension or other disciplinary action is taken, although many LEAs advise this
4. Parents have the right to appeal, e.g. in cases of suspension or expulsion, if it is considered that the governing body and LEA have acted unreasonably
5. Parents, under the Education Act (1944) 'have a duty to secure regular attendance of registered pupils'
6. It is the duty of every LEA to make provision for the education of school-age children residing within its administrative area
9. The Secretary of State has the power to settle disputes which may arise as a result of an appeal made, e.g. by parents in respect of an LEA decision.

As with any aspect of law, application is a matter of interpretation, especially in respect of the 'reasonableness' of any action taken. Also, just as decisions reached by magistrates vary from one court to another, so too will those taken by schools on matters of conduct and discipline.

TOWARDS A CONSENSUS

The Articles of Government indicate that the headteacher is accountable to the governing body for the conduct and discipline of the school. However, the wise headteacher will consult widely before determining the school rules and the application of any sanctions.

For rules to be acceptable and workable they need to be regarded as reasonable and a consensus of opinion is desirable. For example, the headteacher should arrange for teachers and governors to comment and agree the school rules, while being given the opportunity to modify them if required. It is also a good idea to invite the opinion of a PTA when determining school rules.

The headteacher, as the formal legal executive of the school by virtue of his position and contract of employment, represents the only legitimate source of authority within the school. He is free to make the rules, although these must not conflict with those set down by the LEA and must always be seen to be reasonable.

AUTHORITY OF THE HEADTEACHER

The authority of the headteacher is set out in the Articles of Government along the following lines:
1. The headteacher shall control the internal management of the school
2. The headteacher shall control the discipline of the school
3. The headteacher shall have the power to suspend pupils from attendance for any cause he considers adequate
4. The headteacher shall exercise supervision over the teaching and non-teaching staff of the school
5. On suspending any pupil, the headteacher shall notify parents in writing and report the case to the chairman of governors who shall consult with the LEA
6. There shall be full consultation at all times, between the headteacher, the Chief Education Officer and the chairman of governors.

DELEGATED AUTHORITY

In practice, no one headteacher can attend to every minute detail in relation to conduct and discipline. In any event it will be taken as read that the teacher in the classroom will deal with minor offences as they occur, e.g. by issuing extra work, imposing lunchtime detention or giving set chores for completion. Therefore, although the headteacher must always retain overall responsibility, he may delegate specific authority for certain aspects of conduct and discipline to other members of staff.

For example, minor infringements of school rules and occasional trouble-making may be dealt with by a senior member of staff such as the year tutor or deputy head. The sanctions applied could include 'official' detention or initial contact with parents in an attempt to resolve an issue at an early stage.

For his own protection, a headteacher needs to exercise considerable care when delegating authority and setting its limits. Members of staff must be in no doubt that they are accountable to the headteacher for any action they take.

IN LOCO PARENTIS

The term means 'parent substitute' and refers to the duty of care placed on the teacher in respect of children who are in effect transferred into his care by parents. It carries with it the expectation that the teacher will act as any reasonable or careful parent would in the same or similar situations. Direct comparison is difficult, however, in that the teacher has to take responsibility for a large number of children, often of varying ages. Nonetheless, it is expected that the teacher will provide a standard of care compatible with that of a careful parent by, for example, not exposing pupils to danger or injury. Accidents do happen, however, when for example playing games or taking part in PE. In such situations the teacher is not automatically guilty of negligence, since this would have to be shown in any subsequent inquiry.

CONDUCT OF PUPILS

Children operate to some extent in a world of their own, being progressively influenced by fashions and fads such as modes of dress, pop music and culture, much of which is often a mystery to the majority of adults, including teachers. Adolescence in particular can be difficult for young people who often have to choose between the values of school and those of their friends or peer group, who tend to influence behaviour. Indeed, while the school operates an official curriculum there also exists a 'hidden curriculum', an unofficial one. It is through this that the various subcultures of the school operate, as group identities develop, with shared values and codes of behaviour which may be, to a greater or lesser extent, either pro- or anti-school.

PEER GROUP PRESSURE

When dealing with disciplinary problems, governors should be aware of the pressures with which pupils, particularly teenagers, have to contend. No one likes to be rejected by his peer group, and some will go to any lengths to be accepted. The problem is often accentuated when the individual child does not experience the 'official' reward system of the school, through academic or sporting achievements. To be written off as 'thick' or 'stupid' is tantamount to throwing a challenge to such pupils to prove themselves outside the formal reward mechanisms and within the informal ones which are set by the peer group. Consequently, under-achievers often set out to impress their peers. This may result in displays of bad behaviour in order to win the approval of the peer group and enhance status.

Some pupils gain a reputation of being a 'hard case' – afraid of nothing and no one. The more 'success' the individual pupil 'achieves' in the eyes of his peer group, the more notoriety he gains through such a pattern of behaviour, and the greater the distance between the pupil and the values of the school.

CAUSES OF INDISCIPLINE

There are many individual cases of misconduct and indiscipline at schools, some of which occasionally find the national headlines. Indeed, the number of cases has grown over recent years and, unfortunately, this seems likely to be the trend for the foreseeable future.

There are a number of reasons for this, but the main ones are changes in behaviour and values in society generally, and the assertion of the rights of the individual to free expression. The effects of such changes in society have led to a general questioning of the nature of authority. Legitimate authority in schools is necessary, however, in order for them to operate and provide controls within which the educative process may take place for the benefit of everyone.

There is no single cause for unruly or unco-operative behaviour. However, generally speaking, it would seem that pupils who achieve within the school system tend to present fewer discipline problems than those who do not. Consequently, there is probably a connection between success at school and behaviour. In any event, most problems at school tend to occur in the final years of compulsory education, i.e. between the ages of fourteen and sixteen.

Although it is difficult to be precise about where the blame might lie in relation to individual cases, it is nonetheless possible to draw up a list of likely causes, both within a school and outside.

WITHIN SCHOOL

1. Lack of clearly presented rules and procedures
2. Class sizes too big to allow for sufficient attention to each individual pupil

3. Ill-defined policies and poorly developed school plans in respect of pastoral care
4. Insufficient staff with specific training in pastoral work
5. Quality of teaching
6. Level of morale and motivation of staff
7. Curriculum seen to be irrelevant by a significant number of pupils, leading to boredom and indifference
8. Insufficient extra-curricular activity, especially at lunchtime
9. Little opportunity to achieve success other than in the strictly academic sense, namely, passing public examinations
10. Poor home–school links.

OUTSIDE SCHOOL

1. Poor parental support for school work, e.g. little or no encouragement given to homework
2. Home background and domestic circumstances
3. Too much or too little spending power
4. Unsupervised access to the home, especially during the lunch break and in the early evening
5. Lack of parental control, e.g. watching late night television and/or unsuitable video material
6. Mixing in the 'wrong company' out of school
7. Little or no contact by the parents with the school
8. General indifference, by parents, to edcuation.

These are the kinds of factors which governors need to be aware of when dealing with individual cases involving the conduct and discipline of a pupil.

TYPES OF MISCONDUCT

Misconduct and breakdown of discipline within a school can take many forms. While many misdemeanours are trivial, problems may arise if they are allowed to go unchecked. This can result in a decline in standards of behaviour, a disregard for authority and a lack of care and concern for others. Most schools will include among their aims and objectives (see Chapter 4) statements about conduct and behaviour which they expect to be observed.

What constitutes misconduct and breach of discipline is coloured by personal value systems, codes of behaviour, attitudes to things like freedom and authority, and the level of an individual's personal sensitivity. For example, many adults accept the view that 'boys will be boys' and show a great deal of tolerance, while others may favour the Victorian view that children should be 'seen and not heard'. In any event there is a need for all concerned to strike a balanced view, maintain a sense of humour and keep everything in proportion.

The following represent typical examples of what most people would generally regard as constituting the sort of behaviour that would warrant some form of disciplinary action: aggressive behaviour; attacking a member of staff; bullying; deceit; disobedience; disregard for the safety of others; failure to submit homework; fighting; gambling; inappropriate dress or hairstyle; insubordination; insulting behaviour; lateness; misuse of school equipment; possession of an offensive weapon; racism; sexism; smoking; spitting; stealing; swearing; truancy; vandalism.

GOVERNORS' DISCIPLINARY COMMITTEE

In response to problems over conduct and discipline, some governing bodies have set up subcommittees to deal with problems as they arise. The advantage of this is that only a few people need to get involved and they can meet quickly and make decisions. Governors will usually decide to support the headteacher, e.g. in suspending a pupil. However, it is important to think ahead about the possible consequences of any proposed action and to be satisfied that proper procedures have been observed throughout. This might best be done by working through a checklist which could include the following questions:

1. Does the nature of the offence warrant the punishment, e.g. suspension, or might other solutions be tried?
2. Is the headteacher being over-fussy or is he justified in his proposed course of action?
3. Was the pupil warned of the possible consequences of his antisocial behaviour?
4. Have the parents been notified, where appropriate?
5. Are the parents likely to want to appeal against any punishment imposed?
6. Does the pupil show any signs of regret or remorse about his behaviour?
7. Is the issue likely to 'drag on' or can it be dealt with quickly?
8. Do the teachers support the headteacher and his attitude towards conduct and discipline?
9. Does the governors' subcommittee unanimously support the headteacher or are other views expressed?
10. Should the LEA be informed about the proposed punishment?
11. Has the pupil been in trouble before?

12. Has the possibility of seeking advice from the educational psychologist or welfare officer been considered?
13. Is there a 'sin-bin' to which the child could be sent at the school or elsewhere?
14. Is the pupil–teacher ratio too high, thereby making it difficult to establish control over some classes?
15. Have the parents been invited to school to talk to the headteacher about the child's misbehaviour?
16. Have parents and members of the local community been invited to share in deciding the school's policy in respect of conduct and discipline?
17. Is the conduct and discipline policy of the school generally well-managed and supported?
18. Are complete records of offences committed available, reliable and up to date?

SCHOOL RULES

Clear statements of school rules can help provide a code of conduct and discipline or at least establish expectations of what these are to be. They do not of themselves guarantee good behaviour and neither can they cover every eventuality. The purpose of the school rules should be to set the tone of acceptable behaviour and indicate clearly the 'do's and don'ts' of everyday school life, in the best interests of everyone. It is also useful to spell out as clearly as possible, the sanctions which the school may apply in the event of a pupil's bad behaviour. No one can then accuse the school of acting unfairly in its treatment of an individual if the conditions have been clearly stated in, for example, the school prospectus.

Governor's question: **I am a parent governor at a comprehensive school and live quite near to a small shopping precinct, which has the usual small café, a newsagents, bakery and so on. A number of shopkeepers and members of the local community have complained to me about the behaviour of the pupils at lunch-time and I wondered what the position is. Does the school have any authority in this situation?**
Answer: **The school accepts responsibility at lunch-time for the conduct and discipline of those who stay on the school premises. Those who leave the school during the lunch hour are usually required to have permission to do so, obtained by sending a letter from the parent to the school. To some extent, the request absolves the school from any liability in respect of the pupils concerned, but there**

is nothing to stop the headteacher using his discretion when a case such as the one you describe occurs. A possible solution is to place the precinct out of bounds at lunch-time, although notice will have to be given to parents and their co-operation sought. The limitation, once imposed, becomes part of the school rules and thereafter subject to the usual range of sanctions if flouted.

PRIMARY SCHOOLS

Although it is not unusual for primary schools to encounter difficult disciplinary problems, they are usually less severe and infrequent when compared with secondary schools. Consequently, a fairly general statement about rules can be made as the following example, based on an extract from a typical primary school prospectus, illustrates:

> *Discipline:* There are few written rules at the school, and these are mainly for everyone's welfare and safety. We are concerned to create an atmosphere where learning can take place. Children are expected to behave in a courteous manner with consideration for others. Where there is a discipline problem, parents will be asked to visit the school and to discuss the matter with the teacher concerned and the headteacher. Meanwhile, we would like to emphasize the following:
>
> 1. Children should walk, not run, when inside the school buildings
> 2. The car park should not be used as a through-route to and from school
> 3. Children are not allowed to leave the school premises during school hours without a note from parents and proper arrangements made for their collection
> 4. Children are not allowed to bring into school knives or any other object which might be dangerous to other children.
>
> *Uniform:* The school does not have a uniform as such. We do, however, expect a good standard of tidiness and cleanliness. The only special clothing required is a pair of pumps and shorts/leotard for PE. Boys will also need football boots.

SECONDARY SCHOOLS

Rules in respect of conduct and discipline in secondary schools are usually more detailed and specific, as illustrated in the following extract adapted from a typical secondary school prospectus:

> *Discipline:* School rules are aimed at making pupils aware of their responsibilities to themselves and to others. They are also intended to lay the foundations of self-discipline. All teachers have a responsibility to uphold and enforce discipline in and around the school, including journeys to and from school.
>
> In the event of serious misconduct, pupils will be referred to their head of year. The matter may be sent to the headteacher or his deputies and be dealt with by them. Corporal punishment is not used. We do, however, operate a number of sanctions to

Conduct and Discipline

be applied in the event of continued misbehaviour or misconduct. Parents will be asked, where necessary, to visit the school, and to discuss possible steps which might be taken to help remedy the situation.

The rules are:
1. Politeness and consideration are to be shown at all times
2. School uniform must be worn and clearly marked with your name, as must any other property you bring into school
3. All equipment required for the school day, e.g. books, rulers, pens, sports wear, must be brought in a bag with your name clearly marked
4. All school work, including homework, must be presented carefully and tidily
5. If you arrive late, you must report to your form tutor and sign the 'late book'
6. You must not leave the school premises without permission from your form tutor, deputy head or headteacher
7. You must not leave the school premises at lunch-time unless a written request is made by your parents
8. You must not frequent cafés at lunch-time, or go to friends' houses or eat snacks in the street
9. You must bring a note from your parents to explain any reason for your absence from school
10. You must not bring into school chewing gum, cigarettes, matches, lighters, glue, fireworks, radios or tape recorders
11. You are responsible for any valuables brought into school, unless you place them in the care of a member of staff or hand them in at the school office
12. You must bring a letter to school from parents before you can be excused, on medical grounds, from games, PE or showers
13. Ball games are forbidden near windows and cars
14. You must 'keep left' when walking (not running) round the school premises, and keep to pathways outside
15. You must not smoke on school premises, including playing areas
16. Entry to school should be via the Benson Road entrance only
17. You must not cycle on school premises and cycles should be locked and left in the designated area
18. The school does not accept any liability for the safe keeping of cycles and motor cycles
19. You must not take part in any form of gambling while on school premises
20. You must be available for 45 minutes after school hours if you have been put on detention. You will be informed sufficiently in advance to enable you to give your parents 24 hours' notice.

Uniform: The wearing of a school uniform is compulsory for all pupils except those in the fifth year. The colours have been chosen for ease of availability and practicality. Pupils may sometimes tell parents that they can wear different styles of clothing, e.g. denim or corduroy trousers or skirts. This is not the case and we would ask any parents in doubt about the exact nature of the school uniform, particular items, shades of colour and so on to contact the school before buying.

General appearance: Boys' and girls' hairstyles should be in accordance with school standards; boys may not wear boots at school or during journeys to and from; girls must not wear cosmetics or nail varnish; the wearing of jewellery is not allowed, although girls may wear plain sleepers or studs in their ears on written request from parents.

The list of rules could go on and on but they are only there to provide a general framework for the conduct of the school. In any event, they will vary from one school to another, according to any particular problems which may have arisen.

Governor's question: **Our school rules stipulate that all pupils, with the exception of the fifth year, must wear the school uniform. However, one pupil, a third-year boy, insists, with parental backing, on wearing denim trousers and a colourful casual shirt. After a protracted series of discussions with the boy concerned and the parents, the headteacher has suspended him, with the backing of the governors and the LEA. He has been away for six weeks now, and a further deadline has passed for him to comply. Where do we go from here?**
Answer: **Ultimately, there is no law which states that pupils are required to wear a school uniform. Having said that, the headteacher has the legitimate authority, by virtue of his position and under the Articles of Government, to establish a policy for the conduct and discipline of the school, providing that this is reasonable and in line with LEA policy. It is a matter of debate as to where you go from here. It is the parents who have a clear duty to cause their child to be educated, since where a 'registered pupil at a school fails to attend regularly, the parent of the child shall be guilty' (Education Act (1944), section 39).**

On the other hand, the LEA has a duty to provide education. Perhaps the best indication as to the outcome is to be found in a similar case, Spiers v. Warrington Corporation (1954). Here, the judgement was that the child had not been suspended at all, since the headteacher was always willing to accept her back at school providing that she would be 'properly dressed'. The court recognized the duty of the headteacher to maintain the conduct and discipline of the school, including the authority to make the school rules. The onus, therefore, is on the parents to comply with the school or risk being charged under section 39.

FACTORS INFLUENCING THE APPLICATION OF DISCIPLINARY MEASURES

There are many considerations involved when attempting to lay down a precise formula for applying disciplinary measures with any school. These are likely to include: the type of school, i.e. primary or secondary, and the age range of the pupils; whether a co-educational or a single sex school; whether the school is on a single site or split sites; the teaching staff and the number of senior posts available; the local context of the school and its setting; the traditions of the school and the customs and precedents already established; the guidelines, rules and regulations laid down by the LEA: the duties and obligations of the LEA as an employer; the rights, wishes and expectations held by parents; the rights and expectations of the pupils; common law in England and Wales; legislation on education; general applications of the law as it affects the management and conduct of schools, e.g. equal opportunities, health and safety, race relations and EEC judgements affecting corporal punishment.

FORMS OF PUNISHMENT

Schools have a number of options in terms of the sanctions they wish to apply in cases of misconduct and bad behaviour. These range from a mere 'telling off' to the more serious cases of suspension or expulsion. It is useful to have decided beforehand the broad category of offences which would merit the application of the more formal types of punishment. Examples of available forms of chastisement or punishment include: a 'telling off'; extra school work, e.g. lines or homework; being sent to the headteacher or other senior member of staff; being banned from certain activities for a period of time, e.g. games and PE or school clubs and associations; placed on report, i.e. having to report to a particular teacher at a set time every day; being made to clean up or tidy up or rectify any damage; moved to another class; detention, i.e. kept in after school; corporal punishment (until August 1987); short-term suspension; long-term suspension; transfer to another school or special unit; expulsion.

EXPULSION

Expulsion is the last resort in disciplining a pupil. It is at this point that a pupil would be removed from the register. Both the LEA and the headteacher are reluctant to see this sanction applied since, normally, it merely transfers the problem to another school. In any event the legal requirement remains for the LEA to make provision for the education of any child under the age of sixteen and for parents to ensure that their child continues to receive education.

Expulsion is something of an admission of failure on the part of a school, and is only contemplated after a series of events where there appears to be absolutely no other reasonable course of action available or justifiable. Consequently, expulsion will usually be applied following a series of previous incidents, possibly involving periods of suspension. If the governors and the LEA uphold the decision to expel, the parents have the right to make an appeal to the Secretary of State under section 68 of the Education Act 1944. If he overrules the governors and the LEA on the grounds that they acted 'unreasonably', then the pupil would have to be reinstated.

An additional factor governors need to consider is that when a headteacher gets involved in expulsion cases he may very well find that he is expected to reciprocate, i.e. accept another school's problem cases in return.

SUSPENSION

With the abolition of corporal punishment, the application of suspension procedures seems set to grow. As a result, this is an area of activity with which governing bodies, sooner or later, will be called upon to deal. However, if it becomes a regular feature, careful consideration needs to be given to its likely causes and possible remedies.

When dealing with suspensions it is important to recognize that governors are not acting in a judicial capacity, but rather to protect the general well-being of the pupil involved, as well as the school as a whole. Care needs to be taken by governors to ensure that their independence and impartiality is not compromised by being involved in cases of suspension. It should also be recognized that suspension should be seen not so much as a punishment in itself (for some pupils it may even seem to be a reward), but rather as a means of providing a cooling down period for all involved.

A rationale for the use of suspensions is provided in the Taylor Report (1977), namely:

(a) to allow the school to function satisfactorily while problems are solved;
(b) to allow the headteacher reasonable discretion to take very short term action in an emergency without excessive formality but with suitable safeguards;
(c) to avoid unnecessary interruption to the child's education and to keep the period of non-attendance as short as possible;
(d) to bring all relevant considerations and all interested parties quickly together to this end.

(para. 912)

Procedures for dealing with suspensions are usually ill-defined. Typically, however, the headteacher has the right to suspend a pupil for what he considers to be a valid reason, e.g. assault, whether or not a prima facia case exists, and whether or not the school rules have been broken. The headteacher must inform the parents where a suspension is imposed, in writing, as well as the chairman of governors and the LEA. A suspension is usually set for a specific duration, but may last longer if parents and pupils do not comply with a particular request, e.g. to change a hairstyle or mode of dress or appearance to that acceptable to the school.

The LEA may overrule the headteacher and the governing body, though this can lead to difficulties, as in the case of Poundswick School (see p. 89). Direct confrontation between the headteacher and governors and the LEA is, however, unlikely. Given the lack of clarity about where the powers of each of those involved begin and end, it is best avoided if at all possible.

Parental appeals

Parents should always be informed about any suspension, preferably before it is implemented, when circumstances allow. They should also be advised of their right to appeal as well as to the procedures they need to follow in order to do so. The initial appeal will be heard by the governors and if the matter is not resolved satisfactorily, then the next stage is for the appeal to be made to the LEA, and if all else fails, to the Secretary of State, as in the case of expulsion.

DETENTION

This is a fairly common punishment used for misdemeanours at secondary schools. Ideally, details regarding its use should be publicized in the school prospectus. There are a number of implications in applying this sanction: teachers should ensure that parents have been given sufficient notice, e.g. 24 hours, where a detention is to last longer than, say, 40 minutes; they should also be aware of any transport problems which may arise as a result of imposing a detention, although this is not in itself a reason to avoid this type of punishment. Also, in cases where a child lives some distance away from the school, there may be a number of additional important facts, e.g. when the school bus leaves, or the frequency of the local bus service, or of when the school patrol finishes at a particularly busy road. The teacher should also check whether the child concerned is dependent on another for getting home, or is himself responsible for seeing a younger child home safely.

It is a good idea for governors to check the precise procedures used when applying the detention sanction to ensure that the eventualities described are covered, that any LEA rules are being observed and whether the punishment tends to be over-used by any of the teachers.

CORPORAL PUNISHMENT

Corporal punishment will no longer be permitted in schools from August 1987, following a vote on the issue in the House of Commons on Tuesday, 22 July 1986. Voting was 231 in favour and 230 against. The effect of the decision is that

Britain is no longer the 'odd one out' in Europe. The decision to abolish corporal punishment seemed inevitable following the judgement of the European Court of Human Rights in 1982 to the effect that pupils could not be subjected to corporal punishment against their parents' wishes. In the light of this ruling, many LEAs abandoned the use of this sanction before the vote in the Commons.

STAFF DISCIPLINE

Occasionally, the need arises for governors to deal with a staff disciplinary matter, which may even be directed towards the headteacher. The precise nature of the 'offence' can obviously vary considerably, and may or may not be closely concerned with the school. In any event, a disciplinary matter will produce a reaction from parents, teachers, governors and the LEA. As a general rule, the question to be asked is whether the offence, committed within or outside the school, is sufficient to disqualify the teacher from undertaking his duties in a satisfactory way, which is itself open to wide interpretation. For example, it may well be that a fairly trivial offence is sufficient to cause parents to lose confidence in a teacher.

Ultimately, cases involving disciplinary action and an individual teacher, his suspension or possible dismissal, are matters for his employer, i.e. the LEA and not the governors. In the case of voluntary schools, the ultimate responsibility will rest with governors where they are the employers.

IN A NUTSHELL

The issue of conduct and discipline is important for any school since a sense of order must be maintained when large groups of children are gathered together in one place. The headteacher is responsible for discipline and may also use his discretion in terms of the kinds of sanctions to be used in particular circumstances. Most headteachers will consult with their colleagues, governors and parents when establishing the school rules, and aspects of these should be published in the school prospectus.

The range of sanctions a headteacher can apply no longer include corporal punishment (from August 1987), and schools may need to investigate the use of alternative sanctions. Suspension, which is usually regarded as a cooling off period in cases of dispute, should only be applied according to set procedures which need to be established by the headteachers and the governing body, taking full account of any LEA requirements.

Expulsion is the last resort for any school. It should be applied only after careful consideration and consultation between the headteacher, the governors and the LEA. Parents have the right of appeal regarding suspensions and expulsions, initially to the governing body, thereafter to the LEA and ultimately, to the Secretary of State. Whatever the issue, the overriding factor to be considered is whether the sanction used is 'reasonable' in the circumstances.

Governors may also become involved in staff discipline cases. Where this happens full consultation should take place with the LEA, which will have the final say, as the employer.

SELF-TEST

1. Who is responsible for conduct and discipline at the level of the school?
2. What factors should a teacher take into account before imposing detention?
3. Identify six factors which a governor should consider when involved in a disciplinary matter concerning an individual pupil.
4. Ideally, who should be involved in determining school rules?
5. What procedures should be followed by the school when imposing a suspension on an individual pupil?
6. Who represents the last 'court of appeal' in both suspension and expulsion disputes?

POINTS TO PONDER

1. In what ways might the governing body help to establish the rules and procedures to be adopted by the school in respect of its conduct and discipline?
2. Given the demise of corporal punishment, what effect do you consider this will have on your school's ability to maintain satisfactory levels of conduct and behaviour? What alternative sanctions might be developed in its place?
3. In order to reduce cases of indiscipline, what preventive measures might be introduced into the school? For example, could improvements be made in general management by providing smaller classes where needed or improvements made to the curriculum to increase and hold pupil interest?

4. What LEA advice and services might the school use in order to help identify causes of indiscipline and apply effective sanctions?
5. To what extent should parents be involved in the development of your school's conduct and discipline policy? Indicate the kind of barriers you anticipate will inhibit such a scheme and suggest any possible solutions.
6. In what circumstances would you expect your headteacher to impose a suspension on a pupil? Would your governing body generally support or oppose such a move? Where opinions differ, suggest the procedures to be followed in order to settle the issue.

GOVERNOR'S CHECKLIST

1. Does the school have a clear detailed statement setting out its rules and regulations?
2. Are you aware of any delegation of duties to senior members of staff in respect of disciplinary procedures?
3. Is sufficient use made of external expertise and advice, e.g. educational welfare or psychological services, when dealing with the school's conduct and discipline problems?
4. What methods are used to inform parents about the school's policies in relation to the maintenance of good behaviour and conduct?
5. Does your school, or LEA, have a special unit to which difficult children might be sent and, if so, what procedures are to be followed regarding its use in particular cases?
6. Where no such facility exists, what alternative arrangements are made to deal with pupils who persist in behaving badly?
7. Do you know the procedures to be used when imposing either suspension or expulsion?
8. Is there a special subcommittee of the governing body, set up to deal with cases of indiscipline and misconduct? If so, who are its members, what is its remit and how frequently does it meet?
9. What rules are to be followed by pupils in relation to leaving the school premises at lunch-time? What steps are taken to ensure that these are observed?

FURTHER READING

Blackburn, K. (1983) *Head of Year, Head of House*, Heinemann, London.
DES (1984) *The Education Welfare Service: An HMI Enquiry in Eight LEAs*, HMSO, London.
Galloway, D., Ball, C., Blomfield, D. and Seyd, R. (1982) *Schools and Disruptive Pupils*, Longman, London.
Hamblin, D. (1978) *The Teacher and Pastoral Care*, Blackwell, Oxford.

10
THE CURRICULUM

The curriculum is the very basis of education, the *raison d'être* for an individual school and the appointment of staff – in fact everything that constitutes the education system. There are literally thousands of books about the school curriculum and a large number of definitions, among which the following are examples:

The total experience of the child, regardless of whether it is planned or not.

The learning experiences provided by the school.

The subjects taught by the school.

The course a pupil or student studies.

The provision of socially valued knowledge transmitted by the school.

The total scheme of subjects related to an overall rationale.

A total range of subjects or courses designed with specific ends in mind.

Whatever definition is used it is important that it can be translated into action, i.e. that whatever is proposed is realistic and manageable. The definition used here is: 'The curriculum refers to all the school's teaching and learning activities which have been deliberately planned.'

WHO DECIDES THE CURRICULUM?

What finally emerges as a school's curriculum is determined by a variety of influences and pressure from a number of interested parties, as illustrated in

Figure 10.1. Once again, the outcome is the result of a sharing of ideas, with no single group or organization having the power to decide what the curriculum should be for an individual school.

Figure 10.1: Fingers in the curriculum pie

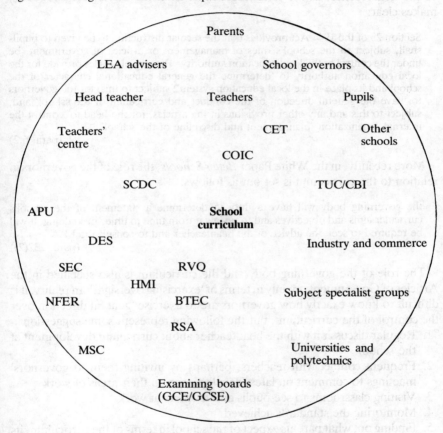

GOVERNING BODIES

The governing body represents the 'lay' interest in overseeing the nature of the curriculum and how it is taught, within any guidelines set out by the LEA. It is important to recognize that the role of the governing body is that of a partner and it is not empowered to tell the headteacher or the teachers what they should do, but rather to take an interest in the nature of the curriculum and the standards achieved.

The statutory position of governing bodies is provided in the Articles of Government which indicate the role of governing bodies and the responsibilities of the headteacher, as the following extract from the Taylor Report (1977) makes clear:

> Section 23 of the 1944 Act provides that the secular instruction to be given to pupils shall, subject to the school's rules of management or articles of government, be under the control of the local education authority. The model articles provide for the local education authority to 'determine the general educational character of the school and its place in the local education system'; subject to this, for the governors to 'have the general direction of the conduct and curriculum of the school' and, subject to this and any other provisions in the articles, for the head to 'control the internal organization, management and discipline of the school'.
>
> (para. 6.2)

More recently, in the White Paper *Better Schools*, the role of the governors in relation to the curriculum is set out as follows:

> the governing body will have a duty to determine a statement of the school's curricular aims and objectives and to review it from time to time. In so doing, it will be required to seek the advice of the headteacher and to consult the LEA.
>
> (para. 232(2))

The role of the governing body and the curriculum is also specified in the Articles of Government, mainly in terms of 'exercising oversight'. In reality, it is difficult to know exactly how governors are to exercise 'general direction over the control of the curriculum', but the following represent some suggestions:

1. Regular discussion with the headteacher about curriculum development at the school
2. Frequent contact with teachers, perhaps by inviting them to governors' meetings to comment on latest developments in their areas of work
3. Visiting classrooms to see pupils and teachers at work
4. Monitoring the standards achieved
5. Finding out what parents expect of the school in terms of the curriculum, its scope, choice and relevance
6. Identifying, with the advice of the headteacher, any particular skill shortage among the teaching staff
7. Recognizing staff development needs in an endeavour to keep the curriculum up-to-date
8. Supporting plans to meet staff development needs in respect of the curriculum (INSET)

9. Finding out (in the case of secondary schools) what industry and commerce requires in respect of the curriculum
10. Determining whether the school is under-resourced and unable to deliver certain areas of the curriculum
11. Identifying funding opportunities for curriculum development, e.g. EEC or MSC money for specific projects
12. Finding out about the standards attained in the school generally, e.g. by checking performance levels at examinations or by the use of standardized tests
13. Keeping in touch with the policies of the LES on all curriculum matters perhaps by inviting specialist advisers to address governors' meetings on latest developments and future trends
14. Keeping up-to-date on current thinking about curricular developments.

THE HEADTEACHER

By virtue of his role and status, the headteacher is in overall charge of the school, how it is organized and managed and what is actually taught. This responsibility involves curriculum development, the schemes of work to be followed, the allocation of teachers, the teaching methods used and the provision of materials. There is no doubt that the headteacher can and does greatly influence the nature of the curriculum. Even so, most exercise tact and recognize the need to maintain public confidence in the work of the school and among teachers, parents and LEA officials, in order to fulfil their expectations. Without this overriding concern, serious damage might be inflicted on the school's reputation.

TEACHERS

The teaching staff are responsible for the delivery of the curriculum in the classroom on a day-to-day basis. They are the professionals 'on the job' and are in a position to influence what is taught and the methods adopted. This does not mean that teachers have total freedom to determine the curriculum, since there are a number of pressures and expectations held by a wide variety of interested parties, as shown in Figure 10.1. Considerable interest is taken by all parties at central and local level in what is taught, how it is taught and the standards achieved, both at primary and secondary schools.

LEAs

Under section 23 of the Education Act (1944), the LEA has a clear responsibility for secular instruction in the schools under its control. In reality, the LEA does not actually develop the curriculum for each of its schools, this being delegated to the headteacher and his colleagues who have to teach according to the requirements of the syllabus. The role of the LEA is to formulate an overall policy for the curriculum, as indicated in section 7 of the Act. This states that:

> it shall be the duty of the local education authority for every area, so far as their powers extend, to contribute towards the spiritual, moral, mental and physical development of the community by securing that efficient education throughout those stages shall be available to meet the needs of the population of their area.
> (Section 7)

A lot of water has gone under the bridge since the 1944 Act. Indeed, LEAs have been required to comply with all manner of directives and regulations issued by central government, through the DES and the HM Inspectorate, many of which have had a direct impact on the curriculum for both primary and secondary schools.

PARENTS

As consumers of education, parents have a number of expectations of schools, although these often turn out to be negative, i.e. they are often more certain about what they do not want than they are about suggesting what they do want. Much of this is born out of unfamiliarity in that change has been fast-moving and has affected all aspects of the school curriculum. Examples of such changes in primary schools are the introduction of new reading schemes, new mathematics schemes and computer literacy; in secondary schools, in addition to these changes, there is a movement towards subjects like information technology and peace studies.

CHANGE

It is not just the subjects themselves which have changed but the whole philosophy of what education is or should be about. This ultimately affects the teaching methods used. As a result, there has been a gradual decline in the authoritarian approach. No longer are pupils viewed as empty vessels waiting to be topped up with information. In its place, the emphasis has shifted away from the teacher and towards pupil-centred learning where the child is encouraged to find out for himself (the 'discovery method'), ask questions and seek solutions to problems.

Given the amount of change which has taken place in education, it is hardly surprising that parents become unnerved about what schools are trying to achieve. Where this happens there is a possibility that the expectations held by parents will break down, as occurred at the much-publicized William Tyndale primary school in 1973/74.

In this instance, teachers, under the direction of the headteacher, introduced what might be termed a child-centred curriculum in which subject divisions become blurred in the face of continuous activities. Parents, whose own experience of junior education was on very formal lines, simply did not accept or understand this new arrangement. Such changes meant, for example, that the structure of the classroom was altered: desks were no longer set out in rows, but in groups to create 'workshops'. Also, the nature of the school day changed from the traditional highly structured pattern of subjects towards the introduction of 'the integrated day', which may be described as 'children in the same class, pursuing different activities which some adults may label as work, others play. Sometimes the whole group or class may be involved in a project' (Auld Report on *William Tyndale, Junior and Infants Public Inquiry*, 1986, p. 145).

Other problems can arise from the differences between the values and priorities of parents as distinct from those of teachers. These can often be difficult to reconcile in that parents will tend to attach more importance to, say, vocational aspects of the curriculum while teachers may value the total development of the child, e.g. in educational, physical and emotional terms. Parental anxiety in respect of primary schools tends to centre on the three Rs: in the case of secondary schools it is more likely to focus on the relevance of the curriculum to the 'world of work'. This is a view which has recently gained support from the DES through the introduction of the Certificate for Pre-Vocational Education (CPVE) and the growing involvement of the MSC in secondary schools.

CAUSES OF CHANGE

Change is a dynamic feature of the curriculum. This is because schools mirror and reflect changes taking place in the world. Governors should, therefore, exercise some caution when looking at what schools do today as compared with their own experience gained ten years ago or more.

Despite changes, however, the curriculum tends to be a mixture of the traditional and the modern. The main causes of change include: the development of new technology; demand by parents, industrialists and others for additional skills or improvements to existing ones; changes in the values of society and their impact, e.g. sex education, community and peace studies; economic factors, e.g. large-scale unemployment; political change, e.g. entry into the EEC and the concomitant demand for foreign languages; introduction of new teaching methods by teacher training institutions, e.g. pupil-centred learning; enhanced provision of teaching materials, e.g. audiovisual aids; changes of national policy, e.g. by the DES or MSC; research by external groups, e.g. APU, NFER and university research departments; entry requirements of universities (UCCA) and polytechnics (PCAS) and professional bodies.

THE GREAT DEBATE

The anxieties of the general public concerning both the standard of education and the nature of curriculum content were fuelled by the changes in the organization of the education system in the late 1960s, especially at the secondary stage and the shift from a selective system to a comprehensive one. So intense was the debate that Prime Minister James Callaghan launched what was to become known as the 'Great Debate', triggered by his now famous speech made at Ruskin College in 1976, when he called for higher standards and the development of a core curriculum. The effect was to raise the temperature of the debate on education and led to an increase in the intensity of DES and HMI intervention in schools. The effects are still felt today.

The argument generated, sometimes fiercely, between those in favour of the new comprehensive system and those against, the main protagonists of the latter promoting their argument by the publication of 'Black Papers'.

INFLUENCE OF THE DES

What schools actually do cannot be divorced from the outside world, especially during times of increasing pressure for accountability. Since the curriculum is the very essence of school work, it is always under close scrutiny by the DES and the Inspectorate. Despite such involvement, however, the decentralized nature of the education system extends to the curriculum.

The DES does not direct what should be taught in individual schools and when, but nonetheless it is increasingly influencing the curriculum in a variety of ways. For example, the Assessment of Performance Unit (APU), established by the DES, was set up to provide information about standards and levels of performance in schools, and has reported on mathematics, foreign languages, design and technology. The data collected is used to modify aspects of the curriculum. The APU publishes a number of leaflets and discussion documents which are available free of charge (see p. 264).

The DES itself also publishes material on curriculum issues, many of which are prepared by HMI and are available for a small fee. Although the DES mainly exerts influence over curriculum development by issuing a variety of different papers, there is nothing to prevent it from applying considerable pressure in more direct ways.

For example, the development of the policy leading towards the introduction of the General Certificate of Secondary Education (GCSE) has been influenced largely by the Secretary of State and the DES. Their continual debate with teacher unions and their persistance in pursuing this policy, albeit with the allocation of additional resources, has finally led to its acceptance and introduction. This demonstrates the capacity of the DES, given appropriate political backing, to directly influence the curriculum.

OTHER INFLUENCES

Other organizations with a finger in the curriculum pie include a variety of examining boards, polytechnics and universities. Higher education depends on a steady supply of well-educated students from secondary schools, i.e. those able to benefit from higher education. In adddition, the Department of Employment, through the MSC, has introduced a number of vocational courses, e.g. Technical and Vocational Education Initiative (TVEI), into secondary schools.

THE PRIMARY CURRICULUM

The curriculum of the primary school may be expressed in terms of aims and objectives (see Table 10.1). Table 10.1 shows the areas of learning activity

Table 10.1: Primary school curriculum

Area	Statement of objectives	Means
1. Language 2. Mathematics 3. Environmental studies 4. Religion and moral education 5. Art, craft, design and music 6. Physical education	These to be presented in a series of brief statements, in terms of what the pupil should be able to do or the level of understanding or appreciation he would be expected to have when he completed any stage of the curriculum	These include: teaching strategies; teaching materials; textbooks; equipment; any special facilities required

provided by the school which will be of general interest to parents, and is the kind of information which could be included in the school's prospectus. Taking it a stage further, the 'statement of objectives' indicate what each child should have learned when reaching a particular stage in each of the six areas listed. The general facilities and techniques to be used would be included in the 'means' column.

Ideally, schools could produce a booklet, prepared by teachers, containing full details in respect of the way in which the curriculum is managed, along the lines indicated in Table 10.2.

Table 10.2: Teaching scheme (languages)

Overall aim	Learning objectives	Teacher's action
Fluent reading	At the end of this stage pupils should be able to:	To achieve the objectives teachers will be required to:
	1. Read books of a standard appropriate for their age	1. Develop a reading scheme linked to objectives
	2. Demonstrate an understanding of what has been read	2. Maintain progress from phonetics to understanding
	3. Use books as a tool to find the answers to questions	3. Provide and encourage use of a variety of reference books
	and so on	and so on

PUBLISHING THE CURRICULUM

There are a number of very good reasons for producing a systematic curriculum according to a well-developed scheme, both from the point of view of the teaching staff and parents. The advantages are that: parents may see what the school is attempting to achieve and the methods it uses; pupil progress is relatively easy to monitor; headteacher and teachers have a sense of direction and purpose which helps foster good staff morale; it encourages teachers to think constructively and to work systematically; it highlights possible areas of overlap or deficiency; it provides the basis for co-ordination between the different year groups, both for pupils and teachers; information presented in tabular form can easily be up-dated as required; the scheme provides an overview of the whole range of the school's activity.

THE SECONDARY CURRICULUM

The secondary school curriculum has a number of complexities in that it must be designed to foster positive attitudes towards study, work and leisure time across a wide variety of subjects. However, whatever subjects and courses are offered, there is no reason why they cannot be treated in a systematic way on the basis of aims and objectives, in the same way as primary schools. Usually, it is easier to view the secondary curriculum by separating years one, two and three from years four and five since the first three years are concerned mainly with what might be described as 'foundation studies', while the last two years are focused on a limited range of chosen subjects or courses which are either vocationally based or academically oriented and leading to public examinations.

Although secondary schools are organized differently and offer a much wider range of subjects and courses, it is still possible to produce some information about the curriculum for inclusion in a prospectus. Lists of subjects and courses are, however, unlikely to provide all the information which is often needed by parents when, for example, selecting the school to which to send their child. It is more likely to be the philosophy of the school and its curricular aims and objectives which will be of direct relevance when making the choice and not just lists of subjects and courses. An example of the kind of general information which might be provided on curriculum aims is shown in Table 10.3.

Nonetheless, secondary school teachers need to provide detailed syllabuses and schemes of work in the same way as primary school teachers. Therefore, where parents wish to have further information, they should be at liberty to approach the school in order to find out precise syllabus detail where they consider this to be necessary. A good school prospectus will make this point clear.

Governor's question: **The curriculum at our school always seems to be undergoing some kind of change or other. There are very few recently trained teachers on the staff and so I cannot help but wonder how they keep up-to-date. What do schools do in this respect?**
Answer: **Your LEA should provide training facilities for teachers to maintain their level of awareness of developments in education in general and in specialist subject areas. This may take the form of specific training courses, perhaps provided by LEA advisers, or through a range of services provided by LEA teachers' centres. The onus tends to be very much on the individual teacher as to whether he is going to avail himself of such opportunities. It is normal practice, in the first instance, for LEAs to circulate information about available courses and conferences so that interested teachers may apply. Raise the question at your next governors' meeting to find out what procedures are used and the steps taken to encourage staff to up-date.**

The list of curricular aims in Table 10.3 is not intended to be exhaustive and could be elaborated or expanded to reflect the setting and context of the

Table 10.3: Overall aims of secondary curriculum

The school's curriculum is designed to enable each pupil to:

Use and apply a range of study skills

Think logically and present coherent arguments on the basis of evidence

Exercise judgements, on the basis of information, on a variety of moral and social issues

Acquire basic knowledge in mathematics and sciences and apply it appropriately

Acquire, through practice, skills in communication

Appreciate art, literature and music

Stimulate imagination and creativity

Gain insight into the world of industry and commerce

Develop tolerance and understanding for others irrespective of sex, class, colour and creed

Develop awareness of the future, as it applies to the individual pupil in terms of his career, vocational training or further/higher education potential

Appreciate new technology and harness it to effect

Develop the skills and abilities for which an individual pupil demonstrates a special aptitude

---

individual school. It will, however, always contain a mixture of knowledge, skills and attitudes. Also, it is a good idea to consider curricular aims in the light of the overall aims and objectives of the school.

FINDING OUT ABOUT THE CURRICULUM

To fulfil their 'watch dog' function, governors should collect as much information about the school's curriculum as they can. The initial step is to become familiar with the subject content and teaching methods, as well as the time allocated to the various subjects and the overall standards achieved. This is unlikely to be a once-and-for-all activity since the curriculum is subject to frequent change.

Teachers will be able to supply governors with outline schemes of work that they have prepared or copies of the syllabuses from external examining boards. Curriculum documents often include jargon and the use of special terms; governors should seek clarification where necessary.

It is unrealistic to expect governors to know all about curricular matters and issues. After all, it is the professional domain of teachers and something for which they will have taken several years of training. All that can reasonably be expected is that governors possess a general awareness of curriculum content and associated teaching methods. Caution needs to be exercised since curriculum is a matter, by and large, for experts. It is all too easy for the lay person to jump to the wrong conclusions, even with the best of intentions, when faced with what appears to be sound evidence.

TEACHING METHODS

Teaching methods may be allocated broadly to one of the two groups, i.e. formal or informal. It is a matter of professional judgement about which method to use and in which circumstances. A tour of the school will reveal whether formal teaching methods are used, since classrooms will tend to be set out in rows of desks, with the teacher at the front. Informal teaching styles will be reflected by classrooms being set out in groups of desks, with the teacher moving around between the different groups.

Subject content will be significant in determining the teaching method. For example, where factual information is to be learned (remembered), formal teaching methods will tend to be used. But where the pupil is required to interpret, exercise judgement or solve problems, then informal discovery methods will be more appropriate.

EQUIPMENT AND FACILITIES

Effective teaching, whatever the style used, will depend upon the availability of adequate facilities and equipment (see Chapter 8). Governors may ask questions about what teachers require in order to deliver the curriculum. Some information may be easily obtained from general conversations with staff and a general knowledge of the school, or it may be apparent from close scrutiny of schemes of work or subject syllabuses.

Governor's question: **We have recently appointed a new headteacher at our school and there is trouble already. He wants to change the traditional methods of teaching and introduce what he calls 'child-centred learning'. This, by all accounts, seems to allow children to do what they want and some seem to play all day. Parents are up in arms and have approached members of the governing body to express their concern. What can be done?**

Answer: **The headteacher is responsible for the day-to-day management of the school, including all aspects of the curriculum. Most headteachers keep their governors well informed about the curriculum, especially about any changes they wish to make. Try to get him to explain his policies both to the governing body and to the parents, perhaps by holding a special parents' meeting. Also, it may be too early to judge the value of his ideas: another option, therefore, is to advise parents to wait a while, observe developments and then act if necessary, e.g. by expressing concern to the education office or the education committee.**

ASSESSMENT AND EXAMINATIONS

While primary schools do not have examinations, they do conduct what are termed standardized tests. These are used to measure the levels of performance and abilities of pupils as they progress through the various stages of a primary school. A standarized test is one which has established normal levels of attainment across the pupil population in order that comparisons may be made, for example, with reference to a particular age group. They are compiled by research-based organizations, such as the National Foundation for Educational Research (NFER) and Moray House, and are used by an LEA to monitor standards across its primary schools. The APU also runs tests on a sample basis across the country, the data collected being used to advise the DES and the Inspectorate.

Secondary schools use a number of assessment techniques which include continuous assessment of course work and examinations. The introduction of the GCSE involves the teacher in the preparation of assessed course work as well as examinations, both of which are under the overall control of one of the examining boards. The CSE and GCE 'O' levels will be replaced by this system. Governors should easily be able to establish how well a school is doing in relation to such examinations, in terms of basic statistics, but care needs to be taken when analysing and interpreting results. For example, it is difficult to judge performance without proper means of comparison.

REVIEWING THE CURRICULUM

Governors can help review the curriculum by carefully considering the following points: the level of interest, support and frequency of contact with the school by the LEA, especially its advisers; areas of possible concern by parents; the scope of the curriculum in terms of choice of subjects and courses; the provision of courses of lower-ability pupils; the extent to which the curriculum reflects equal opportunities, both in terms of sex and race; the extent of curricular development within the school; whether there is any collaboration between schools to formulate policies for curriculum development by sharing and exchanging ideas and so reducing unnecessary duplication of effort; the procedures used to evaluate teacher performance; the method used to evaluate the overall performance of the school; numbers of pupils opting to study different subjects and undertake different courses; the criteria used for allowing pupils to take certain courses and examinations; levels of attainment, e.g. examination successes; the extent of any shortage of teachers in specific areas; information about examination results in the comparison with those of other schools nationally; the numbers of pupils progressing to higher education; the numbers of pupils securing first-time employment.

IN A NUTSHELL

The curriculum comprises the total of planned learning experiences and activities provided by the school. It is subject to a variety of pressures which culminate in constant change and necessitates the provision of systematic curriculum development. Overall, curriculum policy is influenced by the DES and HM Inspectorate, while the LEAs have an obligation to ensure that curriculum policies are implemented across their schools and that they comply with any directions imposed. The headteacher is responsible for the curriculum at school level, including what is taught, by whom and the teaching methods used.

The role of governing bodies is to exercise general oversight of the school's curriculum, while at the same time taking full account of the fact that the curriculum is mainly the concern of teachers. This should not, however, inhibit governors from making suggestions from time to time.

SELF-TEST

1. Identify the organizations and individuals determining the curriculum.
2. Why does the curriculum change?
3. Identify four ways in which governors may keep the curriculum under review.
4. What do you understand by the 'the Great Debate', and what led up to it?
5. How does the DES influence the curriculum?

6. What are the main differences between formal and informal teaching methods?

POINTS TO PONDER

1. 'The curriculum of our school is a matter for the headteacher and teachers and nothing to do with the governors.' Consider this statement. What steps might governors take to overcome this kind of situation?'
2. The curriculum is subject to rapid change. Identify the kinds of changes which have taken place at your school and anticipate any you consider likely in the future.
3. Identify possible barriers to the implementation of curriculum innovation at your school. You could consider, for example, organizational and management factors, facilities and equipment and staff development needs, as well as the local context.
4. Is there any involvement by your community in the school's curriculum? What steps might be taken to encourage and increase involvement, particularly at the 'delivery stage'?
5. Is the governing body generally satisfied or dissatisfied with the overall performance of the school? What methods are used to monitor progress and keep the governors fully informed?
6. The headteacher, as the person direcly responsible for the curriculum, has the right to decide what should be taught and the teaching methods to be used. What action would the governing body take if he failed to take into account the concerns and wishes of parents?

GOVERNOR'S CHECKLIST

1. Are all the subjects provided in your school's curriculum relevant to the needs of today?
2. Does your headteacher invite governors to participate in discussions on curriculum issues?
3. Are you aware of any specific gaps in the curriculum provided by your school due to, for example, lack of expertise or specialist facilities?
4. Is the curriculum managed effectively in terms of the ways in which teachers are deployed in the school?
5. Does your school have some form of regular method of curriculum review?

Is there a particular committee set up for this purpose and, if so, to whom is it responsible?
6. What methods are used to regularly monitor pupil progress at your school?
7. Does your school have a staff appraisal policy in order to monitor teacher performance?
8. What means are used to keep parents fully informed about your school's curriculum?
9. What steps are taken to involve members of the local community in the curriculum at the 'delivery stage'?
10. What staff development opportunities are provided by your LEA to keep teachers up-to-date about curriculum development?

FURTHER READING

DES (1981) *The School Curriculum*, HMSO, London.
DES (1983) *Curriculum 11–16: Towards a Statement of Entitlement. Curricular Re-appraisal in action*, HMSO, London.
DES (1985) (4th impression) *Education 5–9: An Illustrative Survey of 80 First Schools in England*, HMSO, London.
DES (1985) *Quality in Schools: Evaluation and Appraisal*, HMSO, London.
DES/HMI (1985) *Technology and School Science*, HMSO, London.
DES (1986) *A General Introduction to GCSE*, HMSO, London.
DES (1986) *Sex Education at School (a draft circular)*, HMSO, London.
EOC (undated) *Do You Provide Equal Educational Opportunities?* Equal Opportunities Commission, Manchester.
Wheldall, K. and Merrett, F. (1984) *Positive Teaching: The Behavioural Approach*, Allen and Unwin, Hemel Hempstead.
HMI Series, *Curriculum Matters*, HMSO, London.

11
STAFFING SCHOOLS

Governing bodies are usually involved in the appointment of teaching staff, including the headteacher. Procedures vary from one LEA to another but a fairly standard practice is to establish a subcommittee of the governing body to be directly involved in the appointment of staff. All governors are entitled to be members of this subcommittee.

However, this is a contentious area as far as teacher governors are concerned in that sometimes they may be excluded, e.g. where an appointment may leave a vacancy which might be of direct interest to a teacher governor or where a relative of the teacher governor is a candidate. In either of these cases the teacher governor might be considered to have a pecuniary interest in the outcome.

In a recent court case the judgement favoured an LEA's right to exclude a teacher governor from the appointments panel. However, the position is under review by the DES, which appears to hold the view that all governors should be treated equally. New regulations will probably follow, although it is not yet certain whether inclusion or exclusion will predominate.

The following extracts, based on typical Articles of Government, illustrate the formal basis for the involvement of governors in the appointment of teaching staff.

(a) Appointment of headteachers

The appointment of the headteacher of the school shall conform to the following procedure:

The vacant post shall be advertised by the authority and all applications shall be referred to the governors for consideration. The governors shall draw up a shortlist of names and the final appointment shall be made by a joint committee comprising three governors of the school and three members of the education committee, such joint committee to be under the chairmanship of one of the three members of the education committee and all members having the right to vote.

(b) Appointment of assistant teachers

The appointment of assistant teachers shall be to the service of the authority within the limits of the establishment of staff laid down for the current year by the education committee. The appointment of assistant teachers shall be subject to the following procedures:

1 On the occurrence of a vacancy for an assistant teacher, the authority shall advertise the post. If, however, in the opinion of the governors, the vacancy shall not be advertised, the governors shall so recommend to the authority, who shall, if they think fit, not advertise the post. Provided that the authority may, if they think fit and after considering the views of the governors and the headteacher, require the governors to appoint a teacher to be transferred from another school or from any pool of new entrants to the teaching profession.
2. The appointment of assistant teachers shall be made by the governors, in accordance with any procedure of the authority at that time in force.
3. The appointment of assistant teachers shall be made to the service of and under a written minute of the authority.

The most striking difference between these extracts is that the exact composition of the interviewing panel is specified for the appointment of headteachers, whereas no formula is laid down in respect of the appointment of assistant teachers. The term 'assistant teacher' includes all other teachers, irrespective of seniority or degree of responsibility. Governors of voluntary schools need to check the precise arrangements which apply to their school in respect of appointments procedures.

It should also be noted that present arrangements in respect of the procedures to be followed in the appointment of teaching staff will be amended following new regulations arising out of the Education (No. 2) Act (1986). The major change is to be that appointment procedures will no longer be specified individually by LEAs in their Articles of Government, but will be replaced by standard procedures – one set for the appointment of headteachers, another set for the appointment of other teachers. These will be uniform for all LEAs, whose only area of discretion will then be in respect of which of these sets of procedures they wish to apply for the appointment of deputy heads.

WHAT CAN GOVERNORS DO?

The influence governors can have in the outcome of any staffing appointment is dependent on the LEA. Some encourage governors to play an influential part, while others limit their contribution to being little more than a formality. If the opportunity for genuine involvement in decision-making is unsatisfactory, governors should raise the matter at meetings of the governing body and, if necessary, lobby members of the education committee in an attempt to bring about improvements.

Schools stand or fall on the quality of teaching staff and if governors are to influence the general well-being of schools then they must participate fully in appointment procedures. This is more easily said than done. The extent of governor influence depends on a number of factors, including the quality of the relationship between the governors and the headteacher, and governors' knowledge of the school. In addition, the quality of relationships between individual governors is important since this affects the extent to which information is shared among them.

Governor's question: **I have been an LEA governor at a large comprehensive school for almost five years. One of the things which really interested me about being a governor in the first place was the selection and interviewing of teachers, but I have never been involved in the process. What steps can I take to become a member of the appointments committee, for I feel that I have a good contribution to make to this area of work?**
Answer: **Different LEAs and schools have their own procedures for setting up appointment committees. Nonetheless, if the opportunity exists, all governors are entitled to be considered for involvement, though places are usually restricted to two or three, including the chairman. The Articles of Government may also help in that they often make quite specific reference to the procedures to be used in relation to the composition of appointment committees. Have a word with the chairman about your interest, and if you have tried this already to no effect, raise the matter at the next meeting of the governing body. Other governors may feel the same way as you about this and in any case there seems to be no good reason why there should not be a system of rotation to give everyone the opportunity to be involved if they wish.**

THE ROLE OF THE LEA

The LEA has an obligation to appoint qualified teaching staff to its schools. This is to comply with its overall duty to provide 'efficient education' as required under section 7 of the Education Act, 1944. The appointments procedures are laid down in the Articles of Government; therefore, the LEA is the employer and is entitled to have the final word about who it should employ. Nonetheless, many LEAs recognize the importance of governors' local knowledge of a particular school and are happy to call upon this when making appointments.

As any other employer, the LEA has the statutory obligation to comply with and implement, as necessary, legislation relating to its staff. This includes: Disabled Persons (Employment) Acts, 1944, 1958; Remuneration of Teachers Act, 1965; Equal Pay Act, 1970; Superannuation Act, 1972; Health and Safety at Work Act, 1974; Trades Unions and Labour Relations Act, 1974; Rehabilitation of Offenders Act, 1974; Sex Discrimination Act, 1975; Race Relations Act, 1976; Employment Protection (Consolidation) Act, 1978; Employment Acts, 1980 and 1982; Trades Union Act, 1984; Data Protection Act, 1984.

It is common practice for LEAs to publicize their position in relation to the implementation of certain aspects of employment legislation. For example, in advertisements relating to teaching posts, the words, 'an equal opportunity employer' are frequently included, with some authorities choosing to elaborate with their own interpretation of what this means. Three examples are given here:

> The Council is an equal opportunity employer and welcomes applications from members of ethnic minority groups, disabled persons and all other sections of the community.
> (Bedfordshire Education Service)

> Ealing's new Council welcomes applications regardless of sex, race, ethnic origin, sexual orientation, disability or responsibility for dependents.
> (London Borough of Ealing)

> The Council is committed to be an equal opportunities employer and service provider. Applications are invited from women and men from all sections of the community, irrespective of ethnic origin, disability, sexual orientation or marital status, who have the necessary attributes for the post.
> (Calderdale Metropolitan Borough Council)

DISTRIBUTION OF STAFF

There are two basic rules relating to the staffing of schools: (1) Every school has to have a headteacher; and (2) Teaching staff in all maintained schools must have 'qualified teacher' status. This is granted by the DES, which allocates a registration number to those who have completed an approved course of teacher training (see below).

It is important to recognize that it is for the individual LEA to decide the number of staff it appoints to individual schools. This can be done in several ways, for example: according to the pupil–teacher ratio (PTR); on the basis of the curriculum; on an activity basis (Audit Commission terminology, similar to curriculum); and whether it is a social priority area; or on any other criteria which an LEA wishes to adopt. It should be added that some authorities are more generous than others in respect of staffing levels.

The complement of staff above Scale 1 (basic teacher scale) within an individual school is based on the application of a system of units devised by the Burnham Committee, and reviewed every three years to produce an average. Each school has a 'unit total' arrived at on the basis of the ages and numbers of pupils, as illustrated here:

Each pupil under 14 years of age – 2 units
   aged 14 and under 15   – 3 units
   aged 15 and under 16   – 4 units
   aged 16 and under 17   – 6 units
   aged 17 and over   – 8 units

The total number of units then provides the 'group total' of the school. The grouping of schools, according to the Burnham assessment, is shown in Table 11.1. The group total is also used to determine the salary range of the headteacher and those of deputy headteachers.

It is important to remember that the total number of teachers allocated to an individual school is wholly at the discretion of the LEA and has nothing to do with the Burnham grouping or points score, which only comes into play when working out the number of scale posts, i.e. numbers of teachers and levels of posts need to be treated separately. The discretion rests with the LEA as to whether to place a school on the minimum or maximum or somewhere in between the points score range, as shown in column three of Table 11.1.

In working out the allocation possibilities, each teaching post has a points value:

   each teacher on Scale 2– 1 point
   each teacher on Scale 3– 2 points
   each teacher on Scale 4– 3 points
   each senior teacher   – 3 points

Therefore, when allocating scale posts to a school, the LEA does so within the framework of Table 11.1. For example, in a Group 9 school with an average of 2,150 units, between 30 and 44 points are available for scale posts, i.e. posts over Scale 1. A possible allocation, using 40 points, could be as follows (for amendments, see SI 1984/1650 and SI 1986/559):

	Posts	Points
Senior teacher	1	3
Scale 4	2	6
Scale 3	8	16
Scale 2	15	15
	26	40

Table 11.1: Grouping of schools

Unit total or review average	Points score range	Highest scale for teachers below deputy head teacher	Group of school for head and deputy head teacher purposes
(1)	(2)	(3)	(4)
up to 100	0– 1	2	1
101– 200	0– 1	2	2
201– 300	0– 2	2	3
301– 400	1– 3	2	4
401– 500	2– 6		
501– 600	3– 8	2	5
601– 700	5– 11		
701– 800	7– 13		
801– 900	9– 15	3	6
901–1,000	10– 17		
1,001–1,100	11– 21		
1,101–1,200	13– 23	3	7
1,201–1,300	14– 26		
1,301–1,400	15– 28		
1,401–1,600	17– 33	4	8
1,601–1,800	21– 37		
1,801–2,000	25– 40		
2,001–2,200	30– 44	4	9
2,201–2,400	35– 49		
2,401–2,700	41– 55		
2,701–3,000	47– 60	4†	10
3,001–3,300	52– 65		
3,301–3,700	57– 74		
3,701–4,100	62– 79	4†	11
4,101–4,600	68– 83		
4,601–5,100	75– 90		
5,101–5,600	81– 96	4†	12
5,601–6,000	88–103		

Table 11.1 – *continued*

Unit total or review average	Points score range	Highest scale for teachers below deputy head teacher	Group of school for head and deputy head teacher purposes
6,001–6,100	88–103		
6,101–6,600	94–109	4†	13
6,601–7,100	101–116		
7,101–7,600	108–123		
Over 7,600	Proportionately	4†	14

† Including senior teachers, corresponding to column 1, sections 2, 401 to >7,600 inclusive.

Extracts from the *Burnham Scales of Salaries for Teachers in Primary and Secondary Schools, England and Wales* (1977) are reproduced by permission of the Controller of HMSO.

It is important to recognize that whatever the national framework, LEAs still retain autonomy when setting their own staffing levels. This means that they can place their own interpretation on the regulations, by, for example, opting to appoint more Scale 2 posts and fewer Scale 3, or vice versa. Additionally, in certain situations, e.g. the existence of special needs or in circumstances of 'exceptional difficulty' (educational or social disadvantage), an LEA may exceed the maximum number indicated in the range and allocate extra points.

Although LEAs have the final say, headteachers can also exercise influence when deciding the allocation of promoted posts. But where he wishes to switch points within the overall points secured, e.g. remove a Scale 2 post from needlework and enhance a Scale 2 information technology post to a Scale 3, he needs the approval of the governing body.

Similarly, he must have this approval where a Scale 3 post may disappear altogether, e.g. Classics, as a consequence of the pace of curriculum change. Careful consideration needs to be given as to where the points should go in order to maintain a fair and balanced hierarchical distribution of promoted posts, while bearing in mind the implications for staff morale.

VACANCIES

Teaching staff vacancies arise for a number of fairly obvious reasons, which include: retirement; early retirement; promotion; transfer; dismissal; accident or sudden death; pregnancy; resignation.

Whether or not a vacancy is filled will depend on a variety of factors and circumstances. For example, a declining school roll may mean that it becomes unnecessary to consider a full-time replacement. Another example is where an LEA has a policy for early retirement.

Advertising the vacancy

Once it is established that a vacancy does exist and that the position is to be filled, an advertisement is drawn up and placed in the national educational press, i.e. *The Teacher*, *The Times Educational Supplement* and the *Guardian* (Education Section on a Tuesday).

Even where prospective applicants are asked to send for further details and an application form, a good advertisement will include a clear job title, the grade of the post, a brief description of the type and size of school and where it is located. Applicants should be given information of the qualifications and experience required, and the specific teaching skills sought, plus any special responsibilities associated with the post. The advertisement should also stipulate the closing date and the address to which applications should be sent. Many advertisements, particularly those included in a block from an LEA, contain very limited information and can result in an excessive and often unnecessary amount of paperwork, since many would-be applicants fail to respond as soon as they receive fuller details of the vacancy.

'Further particulars'

Once an advertisement has been placed, every enquiry should be regarded as a potential future employee, so it is particularly important to encourage their continued interest. The quality of information sent out will be responsible significantly for either sustaining interest and producing some good applications, or putting them off altogether.

Additional information ('further particulars') should be sent out with the application form. This will fall into four broad categories: about the job, about the school, about LEA policies and about the area (local/regional amenities). It will include: a job description; the organization and management structure of the school, including the number of registered pupils, whether it is single sex or co-educational, age range, two or three form entry; a description of the school's location and catchment area; the school premises and facilities, e.g. split-site operation, special features, library, workshops, laboratories and playing fields; curriculum organization and development, including range, choice and levels of subjects; recent record of public examination successes (if applicable); staffing establishment of the school and the delegation of responsibilities; provision of technical support staff; current pupil–teacher ratio; opportunities available for staff development; extra-curricular activities, e.g. clubs and societies; arrangements and procedures used to provide pastoral care throughout the school; contacts with industry and commerce; contacts with other educational establishments; quality of school–home links, whether there is a PTA and extent of parental support generally; whether the school is currently used as a community resource; future trends (e.g. anticipated increases or decreases in pupil numbers); policy statements by the LEA in relation to aspects of employment legislation (e.g. equal opportunities, disability and rehabilitation of offenders); the nature of the area in which the school is situated (e.g. city, residential, rural); population size and demographic trends; industrial, commercial and economic developments, including job opportunities; proximity to motorway and rail networks and to places of interest and scenic beauty within the region; availability of housing, including details of subsistence allowances and removal expenses; cultural and social amenities.

JOB DESCRIPTION

The job description provides applicants with information about the nature of job and the duties and responsibilities involved. A typical job description would include: job title; job grade, if applicable; where located; to whom responsible; for whom responsible, if applicable; main duties and responsibilities; specific duties and responsibilities; working environment and any special conditions; developmental opportunities. Two specimen job descriptions are shown in Tables 11.2 and 11.3.

Reviewing job descriptions

When any job description is prepared it should not be viewed as a once-and-for-all activity. Such is the pace of change that many schools conduct a regular review of job descriptions. This will be part of the process of responding to curriculum developments or changes in education theory and practice. Also, the management structure of the school may need to be amended in order to effect a change of direction or secure improvements in certain areas of activity. Therefore some job descriptions will be modified in consultation with post-holders, while others may virtually disappear (by the demise of a subject area), and be replaced by new ones.

Where there are changes which affect an existing post-holder, any amendments or modifications will be subject to the consent of the governing body and the Chief Education Officer. However, the opportunity to undertake a

Table 11.2: Job description for a headteacher (abbreviated version)

Job title:	Headteacher
Grade:	Burnham Group 9
Location:	Meanswell County Secondary School
Responsible to:	Governing Body and LEA
Responsible for:	The organization, management and conduct of the school

Specific duties and responsibilities:

1. Determine the aims and objectives of the school in consultation with the governing body

2. To provide academic leadership and foster a high level of staff morale and professional standards

3. To maintain a broad and balanced curriculum relevant to the needs of the full age range and abilities of pupils

4. To ensure the review, modification and development of the curriculum through consultation with the staff, governors and the LEA

5. To ensure that the progress of pupils is monitored in all areas of work and that full records are maintained

6. To make provision for pupils with special educational needs

7. To manage the resources allocated to the school in line with LEA policy

8. To take part in the appointment of staff in consultation with governors and LEA officers

9. To encourage the development of good home–school links

10. To submit reports, as required, to the LEA

---

reappraisal of a job description also arises when a member of staff leaves. In such an event, the job description need not necessarily go forward again as it may be preferable to rewrite it in the light of current and future trends.

PERSON PROFILE

While a job description provides details for prospective candidates, a person profile or job specification is also drawn up to help identify the necessary criteria and characteristics required of the successful applicant. This profile is then used to help match the candidates with the demands of the job as stated in the job description. The type of information included in a person profile is as follows: general education; essential qualifications; relevant experience; special skills

Table 11.3: Job description for Scale 2 teacher

Job title:	Teacher of English
Job grade:	Scale 2
Location:	Meanswell County Secondary
Responsible to:	Head of English
Responsible for:	Student teachers on teaching practice within the department and teachers of English during their probationary year

Specific duties and responsibilities:

1. To teach English throughout the lower school

2. To design schemes of work for English language and English literature for low-ability groups

3. To contribute to the school's 'English-across-the curriculum' approach

4. Maintain records of textbooks and equipment

5. To assist with school drama activities

6. To organize drama workshops for staff

7. To contribute to the liaison activities with local primary schools

8. To take part, as required, in the pastoral aspect of the school

9. To help co-ordinate parents' evenings

10. To undertake other duties as specified by the Head of English and/or by the Headteacher

---

and abilities; achievements; personal characteristics, e.g. appearance, speech; physical make-up; leadership qualities; level of commitment; extent of motivation; degree of ambition; disposition; interests; adaptability and flexibility; personality factors. There are three main things which need to be borne in mind when considering person profile. The first is that some of the items in the list will be statements of fact while others will be subject to personal opinion or judgement. The second is that the relative importance of the items will vary from one job to another. Third, each of the items included in a person profile can be elaborated upon and made more specific, forming the basis of a checklist for interview assessment purposes (see p. 193).

QUALIFICATIONS

Qualified teacher status is the basic qualification required to be employed as a teacher in schools (teachers in further education do not need a teaching qualification). However, all those who graduated before January 1974 may teach in secondary education, while those who graduated before January 1970 may also teach in primary and special schools.

Since September 1984, all new entrants to the teaching profession are required to show that they have achieved a minimum standard of competence in English and mathematics, which means the possession of a GCE 'O' level (at least Grade C) or equivalent (e.g. CSE Grade I).

Therefore, anyone wishing to be appointed as a teacher must:
1. Have a letter of recognition of qualified teacher status from or on behalf of the Secretary of State, which includes the DES number
2. Have been awarded one of the following qualifications
   (a) a three-year full-time Certificate of Education (phased out since 1979)
   (b) a short (one-year) Certificate of Education for those with special but below-degree level qualifications (e.g. craft, art or technology diplomas or certificates)
   (c) a three-year Bachelor of Education (BEd) degree taken at a university, polytechnic or institute or college of higher education
   (d) a four-year Bachelor of Education (BEd) honours degree at a university, polytechnic or institute or college of higher education
   (e) a degree other than a BEd but which includes a teacher qualification following a four-year course (offered on a limited basis by a few universities)
   (f) graduates nominated by their LEA for exceptional recognition as a qualified teacher.

HONOURS DEGREES

Honours degrees are awarded on successful completion of a three- or four-year period of study, whereas ordinary degrees are awarded after three years. Honours degrees are divided into three classes, namely first, second and third; the highest level of attainment is a first class honours degree. The second class category is subdivided into two divisions – upper and lower (when written on an application form this may be represented as a IIi or IIii honours degree).

A pass degree is awarded in circumstances where the candidate failed to meet the requirements of the honours programme but where the work was deemed satisfactory. It is often equated, perhaps somewhat unfairly, with an ordinary degree. An aegrotat degree is awarded to a student, on presentation of a medical certificate, when, for example, final examinations were missed through illness. Different institutions and degree-awarding bodies apply their own rules and use terminology in different ways. Therefore, where uncertain about particular qualifications, governors should ask the headteacher for clarification.

It may sometimes be worth pursuing the question of qualifications at an interview.

DIPLOMAS AND HIGHER DEGREES

Sometimes candidates will have been awarded a diploma, e.g. a Diploma in Education (Dip.Ed.) or a Diploma of Advanced Study in Education (DASE). If this is the case, governors who are members of an interview panel should ask candidates to elaborate on the study involved.

Increasingly, candidates for headteaching and other teaching posts may have been awarded a higher degree. Typically, these include Master of Education (MEd), Master of Arts (MA) or Master of Science (MSc). It is a good idea for governors to probe, not only to find out what was involved in terms of study but also to what extent it provided an opportunity for independent inquiry and, if so, the nature of the topic (dissertation or thesis), the conclusions reached and its relevance to the post applied for.

IN-SERVICE TEACHER EDUCATION (INSET)

In addition to qualified teacher status, degrees and higher degrees, diplomas or certificates, governors should look to see whether applicants have been involved in short courses, since these are likely to be of particular relevance to the actual job. Some short courses are funded by grants from the DES and others by LEAs, or by a combination of both. INSET programmes usually focus on specific training needs, either to overcome particular shortages or to improve existing skills. Courses which are likely to be provided include, for example, the new technologies, including mathematics, science, craft, design and technology (CDT), computing and information technology, as well as management training for headteachers and senior staff.

Governor's question: **A teacher at our school wants to leave at very short notice, in the next three weeks, in fact. This is because her husband has suddenly been asked to work abroad. Her departure would obviously be detrimental to the school, since I doubt whether we could find an instant replacement. In any case, I understand from a fellow governor that there are certain rules about teachers' resignations and that there are only a few times during the year when they can leave. Could you please clarify the situation?**
Answer: **Your fellow governor is right. To be more precise, however, there are also set periods of notice which must be served, as well as set leaving dates to be observed. The rules relating to terminating a teacher's contract, on either side, or that: (1) two months' notice to be given terminating on either the 31 December or**

30 April, or (2) three months' notice terminating on the 31 August. In the case of headteachers, the period of notice is one month longer than for assistant teachers. If there is a valid reason for a teacher wanting to resign quickly, which will nearly always be a matter of opinion, then it makes sense for the LEA and the school to comply if they can protect the situation adequately, e.g. by making a temporary appointment. Otherwise, the teacher will have to comply with the regulations, or, if she chooses to ignore them, suffer any financial penalties which the LEA is entitled to impose.

APPLICATION FORMS

Despite the trend in many organizations to favour curriculum vitaes (CVs), most LEAs still have a preference for the traditional standard application form, which is unique to each authority. A specimen application form is shown in Figure 11.1. The principal advantage of using an application form is that it will ask for certain essential information, so helping to ensure that nothing important is missed. The information provided is always presented in the same order, so making for ease of comparison when shortlisting.

However, the disadvantage, particularly from the point of view of the applicant, is that the same standard form will tend to be used irrespective of the post. This can be problematic in that it will often include questions which are irrelevant to the applicant, e.g. details of National Service, membership of professional bodies, research and publications. The extent to which an applicant can respond to such questions is dependent mainly on age and experience. Consequently, a newly qualified teacher could have many blanks in an application form; governors should bear this in mind when scanning completed forms.

For some applicants the problem is often the limited amount of space provided in respect of the information required. A teacher with many years' experience may find it impossible to include all the relevant information in the limited space given. Where permitted, the applicant will have to use additional sheets.

Applicants are usually requested to type or complete the form in black ink. This is to facilitate photocopying in order that all members of the interview panel may have their own set of papers for each candidate.

ADDITIONAL INFORMATION

Some LEA forms incorporate a space where candidates may include information in support of their application. Specific guidance may be given on what should be included in such a statement. Where the form does not allow for this, applicants would be expected to provide an accompanying letter of application.

Figure 11.1: Specimen application form

MIDSHIRE EDUCATION AUTHORITY	**CONFIDENTIAL**

AS THIS FORM WILL BE PHOTOCOPIED PLEASE TYPE OR COMPLETE IN BLACK INK

Application for appointment as _____

At _____ School

PERSONAL DETAILS (Please complete in BLOCK CAPITALS)

First Name(s)	Surname	Title
Address for correspondence		Age
		Date of birth
Telephone Number		DES Ref. No.

Are you registered as disabled under the Disabled Persons Acts? – Yes/No

If you are, please quote your Registration Certificate number

PRESENT APPOINTMENT

Nature of post, status and grade	School or other organization	Employer's name address and telephone number	Date appointed
			Present salary

EDUCATION AND QUALIFICATIONS

Secondary school	From	To	Successes gained (brief details only where more than five years' experience)
Higher education establishments attended	From	To	Qualifications obtained (please give full details and date of award)

ADDITIONAL EDUCATION AND TRAINING – with dates (including short course attendance)

Figure 11.1 – *continued*

OTHER INFORMATION YOU CONSIDER RELEVANT TO THE POST, e.g. publications, out-of-school activities, special expertise or subject interests
Any additional information you wish to add in support of your application should be included on a separate sheet.

PREVIOUS APPOINTMENTS – Teaching, industrial and commercial (in chronological order)

Name and address of employer	Nature of duties	From	To

Please rule a line below each entry

NAMES AND ADDRESSES OF TWO PERSONS TO WHOM REFERENCE CAN BE MADE, one of whom should normally be a representative of your present employer.

Name
Position
Address

Telephone Number

Name
Position
Address

Telephone Number

Signature of applicant _____ Date _____

Where did you see the advertisement for this post? _____

Candidates please note:

Canvassing, directly or indirectly will be deemed a disqualification.

On completion this form should be returned to the headteacher unless otherwise stated.

This additional information provides applicants with an opportunity to express their ideas, perhaps about their philosophy of education, or to point out particular strengths which they could bring to the school. The care taken in preparing this information can be very revealing. Some applicants will do little more than scribble a few lines, while others will take trouble to develop their ideas in a systematic way, giving careful consideration to the nature of the post advertised and their suitability. The quality of the additional information serves as a valuable clue when drawing up a shortlist of candidates for interview.

SHORTLISTING

Once the closing date has passed the first task will be to sift through all the applications received with a view to drawing up a shortlist of candidates to be called for interview. It is not unusual for one vacancy to attract a high number of applications and a systematic approach needs to be taken using pre-determined criteria.

This will involve a series of steps commencing with the careful scrutiny of each application form and any additional information included. It will usually be possible to reject a number of applications at this stage. For instance, profiles may totally fail to match the job description; qualifications may be inadequate or inappropriate for the job; or experience may be unsuitable for one reason or another.

The next step is to give more detailed consideration to each of the applications. This will include a closer examination of qualifications, participation in INSET courses, noting how recent these are, and an analysis of previous experience, in terms of its direct relevance to the key elements of the job. This should reduce the number of applicants once again.

After further checks of those remaining, it should be possible to draw up a shortlist of those to be invited to attend for interview. The shortlist will usually include several very good applicants, and it can be difficult to decide between them on the basis of paper information alone. This means that there may have to be preliminary interviews in order to produce the final shortlist. These will take place just before the formal and final interviews.

REFERENCES

The usual practice is to take up references only when a shortlist has been drawn up. Referees are usually sent a copy of the job description and are often asked to make specific comments in respect of the candidate. Where specific information is requested and supplied, the value of a reference is likely to be increased substantially. It is also important to alert referees as to the interview date in order that all references are received in time to be photocopied for circulation to the members of the interview panel.

IN A NUTSHELL

Few activities are more important for governors than being involved in the selection and appointment of teaching staff. Usually, a subcommittee of the governing body is established to undertake the duties and responsibilities involved. However, the LEA also has a major responsibility for the selection and appointment of teaching staff, partly because it is the employer and partly because it has to ensure that its schools achieve the standard of performance required. It is therefore necessary to strike an effective balance between the interests of the employer (the LEA) and the interests of the school as perceived by its representatives, i.e. the headteacher (where appropriate) and the governors.

SELF-TEST

1. What is the formal basis for the involvement of governors in the selection and appointment of teaching staff?
2. Give five examples of legislation, outside education, with which an LEA, as an employer, must comply.
3. Name the two minimum conditions with which LEAs must comply in terms of staffing their schools.
4. Which governors are usually excluded from the process of selecting and interviewing teachers? What is the reason for their exclusion?
5. What are the disadvantages to applicants of having to fill in application forms?
6. What do you understand by the term 'job description'?

POINTS TO PONDER

1. Draw up a list of points illustrating the different circumstances in which it is likely to be difficult to recruit suitable applicants for a teaching vacancy. How might the LEA and the school governors remedy this situation?
2. What are the limits within which the LEA must operate when reviewing the establishment of a school's teaching complement above the level of Scale 1 teachers?
3. How much discretion is open to LEAs in determining the number and level of teaching posts in its schools? Suggest ways in which governing bodies might seek to use this to the advantage of their schools.

4. Discuss the kind of criteria which may be used when drawing up a job description. How does the 'person profile' tie in with the job description?
5. Discuss the qualities to be looked for in applicants, when appointing a headteacher of a primary or a secondary school.
6. Obtain copies of application forms and further details which are issued by your LEA to applicants for teaching posts. Discuss any improvements which may be made.

GOVERNOR'S CHECKLIST

1. Has your governing body established an appointments subcommittee?
2. Are you aware of the number of teachers employed at your school and their respective grades?
3. Does your school appear to you to be somewhat 'light' on promoted posts, i.e. those above Scale 1?
4. What reputation does your LEA have in relation to staffing?
5. Are there any existing vacancies at your school and, if so, what is being done about replacements?
6. Are there any longstanding vacancies at your school and, if so, what can governors do about them?
7. Is information available within your LEA with regard to projected trends of pupil numbers for your school? If so, what are the likely implications in terms of future staffing?
8. Has your LEA, as an employer, made a clear policy statement in respect of equal opportunities?
9. Does your LEA have an established recruitment policy in respect of the disabled?
10. Does your LEA stipulate to all applicants the requirements of the Rehabilitation of Offenders Act 1974?
11. Have you seen a copy of your LEA's application forms as used for the appointment of teachers and headteachers?
12. How helpful is the information the LEA sends out to prospective candidates for teaching vacancies?
13. Is there an equal opportunity for all governors to serve on the appointments committee when vacancies occur?

FURTHER READING

Home Office (1975) *Sex Discrimination: A Guide to the Sex Discrimination Act, 1975*, HMSO, London.
LACSAB (1977) *Employee Relations Handbook*, Local Authorities Conditions of Service Advisory Board.

PART 4

GOVERNING IN ACTION

> A school is successful if it has a life of its own, and forms a community commanding the loyalty of its members – the pupils, their parents and the staff. Each school needs to have its own individuality which its members themselves build up, promote and develop.
>
> (Green Paper, *Parental Influence at School*, 1984)

The extent of the impact governing bodies make depends ultimately on action, since it is what governors actually do which matters in the end. Sometimes this will take the form of increasing the level of commitment, e.g. serving on a working party or extra committee, while at other times it might mean preparing a case or undertaking a certain amount of lobbying in order to get things done.

Part 4, although at the end of the book, is hardly meant to be the terminus. Indeed, it is hoped that it will provide a jumping off point. Chapter 12 covers the appointment of teachers, and Chapters 13 to 15 consider the basic principles of meetings and how to make the most of them. Chapter 16 makes a number of suggestions concerning alternative routes for the future, and Chapter 17 provides an ancillary 'route map' which should prove helpful when additional or more specific information is required.

12
INTERVIEWING

ABOUT INTERVIEWS

There are different types of interviews in which governors may be involved from time to time, e.g. those relating to conduct and discipline and those involving contact with parents. However, it is the selection and appointment of staff which is most frequently associated with interviews and it is this aspect which is considered in this chapter. This form of interview directly involves those governors who are members of an appointments subcommittee.

An interview is a two-way process. The intention is to provide a forum for the exchange of information between the interviewers and the interviewee (the candidate). Such a process should enable the panel to check the details already held, fill in any gaps in the candidate's application form and clarify any points. It also provides an opportunity to draw out additional information, explore ideas and attitudes and generally assess how the candidate acts, reacts and interacts in the interview situation. In short, it helps determine suitability for the vacancy. The interview panel can do no more than make a prediction leading to a recommendation based on the evidence and information available.

For the candidate, the formal interview represents the final hurdle and provides the opportunity to 'sell' himself. It also provides the opportunity to ask questions and assess whether or not the job seems right for him.

INTERVIEW ARRANGEMENTS

Arrangements for interviews vary from one LEA to another, with membership of the interview panel being determined partly by the nature of the appointment to be made and partly according to rules and regulations as set out in the Articles of Government.

The appointment of a headteacher is something of a special event in that the main interview is likely to be conducted by members of the education committee and representatives of the governing body and senior LEA officials. Contact with the school will consist mainly of a tour and informal discussion with representatives of the staff.

For all other appointments there will already be a headteacher who will take an active role in the selection process. Furthermore, it is his view as to who should be appointed that is likely to carry considerable weight and in the majority of cases will be decisive.

The arrangements made when appointing a Scale 1 or Scale 2 teacher are usually quite straightforward, being confined to a tour of the school followed by a formal interview. The number of governors present will be determined by local custom and practice but in any event the chairman of governors will chair the interview panel. In addition, an LEA representative will usually be in attendance to answer questions about conditions of service, salary levels and so on.

In the case of more senior appointments (deputy head or senior teacher), the interview process may be conducted over a full day, or even two days. The advantages to be gained from a two-day arrangement include: the opportunity for candidates to have a good look around the school; ample time to meet informally and discuss the school and the nature of its activities with different members of staff; provision for a number of informal discussions with the headteacher and other senior staff regarding the overall policies of the school and its future prospects; the opportunity to interact socially with staff, governors and other candidates.

PRELIMINARY ARRANGEMENTS

Once the selected candidates have been notified of the interview date, the next step will be to ensure that all necessary preliminary arrangements are made. These will be shared by the school and the LEA and include: notification to all members of the interview panel; photocopying of all necessary documentation in respect of each candidate; preparation of an interview checklist; collation of all necessary paperwork appertaining to an appointment; selection and booking of appropriate rooms to conduct the interviews and act as a waiting room for candidates where necessary; ensuring that the environment of the interview room is quiet and comfortable; preparation of an interview programme, e.g. informal meetings with staff and guided tour of school premises; arrangements for the reception of candidates; organizing coffee, lunch and other hospitality; drawing up formal interview schedule; briefing the interview panel by the headteacher.

UNDERCURRENTS AT INTERVIEWS

The circumstances of an interview are peculiar in that they are artificial, bringing together a number of people who have never met before and more likely than not will never meet again. As with all committees, some discussion will have taken place beforehand, even to the extent that some minds may have been made up with regard to who should be appointed. Interviews for jobs often come in for such criticism.

However, few decisions are in reality cut and dried before the interview takes place, since a number of things can happen to produce a perhaps unexpected appointment. There will be a number of undercurrents present in any interview process, including: the best candidate on paper failing to turn up or withdrawing; opinion shifting from favouring one candidate to another as a result of an impressive pre-interview performance, e.g. during an informal session with staff; staff coming down strongly in favour of an unexpected candidate; a promising candidate failing to perform as well as expected during the formal interview; unexpected personality clashes emerging during the interview; strong LEA support for a particular candidate; a candidate emerging as favourite at the last minute by virtue of an excellent formal interview; difficulty in securing consensus with regard to who should be offered the post; the first choice for the post turning it down; no candidate performing really well, resulting in indecision about whether to appoint 'the best on the day' or re-advertise.

The impact of many of these problems can be greatly reduced where care has been taken over shortlisting, the composition of the interview panel and the general preparations leading up to the interview. The standard of interviewing will also be instrumental in reaching a sound decision.

GUIDELINES FOR EFFECTIVE INTERVIEWING

The quality of interviewing varies enormously and very few interviewers will have undergone any formal training in the art of conducting an interview. However, there are certain general guidelines in respect of good interview practice, and consideration should be given to the following:

1. The purpose of the interview
2. The structure of the interview
3. The time allocation
4. The pace and control of the interview
5. The interview style adopted by different panel members
6. The types of questions to be asked
7. The sequencing of questions
8. The extent to which probing questions are required
9. The need to fill gaps found in the application form
10. The need to amplify information contained in the application form
11. The amount of talking done by the interviewers
12. The opportunity given to the candidate to talk
13. The importance of listening
14. The non-verbal signals which are received from the candidate
15. Adherence to the interview checklist
16. The need to respond satisfactorily to any questions posed by the candidate
17. Whether the answers received from the candidate are sufficient to enable a decision to be made.

Interviews are more likely to be successful where panel members have considered the above points.

INTERVIEW CHECKLISTS

Although those conducting interviews will have copies of the application forms, it will also be particularly useful to have some form of interview checklist. The greater the number of candidates the more useful the checklists. They can be used to help assess, evaluate and compare the relative merits of the candidates and will also serve as a summary when reaching a final decision.

It is unlikely that LEAs will have designed a standard checklist and so it will be a matter for individual governors to consider whether they would find such a device useful. If a checklist is favoured, one could be designed by those governors who are members of an appointments subcommittee. The checklist should not be thought of as being job-specific. Once it has been designed and produced it can be used time and time again. It will simply be a matter of making minor additions, amendments or omissions as necessary according to the particular post.

A checklist should cover several areas of information including education, qualifications, experience, skills, abilities, personal attributes, qualities and attitudes. A specimen interview checklist is provided in Figure 12.1.

Figure 12.1: Specimen interview checklist

Position applied for _____ Scale _____

Name of candidate _____

Present post _____ Present salary _____

Key
A = Excellent
B = Very good
C = Good
D = Satisfactory
E = Poor

Details	Comments/Remarks/Impressions	Grading A|B|C|D|E
General education		
Essential qualifications		
Additional qualifications		
Special skills/abilities		
Previous experience (a) General (b) Specific		
Personal characteristics (a) Appearance (b) Manner/attitude/ disposition (c) Confidence (d) Maturity (e) Clarity of voice (f) Fluency of speech (g) Quality of expression		
Adaptibility/flexibility		
Level of commitment		
Self-development		
Ambition		
Leadership potential		

USING A CHECKLIST

In Figure 12.1 a grading system has been included with an alphabetical key. This enables comparisons to be made between the candidates and their exceptional strengths and weaknesses to be highlighted without having to make detailed notes. This provides profiles where a strong candidate will have a high proportion of As and Bs, an average candidate would tend to have a majority of Cs, and a weak candidate would have a profile of Ds and Es.

Some interviewers may prefer to use a numerical grading system. For example, a certain number of points out of total of 100 will be allocated to each area, e.g. so many for additional qualifications, special skills and abilities, previous experience and so on. This technique is more complex, but it has the advantage of making it possible to weight the different items in the checklist according to their importance in relation to the vacant post, while also affording merit to above-average candidates.

Alternatively, it is possible to ignore any scoring system and use the sheet simply as a prompt for asking questions and an *aide memoire* for note-taking purposes.

One other important advantage of this technique is that it helps speed up the interview process in that notes are being made during each interview. Otherwise interviewers will have to make notes after seeing each candidate.

Governor's question: **I am a governor at a comprehensive school and a member of the appointments subcommittee. A few weeks ago, we held interviews for a Head of English. There were a number of good candidates for the post but one who was particularly outstanding on paper. However, he was quite hopeless during the formal interviews and did not get the job, largely on the basis of such a poor performance. The debate as to who should get the job was pretty heated at times, as well as being somewhat confused with everyone forgetting just who the different candidates were and mixing up what they had said. Some of us felt that justice had not been done in that the interests of the school had not been served fully by our failure to agree to appoint the outstanding candidate. What can be done to ensure that this does not happen again?**

Answer: **There can be no guarantees, for every interview situation is different. However, it would seem that little or no effort was made to get the panel's act together before the formal interviews. Neither does it appear that there was any kind of systematic progress, with adequate summing up at appropriate moments. The value of a checklist can hardly be overstated. It provides all the members of the panel with the same source of information which can be used to systematically pace the interview, cover all the important questions and record progress.**

MAKING AN EFFECTIVE CONTRIBUTION

In any panel interview situation the members of the selection committee should meet in advance of the interviews to decide what their approach is going to be. Discussion should include the areas for questioning, who should put which questions, the use, if any, of a checklist and the allocation of time to each candidate.

When there is insufficient co-ordination between members of an interview panel there is a strong possibility that there will be overlap between questions, important questions will be omitted, the time allocation will be inconsistent, and candidates will feel threatened and bombarded from all directions and unfairly treated. Such an approach is hardly conducive to producing a good image of the LEA or the school and is unlikely to achieve the selection of the best candidate for the job.

Assuming that the panel has met in advance, to participate effectively as a member of an appointments subcommittee it is important for governors to: be welcoming in their approach to candidates; take into consideration the 'interview situation', i.e. many candidates will be extremely nervous; be courteous and tactful when asking questions; prepare questions which are fair but capable of testing the candidates; keep an open mind and discard personal prejudices; observe mannerisms; be attentive throughout the entire interview as a lot of useful insight into candidates can be gained from watching and listening; discriminate and evaluate the interviewee's performance on the day against potential; take note of areas about which a candidate appears sensitive or prefers to avoid altogether; 'read between the lines', e.g. does the candidate really want the job, would he fit in with the staff and the philosophy of the school?; judge the level of professional commitment which the candidate displays; contribute as a member of the interview team rather than operate on an individual basis; make notes as appropriate; put forward a point of view when arriving at the decision.

INTERVIEW STRUCTURE

In simple terms, an interview should progress from the general to the particular. It is usual practice, once the chairman has greeted the candidate and introduced the members of the panel, to indulge in some small talk, such as 'Did you have a good journey?' or 'I hope you have had an opportunity to see round the school.' Such questions or statements do not really require an elaborate answer and are included simply to help the candidate gain composure in readiness for the interview proper. The next step might be to ask the candidate to talk a little about himself and to elaborate on his qualifications. This provides a candidate with a chance to relax as there is nothing controversial or difficult about such a question.

As the interview progresses the questions will become more specific and challenging, moving away from those concerned with basic fact to those requiring opinion, insight, critical comment, depth of understanding, judgement, leadership capability, decision-making and problem-solving.

Questions requiring basic fact or description will tend to be prefaced by words like, where, when, why, which and what. More searching questions will tend to be prefaced by phrases like:

In your opinion . . .;
To what extent do you agree that . . .;
How would you justify . . .;
If such a situation arose . . .;
How much importance would you attach to . . .;
Given these kinds of choices . . .;
Faced with these alternatives, which . . .;
On what basis would you decide that . . .;
What would you do if . . .;
How would you compare . . .;
What do you understand by . . .;
How would you define . . .;
In what circumstances would you . . . .

ASKING QUESTIONS

The opportunity which governors will have to ask questions will depend on a variety of circumstances. For example, the headteacher may encourage governors to formulate questions and allow for these during the interview. The helpful headteacher may even suggest the questions he would like governors to ask. Conversely, he may wish to limit questioning by governors. It will depend very much on the quality of the relationship between the headteacher and the governors.

The chairman of the governing body, who will also chair the interview panel, can also exercise some influence here, depending on his confidence and expertise. Where a chairman already has committee experience, e.g. as a local councillor or by the nature of his work, he is likely to wish to exert more influence rather than merely act as a rubber-stamping titular head. This is not meant to imply that a chairman should fail to listen to advice offered by the headteacher.

There will also be representatives of the LEA in attendance and they too will wish to put a number of questions on behalf of the employing authority. Consequently, the opportunity for governors to pose questions will depend on the time available, the number on the panel, the number of questions asked and the length of the answers. Where there are fewer than five members on an interview panel, the individual governor may feel almost compelled to ask questions in order to justify his presence. By comparison, on a large interview panel it will be more a question of taking up an opportunity when it arises. Hopefully, many such problems will have been resolved where members have had the opportunity to co-ordinate questions and procedures before the interviews.

SPECIMEN QUESTIONS

With the exception of framing questions to secure basic information, or where a very specific response is sought, questions which will produce a straight yes or no answer should be avoided. Such questions can seriously inhibit candidates who lack confidence and they will consequently find it difficult if not impossible to expand. It is preferable to go for open-ended questions which permit maximum freedom on the part of interviewees. Such questions will help them to demonstrate their ability to gather their thoughts and generally articulate their point of view. However, it has to be borne in mind that such questions are time-consuming and it will be important to have a balance of questions.

What makes for an appropriate question at an interview will depend on the nature and level of appointment, but a few useful suggestions are:

1. What attracted you to apply for this post?
2. I see from your application form that you have a responsibility for pastoral care in your present position. Could you tell us what is involved?
3. What do you consider to be the aims of a primary school?
4. As a newly qualified teacher how would you go about overcoming any discipline problems?
5. If you were to be appointed today as second deputy head would that be the limit of your ambition or would your be looking towards a headship?
6. If you were appointed head of mathematics what changes do you think you would like to introduce on the evidence of what you have seen of the department?
7. What would be your first priority if appointed to our junior school?
8. Justify the importance you would attach to parents' views of the school.
9. Suggest ways in which the school can become a more useful community resource.
10. How much importance do you attach to keeping up-to-date in your subject area and what plans do you have for doing so?
11. What methods do you think should be used to keep the curriculum under review?

12. What do you consider to be your main strengths and weaknesses?

Governor's question: There has been a vacancy for a teacher of craft and design within my school for over twelve months. I have seen it advertised on several occasions and understand that two sets of interviews have been conducted. An appointment has still not been made. Can you suggest what the reasons might be for this situation?

Answer: First, it would seem that it has been difficult to attract candidates of the right calibre. There are likely to be several possible reasons for this, including a shortage of newly qualified or trained teachers in the subject area, the precise location of the school, poor salary as compared with opportunities outside teaching, linked to limited career prospects in general. As far as the failure to appoint is concerned, this is likely to be because the quality of the candidates may not have been very good, and it may have proved impossible for the interview panel to recommend an appointment. It looks as if the second attempt has been equally disappointing. It may also be something to do with the timing of advertisements. Certain times of year are likely to produce better results than others.

REACHING A DECISION

Who gets the job? To appoint or not to appoint? These are two possible questions which could confront any interview panel. It is the responsibility of the chairman to collect the views and opinions of the panel members on the relative merits of the different candidates.

In the first instance the intention should be to eliminate any candidates who are considered to be unsuitable for any reason. The second stage will involve careful deliberation of the remaining candidates. Taking each candidate in turn, the chairman will ask for comments to try to arrive at a consensus of opinion. Sometimes it will be obvious. On other occasions it may lead to considerable discussion and debate.

It may even result in argument, when, for example, the headteacher prefers one candidate and the LEA representatives favour another. Governors will find themselves somewhat on the sidelines, although they should not hesitate to express their preference.

The situation may be complicated further by having to consider whether to appoint an internal candidate. This is not simply a matter of the relative merits of the candidates concerned, as it could also have repercussions for the school as a whole. Not only might the decision produce yet another vacancy due to the promotion of the internal candidate, but the appointment might affect staff morale.

Yet another possibility is where none of the candidates fully matches the criteria for the post. The dilemma then is whether to take the best person on the day, in the hope that it will work out, or re-advertise. The problem may be further compounded by the urgency with which an appointment is needed. Added to this will be the additional expense involved in re-advertising and conducting fresh interviews. The pressure, therefore, tends to be on making a positive decision.

The chairman should endeavour to reach a consensus among members or at the very least secure a simple majority decision wherever possible. Once the decision is reached, the successful candidate will be called back into the interview room and invited to accept the appointment.

Governor's question: I was recently involved in the selection of a deputy head at a co-educational comprehensive school, where I am a governor. There were six really good candidates for the post, three men and three womam. There are already two deputy heads at the school, both men. There seemed to me to be a good case for appointing a woman candidate in this situation, but the headteacher would not hear of it. Even the LEA advisers expressed that, in their opinion, the appointment of a woman would be desirable. The headteacher dug in, even to the point of suggesting that he would rather re-advertise the position rather than appoint a woman candidate. The LEA advisers finally gave way and a man was appointed. Does the headteacher have so much power? Can the LEA officers, as representatives of the employer, be overruled in this way? Is this a case of discrimination against women?

Answer: Indeed, the LEA, is the employer and could, if preferred, have the final say. However, the LEA will want to maintain good relations with all its headteachers and schools, wherever possible. Also, since it is the headteacher who has to work closely with the person appointed, few LEA officers would want to impose a decision on him with which he patently disagrees, unless they had a very good reason for doing so.

Without knowing further details, it is difficult to know whether this is a case of sex descrimination, i.e. where a woman was not appointed on the grounds of her sex rather than her capacity to fulfil the requirements of the job. Any appointment *should* be made on merit, i.e. the best qualified and experienced candidate in relation to the job description, gets the job. If it cannot be shown clearly that this was not so, then there is no case to answer.

IN A NUTSHELL

The extent to which governors can contribute effectively to interviews will depend partly on how well prepared they are and partly on the support they are given by the headteacher and/or the chairman of the interview panel. Successful interviews do not just happen. They need to be planned carefully in order to decide who is going to ask which questions, how long the interviews are to be and the criteria to be used to decide who is the best candidate. The more systematic the procedures used, the more likely it is that important questions will not be missed out and that each of the candidates will feel that they have been treated fairly. A checklist can be considerably useful to help ensure that not only are all important aspects covered, but that there is a basis for summarizing the relative merits of the candidates at the end of the interview session.

SELF-TEST

1. What is the purpose of an interview?
2. Identify three important opportunities which should be provided for candidates *before* the formal interviews are held.
3. What is meant by the term 'undercurrents at interviews'?
4. Look at 'Guidelines for effective interviewing' (p.191–2). Which items do you think will be difficult to achieve? Suggest ways in which the difficulties you have identified might be overcome.
5. What do you consider to be the main advantages and disadvantages of using an interview checklist, both during and after the interview?
6. Name six approaches a governor might take in order to make an effective contribution during the interview.

POINTS TO PONDER

1. To what extent do you consider that the governors who are members of an appointments committee should be involved in the informal preliminaries before the formal interviews?
2. Consult the interview checklist (Figure 12.1). What do you consider to be the advantages to be gained from using a scoring system along the lines suggested? Draw up your own interview checklist and devise your own scoring system.
3. Draw up a bank of questions which might be used in respect of the appointment of (a) a headteacher (b) a senior member of staff and (c) a classroom teacher.
4. Identify the characteristics of a successful interview.
5. Suggest ways in which governors might influence the final outcome in the

appointment of teaching staff both during and after the interviews. What obstacles are likely to prevent your suggestions from being realized?
6. In cases where there is an internal candidate, give reasons why you think the decision of whether or not to appoint in his favour is likely to have an effect on staff morale within the school.

GOVERNOR'S CHECKLIST

1. Were the interview arrangements made in good time?
2. Were candidates given sufficient time to look round the school and meet with staff and pupils on an informal basis before the interviews?
3. Was there a consensus of opinion about who is going to get the job before the interviews have actually taken place?
4. Has an interview checklist been devised for use during and after interviews?
5. Is your headteacher helpful to governors involved in the appointments subcommittee?
6. Does the chairman have the ability and necessary experience to take an active and positive role during the interviews and give a positive lead to proceedings?
7. Was a briefing meeting held for the members of the appointments committee to decide, for example, the order of questions and the time allocation?
8. How did the interview panel reach its decision in terms of who was to be appointed to the post?
9. Do you consider that, after all was said and done, the right candidate got the job? If not, why not?

FURTHER READING

Croner's Guide to Interviews (1985) Croner Publications, New Malden, Surrey.
Goodworth, C. T. (1979) *Effective Interviewing for Employment Selection*, Business Books, London.
Higham, M. (1979) *The ABC of Interviewing*, IPM, London.
LGTB (1986) *The Most Important Thing We Do*, Local Government Training Board, London.
Morgan, C., Hall, V. and Mackay, H. (1983) *The Selection of Secondary School Headteachers*, Open University Press, Milton Keynes.

13
UNDERSTANDING MEETINGS

The central activity of all school governors is to attend meetings of the governing body. The importance of meetings cannot be overstated. However, meetings are complex because they involve a sound understanding of rules and procedural matters, the application of the full range of communication skills (oral, aural and written), and certain management skills, such as planning, controlling, leading and delegating.

This chapter – the first of three about meetings – explains the essential documentation involved, outlines procedures and introduces the terminology used. A glossary of meetings terminology is included within this chapter.

THE NATURE OF MEETINGS

Meetings range from the very formal to the informal and are held for a variety of reasons (see Chapter 14). The degree of formality is dependent largely upon the existence of rules and regulations governing procedure, e.g. as stipulated by the Instrument and Articles of Government. These will also necessitate the appointment of certain officers and the legal requirement to prepare and circulate official documents. It is essential to be fully conversant with any rules which apply in respect of meetings attended in the capacity of school governor.

CHECK THE RULES

Governors' meetings are generally formal and in order to feel comfortable and make an effective contribution, it is helpful to possess a working knowledge of the rules and procedures. The rules relating to meetings of governing bodies are contained in the Articles of Government which should be consulted while reading this chapter. (See also Chapter 6 for further discussion of the Instrument and Articles of Government.)

DOCUMENTATION OF MEETINGS

The main documents used in connection with formal meetings are: the notice; the agenda; and the minutes. Their purposes are to properly convene the meeting (the notice), outline the topics to be discussed (the agenda) and record the proceedings of the meeting (the minutes).

NOTICE OF MEETING

Before any governors' meetings, participants will each receive a notice of meeting which is usually a statement preceding the agenda. It should include the type of meeting (e.g. a meeting, a special meeting, an extraordinary meeting), the day, date, time and place, and should be circulated in advance of the meeting (normally at least seven days before) to all those entitled to attend. Specimens are included in the examples which follow.

AGENDAS

It is difficult to be precise about the exact nature and presentation of agendas since these will vary not only from one LEA to another but also between individual schools. Nonetheless, there will be a number of common features.

All agendas for formal meetings follow a standard format, beginning and ending with set items (asterisked in the examples that follow). In addition, agendas for meetings of governing bodies will also contain LEA items which will be common to all governing bodies throughout a particular LEA. These are indicated by a double asterisk in the examples. The third aspect concerns those items which are specific to a particular school and it is these which will be of most interest to governors, for it is here that they will be most likely to exercise influence. Two examples of what agendas might look like in respect of both primary and secondary schools follow:

Meanswell Primary School

There will be a meeting of the Governing Body on Tuesday, 27 September at 1530 hours in Room B in the Devonshire Road Annex.

AGENDA
1. Apologies for absence.*
2. Minutes of last meeting.*
3. Matters arising.*
4. Headteacher's report.
5. The Swann Report, 1985 (discussion of the implications arising from the report, circulated to all governors by the Education Department).**
6. HMI School Inspection. A report (to be tabled) by the Headteacher.
7. 'Special Needs Provision' (discussion paper previously circulated by Mr Roberts).
8. School discipline (paper to be tabled by the Headteacher).
9. Appointment of vacancy for the scale 2 teacher post with special responsibility for music.
10. Secondment application (Mrs Harrison).
11. Accommodation problems.
12. Fire drill procedures.
13. Lunch-time supervision.
14. Any other business.*
15. Date of next meeting.*

(Note: If the meeting was the first of the three to be held, then items 1 and 2 would be : (1) To elect the Chairman; (2) To elect the Vice-Chairman.)

Meanswell Secondary School

There will be a meeting of the Governing Body on Thursday, 23 March at 1800 hours in the Senior Common Room.

AGENDA
1. Apologies for absence.*
2. Minutes of last meeting.*
3. Matters arising from the minutes.*
4. Headteacher's report.
5. Minutes of the School Council.
6. The Swann Report, 1985 (discussion of the implications arising from the report, circulated to all governors by the Education Department).**
7. New proposals for sixteen to nineteen-year-olds (discussion document on new policies following the LEA's decision to adopt a tertiary college plan).**

8. Progress report on GCSE syllabus development for Environmental Studies (Mr Boyd).
9. Resources. (Discussion document setting out new facilities required to introduce computing as part of the school curriculum, including accommodation, equipment (hardware and software), maintenance, back-up and staffing.)
10. LEA policy in respect of new INSET arrangements.**
11. The school prospectus (review of revisions for final draft).
12. Governors' Working Party on home–school links (progress report by Dr Woods).
13. New arrangements for pastoral care (Mrs Silverton to report reorganization plans.)
14. Finance – plans for fund-raising activities in the Autumn Term.
15. Vandalism and graffiti.
16. Any other business.*
17. Date of next meeting.*

FREQUENCY OF TOPICS

While these examples provide an indication of the structure and content of agendas at meetings of governing bodies, a number of LEAs have studied the contents of their agendas in detail in order to assess the frequency with which items are discussed. Their findings would tend to suggest that the following items represent the major areas of discussion at governors' meetings: procedural matters; building maintenance; furniture and equipment; safety matters; accommodation; staffing; curriculum; public examinations; extra-curricular activities; school funds; conduct and discipline; school meals provision; use of premises; transport; capitation allowance; vandalism; PTA items.

SETTING THE AGENDA

It is up to the chairman, after consultation with the clerk, to establish the order of the agenda and to ensure that it is not too long for the time allocated for the meeting. Governors can help greatly by thinking carefully about whether the issues they have in mind as agenda items could be dealt with more easily outside the meeting, e.g. by telephoning the school secretary or the education office. However, any governor may ask for an item to be included in the agenda, although it may be advisable to consult with either the headteacher or the chairman before doing so formally. Items for inclusion should be submitted, usually in writing either to the chairman or clerk, well in advance of the next meeting, so that agenda setting may be completed in sufficient time to allow for printing and circulation before the meeting.

The final shape of an agenda will be determined by the following factors: number of LEA items; specific school items proposed by the chairman; the order of proceedings as determined by either the chairman or the clerk; items submitted by individual governors; items introduced by the headteacher; items requested for inclusion by teachers.

In addition, there will be a number of contextual factors which will also be significant, e.g. the time of year (election of officers), organizational changes (new headteacher, school merger/closure), special situations (forthcoming LEA or HMI inspection), national and local issues affecting education (new examinations, industrial action).

Governor's question: **Who decides the date and time of meetings?**
Answer: **Governors are often uncertain of who has the authority to decide the date and time of the next meeting. The answer is that no one individual has the authority to decide, this usually being a collective decision between the chairman, headteacher and clerk. Several factors determine date and time.**

As far as the date is concerned, there will be more freedom for the governing body as a whole to agree a date in those situations where the LEA does not supply the clerk. Where the LEA does provide the clerk to service the meeting, then the date will ultimately have to be set by the clerk according to his commitments in terms of the calendar for all governing body meetings within the LEA with which he is involved. So, the principal factor here is the availability of the clerk.

The time of the meeting is also affected by the points mentioned above. Not many meetings take place in the morning, and while some take place in the afternoon, most are held in the evening. Usually evening meetings are satisfactory to most people, but there are occasions when an afternoon meeting is preferred.

Governors who work during the day are entitled, under section 29 of the Employment Protection (Consolidation) Act (1978), to time off for the purpose of attending governors' meetings. This is limited, under the Act, to what is considered to be 'reasonable in all the circumstances'. Whether the employer pays for the employee who takes time off is a matter for his discretion, but an employee can complain (e.g. to his union) if he thinks he has been treated unfairly.

EXTRA MEETINGS

When it is considered that an extra meeting of the full governing body is needed, all that is required is that three governors make a formal request. The precise procedure will vary, but usually contact should be made initially with the chairman, as a matter of courtesy, or direct to the clerk of the governors. The usual rules apply, i.e. there must be an appropriate period of notice and an agenda, supported by additional papers where relevant.

Calling for extra formal meetings of the governing body should only be considered as a last resort. It is unrealistic to expect LEAs to go beyond providing the statutory number of meetings simply because of the logistics involved. One extra meeting may not seem much to one governing body but if every school within the LEA made such a request the system would break down.

To avoid such complications, the best way forward is to establish a small working party of interested governors with a specific remit, e.g. to investigate home–school links and submit a report to the governing body at the next meeting. There would be nothing to prevent the working party from seeking advice, e.g. from the headteacher, teachers and parents. The working party would have no executive decision-making powers, but could nonetheless make recommendations to the full governing body.

Sometimes it may be unavoidable to call for an additional full meeting of the governing body. This is likely to arise in the wake of the emergence of a specific issue which simply will not wait until the next meeting.

SUBCOMMITTEES

Most LEAs require governing bodies to establish several subcommittees to carry out specific responsibilities in individual schools. The usual subcommittees (though there may well be others) are: staff selection and appointments subcommittee; conduct and discipline subcommittee – set up to settle any disputes which may arise; fabric and buildings subcommittee – to monitor the condition of the building, review plans and so on; admissions subcommittee – to keep under review the application of the school's admissions procedures and to deal with any matters arising therefrom.

The composition and powers of any subcommittee are determined by the full governing body. Any subcommittee must operate within the framework of the Articles of Government and report back as necessary to the full governing body.

POSSIBLE PROCEEDINGS

Before any new business is discussed it will be usual for the chairman to make a few preliminary remarks or present a formal welcome and opening address to the assembled governing body. This will be particularly likely when there are new governors attending for the first time. The chairman will then guide the meeting through the items on the agenda.

The previous meeting's proceedings will always be considered but it is fairly standard practice, where minutes have been circulated in advance, for the chairman to ask the meeting's permission to *take the minutes as read*. If the governors agree that the record is an accurate one *the minutes are adopted* and the chairman signs and dates the copy in the minute book. If any changes are considered necessary the chairman will write them in his own hand and initial them.

Governors will then be given the opportunity to raise and discuss any *matters arising from the minutes*. These are likely to occur when one item has been inconclusively dealt with at the previous meeting and where someone may perhaps have additional information to present. Some chairmen tend to view 'matters arising' with a certain amount of caution as it can provide another opening for a topic previously discussed. However, it will be a chairman's duty to ensure that any discussion is relevant to the meeting.

The next items on the agenda may possibly refer to reports scheduled for presentation to the governing body, e.g. the headteacher's report (see p. 220), LEA standard items or committee minutes or working party reports. It is likely that a chairman may allocate a certain amount of time for such reports, to allow any necessary discussion.

Where an agenda item refers to a particular topic for discussion and ultimate decision, certain stages will have to be gone through before any decision can be reached:

1. The proposal is stated as a *motion* (usually submitted in writing before the meeting so that it may be included in the agenda), plus the name of the person suggesting it (*the proposer*) and where required the person seconding it (*the seconder*).
2. The chairman will read out the motion and call upon the proposer *to speak to it*. Where a seconder is required, he too will speak. Discussion will then follow and usually each member will be allowed to speak once only, should he wish to do so, although the proposer may speak twice as he is allowed *the right of reply* to points raised during discussion. The proposer will in effect have the last word.
3. Should any *amendments* to the motion be proposed, the chairman will deal

with them, taking a vote according to the rules and regulations. Where words are simply added to the original motion, perhaps for clarification, this is referred to as an *addendum*.
4. The revised motion then becomes a *substantive motion* and following his *summing up* the chairman *puts the question*, i.e. he presents the proposal, in its finalized form, to the meeting for their vote.
5. Should a governor other than the chairman wish to bring discussion to a close, he may move that *the question be now put* (this is known as a *procedural motion*). Where the meeting agrees, a vote would be taken at this stage. If there is no agreement the discussion will continue.
6. When the meeting votes, the chairman is responsible (with the help of the clerk) for taking the vote.
7. In declaring the result there can be two basic results. The motion may be *carried or defeated*. However, the nature of the result is relevant and will require to be recorded in the minutes. Once passed a motion becomes a *resolution*, i.e. a decision, and its wording is recorded precisely in the minutes. A motion is passed or carried if the greater number of those entitled to vote agrees to it. How big that *majority* must be may depend on the matter in question and on specific rules which may apply in certain circumstances. Where everyone agrees the motion will be said to have been carried *unanimously*, i.e. all governors were in favour. Where a motion is passed '*nem con*' (*nemine contradicente*) or '*nem dis*' (*nemine dissentiente*) this means that some governors may have *abstained*, i.e. refrained from voting. Where the result of the vote is a tie, the chairman will usually, according to the rules, exercise the *casting vote* in order to secure a decision.
8. Once a motion has become a resolution it is still possible to make an adjustment. This would be in the form of a *rider* which is an addition to a resolution which has already been passed. Such an addition requires to be proposed, seconded and voted upon in the usual way. A rider cannot nullify what has already been decided by the meeting; it may only add to or clarify a point.

When all the items on the agenda have been discussed the meeting will be brought to a close by the chairman. Where a meeting may be unable to conclude all the business on the agenda, the chairman may *adjourn* the meeting until a later date. However, in normal circumstances, well-conducted meetings should not overrun and it is one of the chairman's duties to ensure that they do not. This will be particularly important where there is a lengthy agenda and where agenda items may be such that they will require full discussion by those present at the meeting.

Governor's question: **One of the difficulties our governing bodies has is that**

members do not receive their own copy of the minutes – they are read out by the clerk at the next meeting. They are recorded by hand in a bound minutes book and the only chance we get to see them is when the book is passed round during the next meeting. It is hopeless to keep track of things and impossible to ensure their accuracy. Not only is it difficult to remember what was said, but there are substantial gaps between meetings. Also, there are many complaints by those concerned with the life of the school in general that they have no idea what goes on and what is decided at the meetings. Have you any suggestions?

Answer: It is quite absurd that minutes be kept in this old fashioned way. Given the availability of sophisticated office equipment, particularly the development of photocopying and duplicating facilities, it should be a relatively easy matter to ensure that everyone has their own copy. Additionally, where word-processing is available it is possible and simple to quickly prepare draft minutes which can be checked and modified as required. This is certainly a matter which should be placed on the agenda for full discussion. It would be useful to know what other schools do and what facilities are available at the education offices.

ANY OTHER BUSINESS

One item which appears on most agendas is 'any other business' or 'any other urgent business'. It is important that this item should not be abused by governors or used to air their 'pet subjects' or raise contentious points which may not come within the scope of the meeting.

The chairman must be very strict here and ensure that any topic raised is relevant and could not have been put forward in advance as a proper agenda item. Where a chairman considers that the point raised merits full discussion, he will normally suggest that it be advanced as an agenda item for the next meeting. The chairman should avoid permitting more time being spent on this item than on the rest of the meeting – something not unheard of, but indicative of very poor meeting conduct.

MINUTES

The minutes are the constitutional record of what actually took place at the meeting. It is the responsibility of the clerk to record the proceedings and to set these down in the minute book which is open to inspection by representatives of the LEA, teachers, parents, pupils and others involved with the school.

Minutes do not become legally binding until they have been agreed by the governing body as representing an accurate account of the meeting and signed by the chairman. Minor adjustments or modifications would be made by the chairman and endorsed accordingly.

As many LEAs do not send out the minutes of the last meeting until they circulate the notice and agenda for the next (to save time and money), the time between the meeting and the publication of the minutes often runs into several weeks, if not months. A way round this delay would be for the clerk to draw up what might be termed 'draft minutes' to be published for the general interest of parents, teachers and pupils. Such minutes would be provisional only and it should made clear that they are subject to formal approval by the governing body.

Formal minutes of a meeting should ideally: indicate the day, date, time and place of the meeting; list the names of all those present; record apologies received; follow the order of the agenda; summarize matters arising; summarize reports received; discriminate between fact and opinion; indicate motions put with names of proposers and seconders; provide a brief account of the discussion, with names of principal speakers; record motions carried with the precise wording of the resolutions; provide details of the voting, e.g. carried unanimously, passed by majority vote, passed 'nem con' or defeated; record any follow-up action agreed and identify the individuals undertaking to act, e.g. chairman, headteacher; summarize any other business discussed; indicate the date agreed for the next meeting.

NUMBERING MINUTES

For convenience in referring back through previous minutes it is customary for the clerk to preface all minutes with an appropriate reference number. Referencing techniques will vary but a common one is to adopt the year, followed by the month and then the agenda item e.g. 87.3.3 would normally refer to matters arising at the March meeting of the governing body (assuming matters arising to be agenda item 3). An alternative would be to translate agenda items into a continuous run for minute referencing purposes. For example, where fifteen items were contained on the agenda for the first meeting of the year, the second meeting would commence with minute 87.16, representing the first item on the agenda for the second meeting of the year.

Governor's question: **As a governor I receive a copy of the agenda and minutes of governors' meetings. Recently on visiting the school I heard that anyone interested in governor's meetings is entitled to see these papers. I always considered all such papers to be confidential. Could you advise?**
Answer: **The Education (School Governing Bodies) Regulations (1981) state:**

copies of the agenda and signed minutes relating to any meeting of the governing body of a school shall, in each case as soon as may be, be readily available at the school for inspection by any teacher or other person employed at the school, any parent of a registered pupil or any registered pupil.

(para. 12(1))

The regulations (para. 12(2)) also require that several items be excluded from the minutes to be made publicly available and these include reference to a named teacher or other person employed and named pupils.

GLOSSARY OF MEETING TERMINOLOGY

The following is a list of terms commonly encountered at more formal meetings, including those usually applicable at meetings of governing bodies:

Ab initio From the beginning

Abstention Where a member refrains from casting a vote either in favour or against a motion

Addendum An amendment which adds words to a motion

Address the chair Where a member wishes to speak he must first address the chairman, i.e. 'Mr Chairman . . .' or 'Madam Chairman . . .'

Ad hoc From the Latin meaning 'for the purpose of'. For example, an *ad hoc* committee, sometimes referred to as a 'special committee', is one set up for a special purpose and when that purpose is fulfilled the committee is disbanded

Adjournment The chairman, with the consent of those present, may adjourn a meeting and reconvene it at a later date to complete unfinished items on the agenda

Advisory Offering advice or suggestion and making recommendations, but taking no direct action

Agenda Schedule of items drawn up for discussion at a meeting

Amendment An alteration to a motion by the addition, deletion or modification of words

Annual general meeting (AGM) A statutory meeting held once a year at which governors present a report to parents

Annual report The report presented by governors at the AGM

Apologies for absence Excuses given in advance for inability to attend a meeting

Articles of Government The formal terms of reference of a governing body in relation to its powers and functions

Ballot A written secret vote conducted in accordance with the Instrument and Articles of Government

By-laws Rules governing an organization's activities

Call to order The chairman's action to commence the meeting

Casting vote In accordance with the rules and regulations, a chairman may be granted a second vote when there is an equal number of governors for and against a motion

Caucus meeting An informal meeting of an interest group (usually political) before the formal meeting

Chairman The person given authority to conduct a meeting

Chairman's action Where the chairman, by virtue of his office, is empowered to act on behalf of the governing body

Chairman's agenda A more detailed agenda with space for comment

Clerk of the governing body The official secretary, among whose duties is the recording of minutes

Collective responsibility A convention whereby all members agree to abide by a majority decision

Committee A specific group of people elected or nominated, with collective responsibilty to perform particular tasks and duties

Composite motion An amalgam of several motions into one

Consensus Agreement by general consent without a formal vote being taken

Constitution A document comprising a system of rules, regulations and procedures

Convene Call a meeting

Co-opt To invite an individual to serve on a committee as a result of a majority vote. A person is normally co-opted because of some specialist knowledge or expertise he/she can provide

Debarment The exclusion of a party or parties from the formal procedings of a meeting

Declaration of interests Where a member is required to acknowledge that they may have a personal interest in an outcome or decision

Disqualification Where a member is excluded or prevented from holding office

Election The process of selecting candidates to serve on a governing body or committee

Executive powers Decision-making powers under the constitution

Ex officio One invited to attend 'by virtue of his office' but without voting rights

Hidden agenda The term used to describe undercurrents which are present at a meeting

In attendance Present, on invitation, to give expert help, advice or information but with no voting rights

In camera In private

Instrument of Government Rules prescribing composition and terms and tenure of office of members of governing bodies

Lie on the table Something is said to 'lie on the table' when the meeting decides that no action should be taken on it at the present time

Lobbying The term given to the practice of seeking the support of others prior to a meeting

Majority vote Where the greater number of members voting were either for or against a motion

Mandate Authority to take action on behalf of others

Manifesto Public statement of intention to act

Matters arising Queries raised or clarification provided in relation to the minutes of the previous meeting

Motion Formal proposal moved by a member that a certain topic be discussed and that action be taken upon it

Nem con No one contradicting, but where some members have abstained from voting

Nom dis No one dissenting

No confidence A vote of 'no confidence' may be passed by members of a meeting if they are at variance with the chairman

Notice of meeting Official notification of the day, date, time and place of the meeting

Out of order The chairman can rule a member 'out of order' where the member is not keeping to the point under discussion or speaking improperly

Pecuniary interest Where a member stands to gain financially either directly or indirectly from a decision taken

Point of information Formal way of asking for additional information on a topic under discussion

Point of order A query raised in respect of procedure or a possible infringement of the Instrument and Articles of Government

Proposer A member putting forward a motion for discussion at a meeting

Quorum The minimum number of persons that must be present at a meeting to make it valid, as specified in the Instrument of Government for the school

Resolution Once passed, a motion becomes a resolution

Rider Addition to a resolution once it has been passed

Right of reply A proposer has the right of reply once a motion has been discussed but before it is put to the vote

Seconder A member who supports the proposer of a motion

Standing committee A committee which is permanent and therefore meets regularly

Standing orders The rules by which meetings are conducted

Status quo As things stand at present

Subcommittee A group of members from the main or parent committee appointed to deal with a specific aspect of that committee's work

Substantive motion The final motion proposed once amendments have been made or incorporated

Summing-up The synopsis provided by the chairman at the conclusion of discussion or debate

Tabled The description applied to a document to be presented to committee 'on the table' – not one which has been included with the agenda and supporting papers

Tenure Period of office

Terms of office Conditions under which a person may hold office

Terms of reference A statement of the work to be carried out by a group or committee, providing guidelines as to how it should be done and expressing any limitations in respect of methods

Through the chair The term used to preface a question to be put to another member of a committee

Ultra vires Outside the legal power of authority of the governing body

Unanimous Where all agree

Verbatim Word for word

Vote Expression of preference.

IN A NUTSHELL

The rules, regulations and procedures of meetings help to provide a sense of order in that they establish a business-like approach to making decisions, which is one of the main reasons for holding them in the first place. The agenda presents the list of items in the order in which they are to be considered and discussed. It is the responsibility of the clerk to the governing body to produce the agenda, following discussion with the chairman, who will usually assist in formulating the order of proceedings. The agenda will contain items from the LEA (standard items for all governing bodies within the authority) and items placed by the chairman, headteacher, teachers and governors.

The minutes should provide a detailed record of the decisions taken at the meeting and reference to the various contributions made by individual members. The minutes should be made available in draft form for public scrutiny as soon as possible after the meeting. Formal acceptance by the governing body and authorization by the chairman is required before the minutes become official and legally binding.

SELF-TEST

1. Give four reasons for holding meetings.
2. What is an agenda?
3. List the set items you would expect to find on an agenda.
4. Why is the order in which items on the agenda appear important?
5. Why are some items on the agenda likely to be more important to governors than others?
6. What is the difference between 'draft minute' and 'official minutes'?

POINTS TO PONDER

1. To what extent do you consider that the rules and procedures at governors' meetings get in the way of having genuine and effective discussion?
2. Consult recent agendas relating to meetings of your governing body. To what extent are the items included of direct relevance to your school? What do you think could be done to ensure that future agendas are more relevant?
3. One of the main problems confronting governors is that of maintaining continuity between formal meetings. What policies could be drawn up to overcome this difficulty for your governing body?
4. Consult the list 'Frequency of topics' list on page 205. Draw up a list of the topics frequently discussed at your meetings. To what extent do the two lists compare and what makes for order of priority at your school?
5. Are governors encouraged to submit items to the chairman or clerk for inclusion on the formal agenda? What might be done to ensure more participation on these lines?
6. One of the opportunities available to governing bodies is the setting up of working parties to investigate a particular aspect of the life of the school. What working parties would you recommend to set up by your governing body and why?

GOVERNOR'S CHECKLIST

1. Are you usually satisfied with the order of the agenda presented for formal meetings of your governing body?
2. Do you receive your agenda and other papers in sufficient time to prepare for the next meeting?
3. Is the information provided in the agenda sufficiently detailed to indicate the nature of the content?
4. Do the arrangements made in respect of the date and time of meetings take full account of the needs of all members?
5. Does your LEA tend to crowd your agenda with items of its own?
6. Do your agendas contain too many items for the time allowed?
7. Are you well aware of the procedures used at formal meetings?
8. Does our governing body set up extra informal meetings in order to discuss matters of interest or concern?
9. What arrangements are made for prompt publication of minutes?
10. Does your governing body produce 'draft minutes'?
11. Is a reference numbering system used with the minutes and if so do you understand how it works?
12. Are you clear about the rules relating to the publication of agendas and minutes for public information?
13. Are there any working parties, set up by your governing body, of which you are a member?
14. Has your governing body established any subcommittees?

FURTHER READING

Hall, L. (revised by Lawton, P. and Rigby, E. C.) (1985) (3rd edn.) *Meetings: Their Law and Practice*, M.&E. Handbook Series, Pitman, London.

14
PARTICIPATING AT MEETINGS

Participation in all its forms is part of the way in which we live. The public has developed a 'right to be consulted' about virtually every aspect of society. The accent on public participation on school governing bodies reflects the concern that consumers should have a right to their say in how public institutions are managed. As far as school governors are concerned, the main vehicle for participation is meetings. The success of meetings depends on how well each of the participants is prepared. This chapter considers ways in which governors can prepare themselves for meetings as well as make an effective contribution once they are there. For many, attending formal meetings of any kind is an unfamiliar experience. Consequently, when required to do so, a great deal of uncertainty and even anxiety can arise. Attending governors' meetings can be a daunting and unnerving occasion. Nonetheless, they are important since policies are made and decisions taken which affect the life of the school.

FUNCTIONS OF MEETINGS

Before going on to consider how best to prepare for meetings, it is important to appreciate the functions they serve. These are: to provide information and a mechanism for reporting back; to provide a forum for discussion; to influence others; and to determine policies and make decisions.

INFORMATION

Meetings held at regular intervals provide an ideal means for disseminating information. At a governors' meeting it is the headteacher and his colleagues who will update the governors about a number of factual matters, such as the number of pupil vacancies, examination results or recent spending activities. In fact, the headteacher's report is included as a specific item on the agenda of every governing body.

Other information provided at meetings, such as the average amount of money spent per pupil on textbooks, may also be given in response to a governor's question. Where the information is not available when the question is raised, then the information will be supplied at the next meeting.

DISCUSSION

The purpose of any discussion is to consider basic information already known, to elaborate on it and to evaluate any possible consequences for the individual school. There is an opportunity to put forward ideas, exchange views and modify opinions in the light of comments made by other members. An example would be where the LEA has issued its policy for lunch-time supervision. The headteacher, supported by the clerk, would put forward his interpretation of the LEA document as it would apply to the school. Governors would be free to discuss the implications of the policy and, in the light of advice provided, make recommendations on its adoption.

INFLUENCE

Beyond listening to information and exchanging ideas, the real 'bite' of a meeting is when attempts are made to resolve possible arguments and conflict. This will invariably arise because of the different perceptions and ideological and political values which individuals have on the same issue. For example, some governors will be in favour of a school uniform while others will not. Imagine a situation in which the LEA has asked each governing body to decide its policy in respect of school uniform.

This is where an argument will develop, both sides seeking to convert, influence or persuade the other to abandon its position. The outcome will depend to a considerable extent on the degree of intensity with which views are held and the ability of individuals to persuade and argue a case. It is in situations of this nature where the quality of chairmanship will be vital if conflict is to be reduced to a minimum and an acceptable solution reached.

DECISIONS

A decision is a choice made from competing alternatives, e.g. to suspend a pupil or not, or to open up governors' meetings to observers. Making decisions can often be difficult due to lack of sufficient information or evidence, lack of time allowed for discussion, or lack of consensus. Also, the quality and content of the argument both for and against an issue may be such that it is difficult to come down in favour of one side or the other. Consequently, decisions will sometimes be taken about which some members are unhappy and it is important to remember in such cases that governing body decisions are ultimately a question of collective responsibility.

HEADTEACHER'S REPORT

In many ways the headteacher's report should be the highlight of the meeting since this is the account by the person responsible to the governors for the day-to-day management of the school.

A governor should keep a careful eye on just where the report appears on the agenda. If it is too low down in the order of items then a request could be made that it be promoted to a higher position in order to allow sufficient time for discussion. The ideal situation is where the report is forwarded to governors along with the agenda, which then gives some time for reflection before the meeting. It is a good idea to get in touch with the headteacher if a point of clarification is needed or further information is required.

If governors consider that they are not being given sufficient detailed information about certain topics in the headteacher's report, they should raise the matter by asking for the topic to be included as a specific item on the agenda of the next meeting. Governors simply cannot be expected to accept collective responsibility for decision-making with respect to the conduct and management of the school without being kept sufficiently informed by the headteacher.

The list of topics included in Table 14.1 provides a selection of the kinds of items typically included from time to time in a headteacher's report.

Since headteacher's reports have restricted circulation they are difficult to compare, and thus governors are often unable to assess the quality of the reports they receive. One way to solve this problem is for governors from different schools to compare notes when the opportunity arises, e.g. at a training day or conference, although confidentiality must be maintained during such exchanges. If this is not possible, consider the topics in Table 14.1 together with the question which follows.

WHAT MAKES FOR A GOOD REPORT?

Many governors ask, 'What makes for a good headteacher's report?' This is a difficult question to answer since the composition of a report will vary from one

Table 14.1: Topics for inclusion in a headteacher's report

Conduct and discipline
Levels of attainment
Results in examinations – pass rates (where appropriate)
Class sizes
School roll – at present/future trends
Curriculum – scope, choice, relevance
Curriculum – innovation and change
Special education
School–home links
School–community links
School–industry/commerce links (where appropriate)
New facilities/materials/equipment
Buildings – renewal/improvements/repairs
Alternative use of school premises
School playing fields
Alternative sources of finance
Library facilities
Quality/quantity of school textbooks
Teachers' views expressed
Skill shortage areas
Staff development needs (INSET)
PTA activities (if applicable)
Transfer arrangements to and from school
Extra-curricular activities
Pastoral care
Financial matters, including capitation and fund-raising activities
Health and safety
Transport problems

Note: The list assumes no order of priorities.

school to another. However, the solution may be to pose a number of questions in respect of the two principal factors which affect the quality of the report, namely the content and presentation. Possible questions would include:

1. Are there too many or too few items?
2. Is the information useful or merely a catalogue of facts and figures?
3. Are issues and problems which face the school presented or excluded?
4. Are the views of teaching staff incorporated?
5. Are items of information which have previously been requested included?
6. Are aids used to support the presentation, e.g. handouts, summary sheets, overhead projector, flip chart, whiteboard?
7. Does the nature of the presentation hide more than it reveals, e.g. is the speed of delivery so fast that items are glossed over?

8. Is the presentation clear and coherent?
9. Are teaching staff invited to contribute to the presentation where appropriate?
10. Is evidence used to support an argument, e.g. are ancient textbooks circulated to emphasize the problem of book shortages?

A GOVERNOR'S ROLE AT MEETINGS

How confident an individual governor feels to actually participate in the meeting depends on a number of factors, such as personality, the attitude of the other participants, the amount of knowledge and information available and the complexity of the issues. New governors (whether parent, LEA or teacher) are often put off by the fact that other governors – particularly those who are local councillors – have a wealth of experience of committee work and public-speaking, perhaps as experienced governors or in other forms of public office. It is also surprising how many governors feel inhibited by the presence of the headteacher.

GAINING CONFIDENCE

Confidence at committees is something that can be learned. Although some people find meetings a natural and, therefore, an easy context within which to discuss issues and make decisions, for many others it can be an uncomfortable situation. The answer is to be well prepared. Develop a systematic approach to the job of being a committee member, for that is exactly what it is – a job.

Generally speaking, the more effort spent on systematic preparation then the more confidence is built up and, as a result, an effective contribution can be made.

BEING PREPARED

Preparation will start with the arrival of the agenda and supporting papers. Begin by going through the following sequence of steps: scan the agenda, noting the sequence of the items; scan-read the papers accompanying the agenda; highlight those items which are of most interest or appeal; concentrate energies on studying those items highlighted as important; make a list of any further information or explanation required; identify ways of acquiring the information, e.g. additional reading or asking for advice or clarification from experts; decide whether the views of others are needed to help formulate a point of view, and if so arrange to meet informally with other governors before the formal meeting; return to the agenda and make notes of any comments, observations, or points of information; read again, in detail, relevant supporting papers, making notes as appropriate.

AT THE MEETING

Members of any committee can contribute substantially to the smooth operation and success of a meeting by observing certain well-established conventions. The full range of conditions for ensuring effective meetings is contained in Chapter 15. Some general guidelines which all participants need to bear in mind when attending a meeting are as follows: arrive in good time; have all the necessary papers; be well-versed on committee procedure; listen carefully; speak clearly; keep directly to the point when speaking; refrain from attempting to promote 'pet' subjects; know when to keep quiet; have the information needed if asked to report back; refuse to be drawn into an argument; try to avoid personality clashes; accept the authority of the chairman; help reduce conflict when and if it arises; help new members; resist the temptation to chat to other members; keep cool, no matter how seriously provoked; make notes as appropriate; be supportive when good ideas are suggested; refrain from distracting others, e.g. by shuffling papers, strumming fingers on the table; try to remain until the end of a meeting wherever possible, or choose an appropriate moment to leave, e.g. between agenda items, and preferably advise the chairman in advance.

These points represent what might be termed the 'protocol' of meetings, which are easy to comply with. However, more specific advice is necessary to help demonstrate how individuals may ensure that they play an effective part at meetings.

ASKING QUESTIONS

If you are reluctant to speak at meetings a good way of breaking the ice is to ask a question requesting more information. The usual way to do this during a formal meeting is to address the chairman or another member 'through the chair'.

For example, imagine that a governor would like to be clear about the number of pupils on the school register at the present time and the trends for the next three years. It is unlikely that the chairman would himself be in possession of such details, but the headteacher would almost certainly be able to advise.

Using the correct terminology, the governor would ask the question in the following way:

Point of information, through the chair. I would like to ask the headteacher, first, what are the numbers of pupils currently registered at the school and, second, what are the trends likely to be over the next, say, three years?

The correct procedure is italicized, and should be used regardless of the actual question. Experience suggests that asking for information is a relatively straightforward way of making a first contribution at meetings. Governors should not worry too much about the nature of the question since it is actually speaking that is the important thing.

Asking questions can and does improve morale, for having actually said *something* can be important in the first instance. While asking questions can be a decisive way of making a start at formal meetings, one should be aware that asking questions – especially awkward ones – can put people on the spot and may make the persistent questioner unpopular with some of the 'old hands'. Asking questions is, therefore, not necessarily going to increase one's popularity – and it may have quite the opposite effect in some circumstance, especially if long-held traditions are disturbed.

INFLUENCING EVENTS

To restrict participation to asking questions may initially go some way towards securing the acceptance of fellow governors. Nonetheless, it is generally a limitation in that it does not necessarily increase the influence and credibility of a governor. This is simply because the initiative is always with someone else, i.e. the individual with the answers.

There are two main ways of influencing events at meetings. The first is to support the arguments of other governors if in agreement, particularly by seconding any motion they might put forward. The second and most important way of exerting influence is to put forward, as clearly as possible, a point of view which may take the form of a statement or motion. The nature and extent of preparation required to put forward a point of view will be determined by the complexity of the issue and the facts already known.

It may well be worthwhile lobbying fellow governors who are known to be sympathetic, to enlist their support *before* the meeting actually takes place. To talk things over with other governors may raise points which can be added or, and just as important, bring out any unanticipated problems or difficulties.

Not everyone lacks the confidence to speak at formal meetings. Over-confidence can easily result in thoughtlessness where the speaker continually interrupts proceedings and generally does not know when to keep quiet. It is of particular importance for governors to ensure that their contributions are constructive and brief. This may be a matter of self-discipline, especially when the chairman is too easy-going.

ARGUING A CASE

Governing bodies will want to generate their own policies on a wide range of issues following consultation with the LEA and the headteacher and his colleagues. In order to argue a case or put forward policy proposals there will need to be sufficient evidence and information of the following kind: a definition of the problem or issue concerned, including its application and limitations to the situation; people's views, e.g. teachers and parents, whether collected by consultation or questionnaire; whether any legal provisions apply in relation to a particular issue, e.g. data protection regarding the disclosure of examination marks; reference made, where relevant, to any moral questions involved, e.g. in respect of the school's approach to conduct and discipline; 'hard' evidence, e.g. a trip to the playing fields and photographs of the damaged changing rooms; credible witnesses where required, e.g. experts or eye witnesses, as appropriate; how the argument fits in with the existing policies of the LEA; evidence of successful implementation of similar policies elsewhere, e.g. in other schools.

In short, when arguing a case governors need to be in full possession of the facts. This takes time and it is important to realize that new ideas are rarely accepted without considerable discussion and perhaps even argument, so the stronger the case the greater its chances of success.

MAKING DECISIONS

It would be misleading to suggest that governors' meetings are fraught with highly contentious issues which inevitably spark off heated discussion and argument. The reality is that most meetings are quite routine, dealing with what might be regarded as fairly mundane matters which require straightforward decisions.

These are usually taken by a show of hands so there is nothing secret about the procedure. Governors may sometimes feel inhibited or uncomfortable, particularly where they may be at variance with others round the table or even represent a minority point of view. When faced with having to decide which way to vote, and clearly this applies only where there is a serious doubt, the following questions may be helpful; Who will benefit from the decision, e.g. pupils, parents, teachers or, the local community? Do the advantages of voting in favour outweigh any disadvantages, or vice versa? How strong is the argument for and against the proposition or issue under discussion? Is there sufficient information upon which to base a decision? Are there any possible alternative courses of action which have not been explored? Do the ends justify the means, e.g. the course of action to be followed?

MAKING NOTES

When attending any formal or informal meeting, paricipants should always be prepared to make their own notes, irrespective of whether official minutes will be circulated later. Effective notetaking is a skill and yet relatively few people have been trained formally to take notes, either in longhand or shorthand. Nonetheless, anybody can improve their ability to take notes, to the point where meaningful notes become a matter of habit.

Selective notetaking can be extremely useful, both as an aid to concentration during the meeting and as a summary and *aide-mémoire* afterwards.

An agenda will form the basis for making notes because the numbered items will serve as a useful abbreviated form of cross-reference to the notes. Where space permits it may even be possible to make brief notes on the agenda paper itself.

Notes are a very personal thing and how individuals choose to make them will be a matter of preference. However, the following are a few suggestions which may prove useful: try to keep them brief; resist the temptation to write too much; use headings wherever possible; make use of block capitals to give something prominence; use underlining as an alternative device for drawing attention to something; incorporate symbols, e.g. asterisks, to highlight important points; make use of different coloured pens to 'flag' items for personal action or for the action of someone else; make maximum use of abbreviations and initials to represent individual speakers (where appropriate); devise personal shortcuts for common words and phrases; be generous with the spacing allowed for making notes, so that additional points may be added if required; use a size of paper which can easily be incorporated with all official papers afterwards, unless it is intended to revise rough notes after the meeting; try to keep notes reasonably neat, otherwise they may prove difficult to decipher afterwards; always date notes.

FILING NOTES

When meaningful notes are taken at a meeting they should be filed away with the official minutes of the meeting. Governors should keep a special file for all documentation in respect of governors' meetings. This will be a useful source of reference, as well as helping less experienced governors to familiarize themselves with the procedures involved. Where there is a substantial quantity of paper, a lever-arch file will be appropriate for storage purposes.

Personal notes will help to add to the flavour of official minutes and emphasize the points which were considered particularly relevant by the notetaker. It may even be that these 'unofficial' notes will prove useful in clarifying something at a later meeting for the benefit of all members of the governing body.

PREPARING AND WRITING A REPORT

Sometimes it will be necessary for governors to prepare and write up reports. This may arise out of serving as a member of a working party or subcommittee or following some form of enquiry or fact-finding activity, and will usually conclude with certain recommendations which will be placed before the governing body.

Alternatively, a report could take the form of a narrative account of some particular event or activity, which has been organized by governors, perhaps in an attempt to raise funds or integrate the school into the community via a social event of some kind. The main thing to remember when preparing any report is that it should be clear to those who read it.

Just as different types of meetings have different degrees of formality, so too do reports. However, as far as the reports considered here are concerned, it will be sufficient that they are clear, concise and factually accurate. It is often helpful to consider a report as being made up of several constituent parts. Where it is a report giving a narrative account of some event or activity, it will be sufficient to break it up into an introduction, a description of what took place, reference to any special aspects and a final section indicating success or otherwise.

Reports which are required following the activities of a working party, or investigations carried out by a group of governors on behalf of the complete governing body, are slightly more complex and will be broken into five main parts:
1. *The terms of reference,* e.g. what the working party or group sets out to do, under whose instructions and within what timescale, taking account of the framework within which work was to be carried out and acknowledging any limitations agreed beforehand;

2. *The procedures applied*, i.e. how the working party or group sets about its task, the steps it took, the type of activities it engaged in, e.g. consultations with experts, interviews with groups of interested parties, the use of questionnaires;
3. *The findings*, i.e. a synopsis or full details (dependent on the nature of the investigation) of the information and/or facts gathered during the exercise;
4. *The conclusions reached*, i.e. the opinions formed by the working party or group based on its findings and the information at its disposal:
5. *The recommendations*, i.e. suggestions as to what sort of action might be taken by the governing body following submission of the report.

REPORT-WRITING STYLE

Reports sould be written in the past tense and should always adopt impersonal constructions, i.e. 'it was evident', rather than 'we noticed' or 'we observed'. This technique helps lend objectivity to the report, which should be confined to the facts and be devoid of any suggestion of bias, emotion or self-interest. Even where it is necessary to draw conclusions and make recommendations, it should still be possible to do this in an informed manner which is as far as possible free of subjective value judgement. The style adopted should also take account of the audience it is aimed at in the language used, the background information included and the extent of specialist or technical jargon.

PRESENTATION

In terms of presentation, a report should be displayed in such a way that it is easy to follow, i.e. it should contain sufficient headings and subheadings and incorporate numbered points where this would facilitate the reader. Where a report is particularly lengthy it is useful to include a contents page and also provide a brief synopsis at the beginning. Completed reports will normally be circulated to members of the governing body and other interested parties, bearing in mind any element of confidentiality involved.

Circulation would usually be with the agenda and other relevant papers in order that governors should have sufficient time to study its content before the meeting. At the meeting a member of the working party or group would normally be called upon to 'speak to the report' and answer any questions.

BETWEEN MEETINGS

The time between full governors' meetings can create something of a problem. The real difficulty is in terms of maintaining continuity, since meetings are often

well spread-out over the school year – although in certain situations the problem is reversed in that that they are held too close together with not enough time between to allow for decisions taken at the earlier meeting to take full effect. There are a number of ways in which such problems can be reduced, the following being examples:
1. Discuss at the earliest opportunity the date of the next meeting with the chairman, the clerk and the headteacher. Try to ensure that it takes place at what is collectively agreed to be at a sensible time in the school term;
2. Consider the possibility of creating and establishing several appropriate subcommittees of the main governing body, in addition to those usually set up and preferably ones which will reflect main problem areas or items of concern which affect the life of the school;
3. Try to arrange with the headteacher and his staff to attend staff meetings, either of the whole school staff or of departments, in order to maintain regular contact and increase awareness of current issues and difficulties;
4. Liaise with the PTA to keep informed of parental views of in order that these may be more effectively represented at meetings of the governing body;
5. Attend as many of the school's functions as possible to help substantiate the role of school governor underlined by the visible interest displayed in the various activities of the school;
6. Maintain contact, as necessary, with the headteacher, the chairman and fellow governors.

IN A NUTSHELL

There are several reasons why meetings are held. The main recipe for success is the extent to which all participants are thoroughly prepared. An attempt should be made to formulate a point of view on important topics, as well as to observe a few simple conventions when at the meeting. The headteacher's report should be given careful scrutiny since this is the 'site manager's' account of the progress of the school. Governors should also endeavour to keep notes and maintain systematic records of governors' meetings; if asked to prepare a report, e.g. as a member of a working party or subcommittee, care should be taken to ensure that it is developed in a logical and sequential way in order that its point or argument is made effectively.

SELF-TEST

1. What are the main reasons for holding meetings?

2. How would you define a decision?
3. Identify the main conventions to be observed in order to help facilitate effective meetings.
4. What are the characteristics of a 'good' headteacher's report?
5. Why is it important for governors to keep their own notes in respect of meetings?
6. What is the easiest way in which a new governor can make a contribution at a first meeting?

POINTS TO PONDER

1. What positive steps can governors take to influence the outcomes of meetings?
2. Discuss the relative strengths and weaknesses of your headteacher's reports. Suggest ways in which any improvements might be brought about.
3. One of the main reasons for having meetings is to determine policy for the school. Do you think your governing body fulfils this function? What action may be taken to ensure that important items are dealt with by the governing body at its meetings?
4. What main factors do governors need to take into account when voting on a particular issue raised at the meeting? What priorities should be used? In whose interests should they vote?
5. What tactics or strategies are open to a governor seeking to influence other governors both before and during the formal meeting? In what kinds of situations should such approaches be used?
6. 'Governing bodies exist, in part, to ensure the individuality of the school.' Discuss this view and suggest ways in which governors may give effect to it and bring it to life, especially at governors' meetings.

GOVERNOR'S CHECKLIST

1. Are your meetings more concerned with exchanging information than they are with making policy decisions?
2. Are the 'official' papers you receive before a meeting of the governing body sufficiently detailed to enable you to contribute effectively?
3. To what extent are the items on the agenda mainly routine?
4. Is an opportunity provided at your meetings to discuss and argue points of policy?

5. How useful is the headteacher's report?
6. How much trouble does the headteacher go to when presenting his report?
7. Does the report include reference to important items, e.g. curriculum development, staffing matters, special needs, community links, school–home links?
8. Do members appear to be generally familiar with the conventions of meetings?
9. Is there usually a general feeling among members of the governing body that the meetings have been constructive and worthwhile?
10. Do you take notes and keep records, including official papers, of all matters relating to meetings of your governing body?
11. Are you aware of the procedures to be followed when preparing a report on behalf of a working party or subcommittee?

FURTHER READING

Adair, J. (1985) *Effective Decision-Making*, Pan Books, London.
Evans, D. W. (1978) *People and Communication*, Pitman, London.
Maude, B. (1974) *Practical Communication for Managers*, Longman, London.
Stanton, N. (1982) *The Business of Communicating*, Pan Books, London.

15
MANAGING GOVERNORS' MEETINGS

There is little doubt that successful meetings rely to a great extent on the management qualities of the main officials. In the case of governing bodies these are the chairman and the clerk, who is the committee secretary. In order to play effective roles they need to be fully involved before, during and after meetings. It is their joint responsibility to ensure that agendas comprise relevant items and that all necessary follow-up action is taken after meetings. It is the duty of the chairman to see that well-controlled meetings take place, with all participants taking part in the discussions which lead to generally acceptable decisions on behalf of the school. This chapter concentrates on the nature of the two official leadership roles and the ways in which they are able to control events or, at the very least, exercise influence.

CHAIRMAN OF THE BOARD OF GOVERNORS

One of the first tasks of a newly constituted school governing body is to appoint the chairman. In many local authorities chairmen of governors will be members of the ruling political party, perhaps local councillors and members of the local education committee and/or one of its subcommittees. None of these roles constitutes a condition for the appointment of chairman but simply reflects the way in which things have been done over the years.

BREAKS WITH TRADITION

There is absolutely nothing to prevent a parent governor being elected as chairman. All that is required is a majority vote which, of course, may be difficult to secure within a context which is so politically orientated. It is likely but not inevitable, for example, that the local opposition parties will vote with the dominant party to ensure political control of a governing body. They assume on the basis of custom and practice and by agreement that should they be put in power at the next local election, then the new opposition would do the same for them, i.e. return the favour. All of this will change following the Education (No.2) Act (1986), which has the effect of reducing LEA control of governing bodies by altering their composition.

THE APPOINTMENT OF CHAIRMAN

The election of chairman is in the collective hands of the members of the entire governing body. Parent governors, therefore, should be particularly alert at the first meeting to see that the appointment of chairman is dealt with properly. Many parent governors have been caught out by this, in that the decision about who is going to be chairman is taken before they, the parent governors, have fully appreciated what was actually happening.

Defects of procedure should not, however, be confused with poor chairmanship. A school governing body will often end up with a perfectly good chairman despite the sometimes dubious process of his election.

BARRED FROM BEING CHAIRMAN

The headteacher, as an *ex officio* member, is ineligible for election as chairman of the governing body. Teachers are also barred from election as chairman by virtue of being LEA employees. This does not mean, however, that headteachers and teachers cannot be elected chairmen of the governing bodies of another school, in another authority, since the basis of their membership there will be different, e.g. as a parent with a child registered as a pupil of the school.

Governor's question: **Last week I attended my first governors' meeting which was also the first meeting of the newly constituted governing body at my son's school. Somewhat to my surprise the chairman was elected at the start of the meeting, although there was no advance notice, and quite honestly I felt that I had absolutely no voice in these proceedings, yet felt that I ought to have. Did I have any rights and if so what could I have done about things?**
Answer: **All governors, with the exception of the headteacher and any employees of the LEA at the school in question, have the right to stand and be elected as**

chairman. However, it would seem that custom and practice has prevailed in the situation you describe, in that the position of chairman has gone to a member of the local political party, perhaps by tradition. New governors are often caught out by this kind of practice, although technically there is no reason why a new parent governor cannot be chairman. This practice is likely to be less prevalent in future due to the new composition of governing bodies.

ROLE OF THE CHAIRMAN

The role of chairman is clearly an important one, both for the actual governing body and for the school community as a whole. Therefore, the appointment should be one which inspires the confidence of everyone, including the LEA, the headteacher and his staff, the parents and pupils as well as the local community.

There are as many different styles of chairmanship as there are meetings. Much will depend on the personality of the individual. Some chairmen, for example, will be especially cautious at all times and will tend to be 'committee men', fussy about procedures rather than being charismatic, open and friendly, and capable of inspiring confidence and commitment. For those favouring the latter style, issues will tend to be more important considerations, with procedures viewed perhaps as something of a necessary evil. Consequently, certain chairmen will be ideal for some situations but less good in others. This is, of course, the same for all leadership roles, since no one individual can be good at everything.

GENERAL DUTIES OF THE CHAIRMAN

The chairman's role is more extensive than that of the other governors since in addition to chairing meetings, he has a number of general duties to fulfil, which include: acting on behalf of the governing body, as required (the chairman is the only governor with this responsibility), e.g. he may take decisions between meetings; having the final word in deciding whether an issue comes within the terms of reference of the governing body; maintaining frequent contact with the headteacher to discuss important issues; keeping in touch with the clerk to the governing body, e.g. to prepare the agenda for the next meeting; contacting, on behalf of the governing body, political representatives serving on the education committee or subcommittees; establishing and maintaining contacts with officers of the LEA as required; keeping in touch with other governors between meetings of the governing body; drawing up procedures in relation to confidentiality, including the stipulation of what is to count as confidential and deciding the length of time which confidentiality is to apply in any particular instance.

These duties will be ongoing between meetings and help to demonstrate the characteristics found in an effective chairman.

WORKING BEHIND THE SCENES

Thus the effective chairman will be working behind the scenes between meetings, holding discussions with the headteacher, with members of his political party (if relevant) and with other governors, as required. Indeed, while there has to be a formal agenda placed before the governing body at its meeting, there may well be an 'informal agenda' i.e. issues, topics and decisions which have already taken place before the actual meeting. There is nothing necessarily sinister about this. Many formal meetings are preceded by interested parties getting together to discuss points of view. It is unlikely that any formal meeting in whatever context will merely comprise the procedures and processes which are actually seen to take place on the day.

INFORMAL CONTACTS

As in any other business activity, the success of the chairman often depends on the nature and extent of his network of associates and colleagues. This will involve meeting people within both informal and formal situations. The chairman who arranges to have lunch or a drink with the headteacher is likely to discover as much about the problems and issues currently affecting the school as he does about the headteacher.

The danger arising from informal situations is that decisions are often taken before the actual meeting of the board of governors, i.e. minds are made up before discussion has taken place. Decisions taken outside the meeting, e.g. about the nature and format of the agenda itself or on specific items, can undermine the democratic process of the actual meeting, but it is virtually impossible to prevent this kind of activity.

WHEELING AND DEALING

It is important for the chairman to possess strong qualities in terms of interpersonal skills if he is to do the 'wheeling and dealing' necessary for the effective running of meetings and for the benefit of the school. After all, no one would imagine that government ministers or managing directors of large companies would simply turn up to their meetings without being fully briefed about the different positions members might take or the way in which they might vote on certain topics, and risk having all the important decisions taken there and then. In the same way, the chairman may 'wheel and deal' quite legitimately within local politics, and subsequently form opinions based on his understanding of a whole range of policies in so far as they affect a particular issue.

PREPARING THE AGENDA

The shape and length of the agenda will depend on a number of factors. Individual members of the governing body are entitled to suggest topics for inclusion, as is the headteacher, and there will also be items from the LEA. This does not mean that all topics suggested will necessarily get on to the agenda. Too many items can present problems in terms of time and so some may need to be deferred until a later meeting. It is up to the chairman to decide the nature and format of the agenda, in consultation with the clerk and the headteacher, and based on the importance of the various items under consideration.

AT THE MEETING

Where meetings are held without formal procedures or written rules, the chairman's role is often very loosely interpreted, but in formally structured meetings, such as those of a governing body, the chairman's responsibilities become much more complex, requiring him to implement a code of written rules.

Whatever the preferred qualities of the chairman, there is no doubt that his main responsibility is to conduct the meeting of the governing body according to the rules and to ensure that decisions are reached.

THE IMPORTANCE OF TIMING

The effective chairman will plan, in advance of the meeting, the time he will allow for discussion on each of the items on the agenda. Great care needs to be taken here in terms of balance. For example, too rigid a timescale will tend to stifle discussion and lead to governors feeling frustrated because they have not been allowed enough time to consider all the points in detail. On the other hand, governors like to feel that the meeting is making progress and not wasting too much time on trivia. Sustaining momentum adds a sense of purpose and achievement.

PACING THE MEETING

Pacing a meeting well keeps members on their toes. In starting the meeting, the chairman might wish to say something on the following lines:

> It is good to see you all again. I hope everyone has had time to read through the agenda and papers and that you have copies in front of you. I am not aware of any particularly contentious issues, but items 5 and 11 could, I think, be taken together in the light of information which I now have; so I propose to do this, unless there are any objections, when we reach this point on the agenda. Also, given the length of the agenda, I propose to limit discussion on the major items to around 20 minutes in each case. It is my intention that the meeting close at 8 p.m.

This kind of approach helps to alert participants at the outset on how the meeting is to be managed, as well as when they are likely to get a chance to express their views. It may also encourage participants to select the more important contributions they wish to make and to scrap any general points which could be dealt with elsewhere.

Timing should not be used simply as a guillotine or to bully members and curb discussion, but rather as a means to concentrate the minds of members onto important issues, rather than allow the meeting to degenerate into casual conversation. In short, timing should not be severe.

A sensitive chairman will want to sustain rather than limit useful discussion, even at the expense of any time reference set. Therefore, where necessary, members should be encouraged to request additional time, and the chairman should allow it, if it is apparent that by doing so the meeting will benefit.

When the chairman feels that discussion is exhausted, i.e. where there is a tendency towards repetition, the topic should be brought to a close. He may intervene by suggesting something on the following lines:

> Well, I feel that we have covered a number of important points and issues in relation to item 8. I am sure, with one or two minor reservations perhaps, that something on the lines suggested by the headteacher represents an appropriate course of action. So, unless anyone objects, may we proceed to item 9?

TAKING A VOTE

When a formal motion has been presented and reaches the stage where a vote needs to be taken, the chairman should bring discussion to a close, giving the proposer the opportunity to have the final say. He should then repeat the precise wording of the motion (or substantive motion) and take it to the vote in the usual way. This would normally be by a show of hands and the chairman would first call for those in favour. A hand count would be taken, followed by a hand count for those against. Full details of the votes 'for' and 'against' would be recorded for the minutes, including any abstentions.

RUNNING THE MEETING

The following guidelines summarize the chairman's main duties and responsibilities with reference to his conduct and management of meetings. He should:
1. formally declare the meeting open for business;
2. establish the order of the meeting and time reference;
3. ensure that the minutes of the previous meeting are an accurate reflection of what actually took place, and sign to this effect;
4. work consistently through the printed agenda;
5. maintain order as required, and ensure that comments made are relevant to the items under discussion;
6. keep discussion to the point and ensure that it stays within the powers and remit of the governing body;
7. ensure that the more talkative members of the governing body are kept in check in order to keep discussion relevant and give others a chance to contribute;
8. encourage, perhaps by invitation, the quieter members to express their opinions and put forward suggestions;
9. formulate proposals and amendments as required;
10. control the flow of discussion generally;
11. give decisions on points of order;
12. sum up the argument or discussion to reflect the consensus view before allowing a vote.

He should also:
1. put matters to the vote, as required, declare the results and ensure that they are subsequently recorded accurately;
2. rule on the extent of discussion allowed and defer or adjourn either the meeting or a particular topic;
3. clarify points of difficulty as they arise, provide a résumé of the argument to help governors crystallize their thoughts and, at the close of discussion, sum up conclusions reached in an unbiased manner;
4. exercise authority, where appropriate, in taking decisions such as setting up subcommittees, or asking a governor to carry out some sort of research and report back to the governing body as a means of disseminating information;
5. exercise tact and diplomacy and generate a climate of co-operation throughout meetings;

6. agree to chair subcommittees, as required, e.g. for the appointment of staff;
7. exercise a casting vote, i.e. a second vote, in the event of a tied decision;
8. declare the meeting closed.

CLOSING A MEETING

The penultimate task of the chairman is to consider 'any other business'. This should be confined to minor items which have not appeared elsewhere on the agenda and which are of relevance to the governing body. These will be items which may have come to light after the preparation of the agenda or which are of a minor or perhaps social significance.

Where the chairman considers that the topic is too important to be dealt with without prior notice or accompanying details, he may suggest that it be placed on the agenda for the next scheduled meeting. However, if it has a degree of urgency there are two courses of action open to him. He may suggest that an additional formal meeting be called. This would require the support of three members of the governing body. Alternatively, and where appropriate, he may offer to 'take chairman's action' (take decisions between meetings). A date and time will be set for the next meeting before the meeting is closed.

FOLLOWING THE MEETING

At the conclusion of meetings it falls to the chairman to ensure that all necessary action is taken on matters decided upon during the meeting. This may sometimes fall to the chairman himself; on other occasions it will be his responsibility to see that the action is taken by other governors in the period between one meeting and the next.

It is also the chairman's ultimate responsibility to agree, as soon as possible, any draft minutes as prepared by the clerk to the governing body. Another duty is to begin to prepare the agenda for the next meeting. Effective chairmanship is an ongoing process and the good chairman will achieve the objectives of the governing body through securing the confidence and co-operation of all other individuals concerned.

CRITERIA FOR EFFECTIVE MEETINGS

The following points represent the main criteria associated with the management of effective meetings:

1. There is a specific purpose for having the meeting;
2. The agenda is more than just a 'menu' of topics, but also indicates the approach to be taken, adding any factual information required;
3. Individual governors are clear about what is expected of them at the meeting;
4. The agenda is not too long to get through in the time available for the meeting;
5. Sufficient time is allowed for important items to be discussed in detail;
6. Minor items are dealt with quickly;
7. The meeting is kept under control, the pace is business-like, it maximizes involvement and does not allow it to stray from the point;
8. Expertise is available to provide advice on technical matters beyond the competence of the lay governor;
9. There is a good atmosphere based on team spirit and leading to a collective approach to problem-solving and decision-making;
10. Conclusions reached and follow-up action plans are carefully monitored to see that they are implemented.

THE CLERK TO THE GOVERNING BODY

Although technically anybody could be appointed as clerk to the governing body, most LEAs provide an officer from the education department to clerk governing bodies in each of the schools under their control. This is one very effective way of ensuring that a link exists between each school and the local education office. The status of the officer varies from one LEA to another. Some LEAs have appointed officers with specific responsibility for clerking governors' meetings. In others, senior education officers clerk a number of governing bodies in addition to their usual duties.

The question of the status of the clerk is an important one, since the more senior he is within the education office the more likely it is that the decisions taken by the governing body will carry more weight.

It is also worth remembering that unlike governors, who for a variety of reasons come and go, an LEA official is quite likely to have long-term contact and commitment to the school. This can be a considerable advantage, not least in providing a sense of continuity.

LEGAL ASPECTS

There is no requirement under education law for any of these particular procedures to apply. Such rules as there are operate under LEA rules or by-laws. Where this applies, a formal meeting of the school governing body can only take place when the official LEA clerk to the governors is present. Where no such provision is made, as is usually the case for smaller local authorities and in most voluntary schools, then the role of clerk can be fulfilled by anyone, but is usually undertaken by, for example, the school secretary, a teacher or even one of the governors.

This is obviously a very unsatisfactory state of affairs, since it tends to devalue the status of governors' meetings. Furthermore, the role of the clerk requires a certain amount of professional competence and general expertise on educational matters which can only be provided by an LEA officer.

Whatever the status of the clerk, other than where he is a governor, he cannot take part in the meeting. He cannot put forward propositions or vote, although there is nothing to stop him from making a contribution by providing information or generally adding to debate.

ADVANTAGES OF LEA CLERKS

There are a number of definite advantages to be gained form having an LEA clerk:
1. The clerk is often an expert on the procedures of formal committees which helps to ensure that meetings of school governing bodies are run smoothly and efficiently;
2. The clerk can usually answer any technical questions and put forward the LEA policy on different issues as they arise;
3. The clerk, by virtue of attending many schools within the local authority, builds up a wealth of experience and is often in a position to put forward his own ideas, having seen them work perhaps in other schools;
4. The clerk will have a direct contact with other officials within the education department and across the authority as a whole, who may be able to deal with problems and issues discussed by the governing body.

Governor's question: **When I went to the last governors' meeting, it all seemed to be a complete waste of time. Everyone was talking at once, the clerk seemed to be in a hurry – apparently he had to go to another meeting – and the chairman provided no sense of direction. Frankly, I am horrified at the way the whole thing is conducted. What can be done about this?**
Answer: **The two principal officials are at fault here and unfortunately the success of meetings depends very much on their contribution. First, its seems likely that your governing body is serviced by an LEA clerk. If this is the case then he may**

very well be working to a tight schedule of several governors' meetings and be under some pressure to see them all through in the time available. There is, of course, no excuse for this but, frankly, some LEAs do not provide enough support in the form of clerks for their governing bodies. If this situation is a regular feature of your meetings the only course of action would be to register a complaint, stating the exact details and circumstances, preferably in writing, to the education committee.

As for the chairman, it looks as though you are stuck with him, at least until the elections come round again. Meanwhile, the best that can be done in such a situation is for members themselves to get together and find ways round their problems. This can be done by having informal 'caucus' meetings, before and between formal meetings. At least that way the other participants will each now the others' points of view in advance and much fruitless discussion during the meeting, which can be difficult to control, will be avoided.

THE CLERK'S ROLE

The role of clerk, particularly where it is undertaken by a senior officer of the LEA, can be a dual function. As well as taking responsibility to ensure the effective servicing of the meeting, he may act in an advisory capacity, answering questions, providing the LEA perspective and clarifying policy matters during the meetings. There can be such a lot to do at a secondary school meeting that 'double manning' will not be unusual, the officer being accompanied by a committee clerk, whose responsibility it will be to take notes for the compilation of the minutes, so enabling the clerk to the governing body to devote his attention to procedural matters and generally taking a more active role in the proceedings of the meeting.

The role of clerk is an important one, involving several skills, and the quality of minutes will be a reflection on the level of clerking. However, there are considerable resource implications if it is considered necessary to have a committee clerk supplying technical back-up for every governing body meeting within an LEA, although some LEAs have made special appointments in this connection, following the increased work after the 1980 Act. Alternatively perhaps, e.g. in smaller primary schools, it may be that a retired teacher or interested parent will be willing to attend meetings purely to take notes.

Whatever the particular circumstances, the duties of the clerk to the governing body will include: formally arranging the next meeting, setting the date and time, and allowing sufficient notice; distributing the agenda to all members of the governing body, including the headteacher (whether he is a governor or not); attending *all formal meetings* of governors, whether full meetings or subcommittees, where official business is to be conducted; recording the names of those present and any apologies received; taking notes of the proceedings of the meeting; noting any follow-up action required, and who, if anybody, has accepted responsibility to undertake further work; undertaking any essential correspondence and paperwork between meetings; preparing the draft minutes and final minutes, i.e. to record what happened at the meeting and the decisions taken, noting the main points of what was said and by whom.

IN A NUTSHELL

The chairman and clerk have the main roles at governors' meetings. Effective meetings owe their success to the level and quality of their management and contributions. The chairman directs and controls the meeting and generally attempts to ensure that it works effectively to reach the decisions necessary to govern the school. The clerk, usually an LEA appointment, manages all essential documentation, ensures that the proceedings are recorded accurately and provides information and advice where appropriate.

SELF-TEST

1. Which governors cannot become chairman?
2. Why should the chairman pay particular attention to the pacing of meetings?
3. Give three specific examples of the kinds of duties performed by the clerk to the governors.
4. Give three specific examples of activities associated with the chairman, before, during and after meetings.
5. Identify the main characteristics of a successful meeting.
6. What advantages are there in having an LEA clerk to the governors?

POINTS TO PONDER

1. Suggest ways in which the chairman may:
    (a) control over-talkative, domineering governors
    (b) encourage more reticent members to contribute.
2. What are the main advantages and disadvantages to be derived from manag-

ing the meeting according to a pre-determined timescale? Are there any alternative styles of approach which you would like to see used?
3. What specific courses of action would you recommend that a governing body might take when it is faced with a weak, ineffective chairman?
4. What steps might be taken to ensure that the person appointed chairman has the necessary leadership qualities to manage the meetings effectively?
5. How might an LEA clerk best serve the interests of the school and promote the policies of the governing body within the education department?
6. What do you understand by the term 'wheeling and dealing', and what kind of activities do you consider a chairman could reasonably justify?

GOVERNOR'S CHECKLIST

1. Were all the governors well-prepared to take part in the election of chairman?
2. Was the election of chairman conducted fairly?
3. Was the person elected chairman an LEA or a parent governor?
4. Are governors' meetings conducted in a business-like way?
5. Is the chairman able to lead the committee effectively and achieve a sense of direction and purpose?
6. Do some members say too much at meetings?
7. Are some members reluctant to speak out?
8. Does your LEA provide the clerk to the governing body?
9. Do other LEA officials attend your meetings? If so, for what purpose and who are they?
10. Does the chairman carry the confidence of the governors as a collective group?

FURTHER READING

Citrine, Lord (1952) (3rd edn.) *ABC of Chairmanship*, NCLC Publishing Society, London.
Locke, M. (1980) *How to Run Committees and Meetings*, Macmillan, London.
Palgrave, R. F. D. (1964) (revised by Abraham, L. A.) *The Chairman's Handbook*, Dent, London.

16
FUTURE TRENDS

Any chapter entitled 'Future trends' is bound to be somewhat speculative. However, given that education is subject to ongoing and far-reaching changes, some indication of what these might entail seems justifiable. Whereas the preceding chapters have attempted to adopt a balanced viewpoint based on an interpretation of appropriate facts, this chapter must necessarily be predictive and based on personal opinion.

The intention of the chapter is to highlight areas of possible change which seem set to take place towards the end of the decade or maybe even towards the twenty-first century and which are likely to affect the role of governing bodies. The structure follows that of the book, i.e. covering changes affecting the education system as a whole, to those affecting the powers and functions of governing bodies in particular.

GOVERNMENT OF EDUCATION

At national level the trend towards increased centralization of control over education seems set to continue. Although such moves may be considered to have the effect of reducing local democracy, centralization may help to ensure that the provision of education across the different LEAs operates according to given procedures and achieves parity of standards. Controls will continue to be imposed in respect of levels of public expenditure. This is likely to take the form of awarding specific grants, e.g. education support grants. These will, by degrees, increasingly replace elements of the rate support grant, which has the effect of reducing the spending autonomy of a local authority. Perhaps, even more controversially, centralization could also be applied to issues affecting the very heart of education, e.g. the introduction of a core curriculum, the assessment or appraisal of teachers and new rules in relation to school government.

THE IMPLICATIONS OF MORE CENTRAL CONTROL

While moves towards a more centrally controlled system would seem, on the face of it, to have much to commend them, the difficulties of implementation cannot be emphasized enough. No amount of legislation or central directives can eleminate the vast differences which exist between LEAs.

Even though the country is geographically small, central government control of education would need to be operated through the means of regional and district offices, which would probably fail to reflect local needs and preferences and therefore be inferior to the existing situation. Indeed, there is no evidence to suggest that an education system run by bureaucrats would necessarily be more efficient (however that might be defined) than one run by locally appointed officers and elected representatives. For any service to be effective and valued, local groups and individuals need to feel that they have a legitimate right and the opportunity to influence and show concern and interest in the way in which it is to operate if it is to reflect their needs and priorities. The education service in particular belongs to local communities.

INFLUENCE OF AGENCIES

Nonetheless, central government agencies, especially the Audit Commission and the Manpower Services Commission, will undoubtedly be increasingly dominant at the education policy-making stage for the foreseeable future. The Audit Commission is likely to exercise more financial controls on local education policy-making as it continues its quest to secure value for money for the education service as a whole. Similarly, the MSC continues to gain momentum by securing even more influence through its involvement with secondary schools in respect of vocational education and training programmes. Indeed, long-term high levels of unemployment will continue to underwrite its position.

AND THE DES?

The position of the DES, which was until the mid-1960s unchallenged in the field of education, has gradually been eroded in the face of inroads made by the

MSC and the Audit Commission. It has even been suggested that the DES be replaced by a new central government department entitled the Department of Education and Training, which would presumably embrace current activities of the DES and MSC.

Whatever the case might be, it has to be acknowledged that central government departments will continue to need to implement their policies through institutions and organizations which are provided and owned locally – however diversified these might be from one area to another. In other words, central government departments will continue to rely on local authorities to 'deliver the goods' and as a result, LEAs will rightly retain considerable influence over the way in which they choose to provide education.

DIFFICULTIES AT LOCAL LEVEL

At local level, authorities seem set to encounter a number of major difficulties as they approach the end of the century. Not all of their problems relate specifically to education. For example, as a result of the contraction of industry and falling levels of the population as a whole, coupled with an increase in the number of elderly people, local administration will find its resources stretched. Added to this is the possibility of major changes taking place in terms of the local rates system – even its eventual abolition.

As far as education is concerned, chief education officers will continue to experience tensions produced by having to implement national policies according to national directives, while at the same time, serving their political masters at local level. Education committees, too, are likely to be subjected to a number of changes in the light of continued reappraisal of their roles.

Major political parties are contemplating the introduction of a local Ombudsman, while the effects of open access to information and the implications of the Data Protection Act (1984) are yet to be fully realized. Both developments will have a bearing on the activities of education committees. In any event, they seem set to have to deal with a number of unpalatable decisions affecting school closure as the school population as a whole continues its downward spiral and thereby produces an over-capacity in terms of school buildings.

SCHOOL FINANCE

Despite the limitations imposed by the complexities inherent in the system of education finance, i.e. the fact that most of the costs are paid direct by the LEA, this should not be taken to mean that governors cannot exercise influence.

Indeed, this particular topic receives special attention in the White Paper *Better Schools* (1985) and in the Education (No. 2) Act (1986), both of which require that new procedures relating to school finance be introduced by the LEAs and that these directly involve governors.

These are to include: the annual provision to governing bodies of a detailed statement of recurrent expenditure – i.e. day-to-day running costs; the annual provision to governing bodies, by the LEA, of a detailed statement of expenditure on capital equipment for each school; delegation to the governors of an annual sum of money, to be spent at the discretion of the governors, on books, equipment, stationery and so on.

In addition, governors will be required to include details of the finances of the school within their annual report to parents, another new provision contained in the White Paper and the Education (No. 2) Act (1986). The report is to provide information to parents on how the sums of money made available by the LEA to the individual school were spent, as well as information on any other sums received, e.g. through fund-raising activities or gifts.

Although these new procedures have yet to have the force of law behind them (this will have to wait until the new Education Act is passed and consequently when paragraph 23 and certain subsections of paragraph 24 of the Education Bill 1986 become a part of education legislation), there is no doubt that the climate of opinion will become increasingly receptive to governors and headteachers having more of a say and influence in the area of school finances.

SCHOOLS TO DECIDE SPENDING

Some LEAs have already started to experiment with new ways of dealing with the finances of individual schools, with the emphasis firmly on devolving decision-making to the headteacher and the governors.

For example, since the early 1970s ILEA has developed a scheme known as the 'Alternative Use of Resources' (AUR) 'designed to allow heads, teachers and governors flexibility and discretion in how resources are to be allocated within their school'.

Cambridgeshire County Council has also developed its own new policy, know as the 'Local Financial Management' (LFM) scheme of almost total devolution of decision-making powers to heads and governors in relation to use of finance in individual schools.

SCHOOLS AS 'COST CENTRES'

The Cheshire Local Education Authority is experimenting with the idea of schools as 'cost centres'. The school is provided with finance to cover all its costs with the advantage of virement, thereby leading to opportunities of making a saving on some items in order to be able to spend more on other preferred items.

While such cost-conscious schemes can never be perfect, they do offer nonetheless the potential for achieving greater levels of efficiency by giving the responsibility for important decisions to those most directly involved. Also, devolution of decision-taking direct to the schools helps firm-up their individuality in the minds of governors, teaching staff and parents. This applies with even more force, perhaps, to both elected members and officers of the LEA. In any case, there is no real reason why the many decisions which involve finance and which are unique to the individual school need to involve the officers from city or county hall. Standardization of financial policy can and often does lead to wasteful use of resources since they are often wholly inappropriate for some schools within the authority.

Strong traditions are not easily broken, however, and consequently it will be some time before such schemes become common place.

SCHOOLS AND THE COMMUNITY

This is another area for development in the future, particularly in the light of falling rolls. Spare capacity, although usually associated with school closure, can provide a number of opportunities for increasing community use of premises, as illustrated in Chapter 8. The major problem to confront an LEA is how to continue to finance those schools facing a serious decline in numbers.

It is certainly a good idea for governors to try to establish future school population trends in the areas of their schools in order to anticipate any problem, and to try to secure survival by harnessing schools to the needs of local communities. This is where a great deal of creativity is needed by the governors, the LEA and local groups if they are to seek collectively to solve the problem to the mutual benefit of all concerned.

CURRICULUM

Future trends for the school curriculum, for both primary and secondary schools, will almost certainly be linked to achieving more relevance as well as the continued quest for improving standards. Relevance is increasingly attached to information technology and all schools will give pride of place to the application of computer literacy. Courses and programmes will operate partly as a result of DES initiative and partly through MSC support.

Anxiety about standards in education has led to the suggestion that grammar schools be reinstated, supported and perhaps funded by industry. In addition, proposals to introduce a voucher system aimed at making schools more aware of the quality of their work, as well as increasing parental choice, remains a possibility for the future.

In addition, concern has already been expressed by the Secretary of State and the DES with regard to the place of foreign languages in the curriculum. While not part of established policy at the time of writing, strong views are held that a second language should be taught to every pupil. Present figures based on applications for graduate places to train as French and German teachers would suggest that languages could be about to join mathematics, physics, craft, design and technology as subject areas where there is a shortage of trained teachers. The teaching of foreign languages is particularly important given Britain's membership of the Common Market.

Standards are likely to become criterion-referenced rather than norm-referenced, with the emphasis being placed on the pupil's achievement in terms of specific behavioural objectives and based on specific knowledge, techniques or skills. The introduction of the GCSE already points the way ahead. So too do new methods of assessment – profiling, on-course assignments and teacher-marked examinations.

Since the curriculum is largely the preserve of the teachers it remains unlikely that governors will be able to influence it to a large degree. However, the curriculum belongs to everyone in a sense, hence the concern expressed by all sections of the community on such matters as moral and sex education, environmental studies and peace studies. Thus governors should continue to ask questions about the curriculum, not only to ensure that they are as well informed as possible but also to ensure that the school is responding effectively to parent and community expectations. Knowing the right questions to ask, where to find out and how to bypass any obstructions, deliberate or otherwise, will remain critical features of the role of governors in the future.

TEACHERS

Teachers are likely to feel the effects of changes in education more than any other group. Teachers, as professionals, commit themselves to education in general and to their school in particular, being closely involved and concerned with its everyday life. However, they are under continuous pressure from all sides, such as parents, employers, LEAs, DES/HMI, the Audit Commission, and so on. They usually express concern about the nature, content and relevance of the curriculum and the standards achieved at their schools. Part of this concern has led to the suggestion that teachers be subjected to some form of staff appraisal. Details have yet to be agreed and finalized.

Nonetheless, it is naive to hold the teachers themselves responsible for everything that goes wrong. They do not determine the level of resources allocated to their schools, the level of PTR, nor the number of books they can buy or the equipment they can get hold of. Such decisions are in the hands of LEAs. Neither is it any use blaming teachers about the lack of relevance in the curriculum if the LEAs and the DES are not prepared to finance and support extensive staff development and training programmes, which go a considerable way to improving the standard of teaching as well as staff morale in general.

INSET

However, following the introduction of GCSE, significant improvements have been made in respect of the level of resources for INSET, and these are likely to be sustained in the future. This will be necessary if the teaching quality needed is to be obtained and maintained. Governors will also need to add their support to staff development proposals, by listening carefully to future plans and linking teacher secondments to the overall aims of the school and its future needs, particularly in terms of benefits likely to be accrued for school management and curriculum development.

Teachers' pay and conditions of service, such a major issue in the latter half of the 1980s, has hardly been finally resolved, with there being rather more of an uneasy truce. Also, the fundamental pay structure laid down by Burnham and for so long the basis of teachers' pay, has been brought into question; if new proposals are implemented fully in the future, this will mean an end to the scale posts as described in Chapter 11 and the introduction of, for example, professional grades and principal teachers. Pay negotiations and those affecting conditions of service are also likely to be brought together for the first time.

TRAINING FOR GOVERNORS

The provision of training courses for governors has until now at least been a somewhat haphazard affair: some authorities commit significant resources to it, while others tend to virtually ignore it. Hopefully the day is not too far off when

LEAs are required to make provision for training, and anyone wishing to become a governor will need to undertake some form of approved training. In addition, adequate provision may well be made for the purposes of providing travelling expenses and subsistence allowances to governors, which in itself would be recognition of the increasing importance attached to the role.

AND ...

So much for speculation. When you next pick up your copy of the *Times Educational Supplement* or local newspaper, or switch on the television news, there is every likelihood that you will come across many other issues for inclusion in a chapter such as this. All that can be done here is to scratch the surface, so now it's 'over to you'.

POSTSCRIPT: THE 1986 EDUCATION ACT

The Education Bill (1986) finally received Royal Assent on 7 November 1986. According to Mr Kenneth Baker, Secretary of State for Education, the 62 sections contained in the new Education (No. 2) Act (1986) would 're-establish school governing bodies as the main focus for the school's life and sense of purpose' (*Education*, 14 November 1986).

The 1986 Act is devoted almost entirely to the development of a policy for school governors and consequently is bound to have an impact on the work governors do in the future. However, it is difficult to predict whether the Act will have the desired effect of strengthening the position of school governing bodies since there is much which remains to be tried and tested.

Changes in the composition of governing bodies, together with clarification of their powers, duties and functions, will require the formulation of new Articles and Instruments of Government. LEA representatives will no longer have a built-in majority in county schools since they will have parity with parent governors, following the principle offered in the White Paper *Better Schools* 'that no one interest should predominate'.

The formula relating to composition is geared to the size of the school and provides for maximum rather than minimum forms of representation as was the case with the Education Act (1980). Consequently, at the level of the school–LEA interface, new relationships will have to be developed in the light of what amounts to a break with tradition, i.e. the ending of local political domination of governing bodies.

Furthermore, LEAs are to provide governors with training courses which will help ensure that new and experienced governors are better informed about education matters generally and about their own schools and the individual problems each has to face.

It is bound to be difficult to predict the outcome of what amounts to travelling through uncharted waters. In any event, more may depend on the quality of the people persuaded to become governors, regardless of the basis of their membership, than on rules and procedures. Whatever the case, it is likely to be some time yet before any objective assessment can be made of the role of new governing bodies as 'consumer watchdogs'.

MAIN PROVISIONS OF THE EDUCATION (NO. 2) ACT (1986)

The main provisions of the Act are summarized as follows: end of political control of governing bodies; co-opted members to include representatives from the local business community; a written statement to be produced by the governing body in respect of sex education, in the light of which subsequent decisions relating to a parent's request to withdraw a pupil may be made; governors to have a majority on appointments panels; right of appeal to be given to governing bodies in cases where the headteacher is instructed by the LEA to reinstate expelled pupils; when reviewing the curriculum the governing body is required to consult the headteacher and take account of community interests; LEAs to make provision for the training of governors; governing bodies to be required to produce an annual report for parents to be presented at an annual meeting.

ADDITIONAL ITEMS IN THE ACT

Other items in the Act, but not directly involving governors, are: school transport – which requires that LEAs take account of the age of pupils and the nature of the route they have to take when considering the issue of bus passes; teacher appraisal – the Secretary of State is set to introduce, with or without teacher consent, the regular appraisal of teachers (the Act leaves the way open for its imposition in the event of a breakdown in negotiations); freedom of speech (within the law) in higher education – i.e. at universities, polytechnics and institutes of higher education – as applied to students, staff and visiting speakers.

TEACHERS' PAY

At the time of writing, the structure of teachers' pay and conditions of service seems set to undergo something of a fundamental change. Indeed, the teachers' pay dispute rumbled on into 1987 amid unprecedented moves by the Secretary of State, Mr Kenneth Baker, to impose a deal. His pay offer was publicized by using full page advertisements in the daily newspapers and heralded an attempt to impose a pay settlement from the centre.

The teacher unions, however, came up with their own proposals and the dispute finally arrived at a choice between two alternatives – the deal proposed by Baker v. that concluded by the unions and the employers – LEAs – when they met at the offices of ACAS. Whatever is ultimately decided, it seems certain that the Burnham Committee will be scrapped since it is agreed that this mechanism is outdated and that future negotiations should include both pay and conditions.

CENTRALIZATION

Centralization also gathers momentum as the government seeks to establish more direct control over local authorities, particularly with regard to how they spend central government money. It now seems more than likely that the Rate Support Grant will be yet further eroded and that direct grants, in one form or another, will be increased in order to ensure that local spending reflects national intentions if not priorities. (New arrangements for In-Service Education of Teachers – INSET – (see Circular 6/86) together with ESG spending categories are examples of central pressure towards specific local spending priorities.)

By the time this book reaches your hands doubtless many other changes will be in the melting pot. Therefore, the message has to be 'keep your eyes and ears open if you want to keep up to date'. As one retiring headteacher was heard to remark, 'it would be wonderful if the DES, the LEAs and everyone else concerned with education would freeze all recent and impending changes and give schools a chance to digest all that has happened to them in the last five to ten years'!

17
RESOURCES FOR INFORMATION

Education is constantly undergoing change. This makes it particularly difficult for anyone to keep up-to-date with everything that is going on, both at national and local levels, as well as within individual schools. While training courses go some way towards helping, they only last for a few weeks. 'How are we going to keep ourselves informed now?' is a typical question at the end of a course. This chapter has been designed to help governors sustain their involvement by familiarizing them with the range of information-providing sources and facilities which is at their disposal.

Every governor will have different interests and in a book of this nature it is only possible to scratch the surface and provide signposts. Thus the aim of this chapter is to provide governors with the key to information so that they can find out for themselves.

There is a wealth of valuable information available to governors – if only they knew where to look. Sometimes the source of information may be pretty obvious, such as the school prospectus or the Instrument and Articles of Government but at other times it may be quite obscure, as with a point of law or the exact procedures to be followed in certain circumstances. Collecting information is an ongoing activity in an area as dynamic as education. But providing there is a solid foundation based on facts, keeping up with changes as they arise should be easier. Indeed, it often pays to 'get back to basics' on a particular topic.

Finding out can also be an enjoyable experience. Tracking down a vital piece of information or discovering something new can be stimulating. As with all detective work, however, a certain amount of persistence is often required in order to solve the problem.

This chapter is divided into a number of sections, each of which deals with a particular information resource. It will depend on your own purposes and the nature of your enquiry as to which of the sources will be most relevant. For example, if you want to further your knowledge of school governors in particular or education in general, browsing through textbooks is the obvious way to do this. However, where you need to have up-to-date and factual information you are likely to need to consult official papers, documents, indexes, journals or even experts on the subject.

USING A LIBRARY

A library is the obvious source for most of the information which you will be likely to require. Generally, branch libraries tend to be rather limited, although they will be willing to get information for you. A main central town, city or county library will be able to meet most of your immediate resource needs quickly, particularly in terms of government reports, indexes/abstracts, journals and textbooks.

If you live nearby or have easy access to a university, polytechnic or college or institute of higher education, you will almost certainly be able to browse around and use the facilities they have. They will keep copies of all government circulars and a wide range of journals, indexes and so on. You may even be able to borrow textbooks, but check with the particular library as practice varies from one to another.

An added benefit will be access to things like photocopying facilities, quiet rooms, video and audio material and expert help and advice from the librarians. Try to be as specific as possible when asking for advice. The more information you are able to provide, the speedier the process. Where you have very little information for the librarian to go on, try to visit when the library is quiet and the librarian will have more time to help you.

If you are offered the opportunity to join a training course an introductory library session may be included. If not, it is something you could usefully suggest.

OFFICIAL DOCUMENTS

Although a number of official documents have already been mentioned in the text, the following represents a complete summary for easy reference of those which will be of immediate interest and value to the governor.

STATUTES

Education Act 1944
Education Act 1980
Education Act 1981
Education (No. 2) Act 1986
Health and Safety at Work, etc. Act 1974
Sex Discrimination Act 1975
Race Relations Act 1976
Employment Protection (Consolidation) Act 1978
Local Government Planning and Land Act 1980
Employment Acts 1980 and 1982
Data Protection Act 1984
Local Government (Access to Information) Act 1986

STATUTORY INSTRUMENTS

Education Act 1980 (Commencement No. 1) Order SI 489 (1980)
Education (Publication of School Proposals No. 2) Regulations SI 658 (1980)
Education (Areas to which pupils belong) Regulations SI 917 (1980)
Education Act 1980 (Commencement No. 2) Order SI 9659 (1980)
Education (Areas to which pupils belong) (Amendment) Regulations SI 1862 (1980)
Education (School Information) Regulations SI 630 (1981)
Education Act 1980 (Commencement No. 3) Order SI 789 (1981)
Education (School Governing Bodies) Regulations SI 809 (1981)
Education (School Premises) Regulations SI 909 (1981)
Education (School Governing Bodies) (Amendment) Regulations SI 1180 (1981)
Education (Teachers) Regulations SI 106 (1982)
Education (Special Educational Needs) Regulations SI 29 (1983)
Education (School Information) (Amendment) Regulations SI 41 (1983)
Education (Approval of Special Schools) Regulations SI 1499 (1983)
Remuneration of Teachers (Primary and Secondary Education) (Amendment) Order Regulations SI 1650 (1984)
Remuneration of Teachers (Primary and Secondary Education) (Amendment) Order Regulations SI 559 (1986)

ADMINISTRATIVE MEMORANDA

AM/2/81   Education (School Premises) Regulations 1981

AM/4/84   Proposals made under Sections 12 to 16 of the Education Act 1980 (School Closures)
AM/2/86   Children at Schools and Problems related to Aids
A/M25/45 Model Articles and Instrument of Government

CIRCULARS

10/65   The Organization of Secondary Education
10/70   The Organization of Secondary Education
1/73   Local Government Act (1972). Reorganization of Local Government – The Education Function
4/73   Staffing of special schools and classes
8/73   Local Government Reorganization: Arrangements for the establishment of education committees
11/73   The qualification of teachers
1/74   The NHS Reorganization Act 1973. Future arrangements for the provision of school health services and services to LEAs
11/74   Health and Safety at Work, etc. Act 1974
13/74   Education Building after 1974/75
2/76   Sex Discrimination Act 1975
4/77   Race Relations Act 1976
5/77   Falling numbers and school closures
14/77   LEA arrangements for school curriculum
15/77   Information for parents
1/80   Education Act 1980
2/80   Procedures affecting proposals made under sections 12 to 16 of the Education Act 1980
1/81   Education Act 1980: Admissions to schools, appeals, publication and school attendance orders (sections 6 to 11 and schedule 2)
2/81   Falling rolls and surplus places
4/81   School Government
6/81   School Curriculum
7/81   Education Act (1980) – sections 27 and 33(S) Regulations
8/81   Education Act (1981)
3/82   Discontinuance of maintained special schools
4/82   Secondary schools and falling rolls
1/83   Assessment of special educational needs
6/83   Approval of special schools
7/83   Education Act 1980: Application of section 2 to maintain special schools
8/84   School Curriculum

1/86 The In-service Teacher Training Grant Scheme: arrangements for the academic year 1986/87 and revised arrangements to support GCSE in the academic year 1985/86
2/86 School Attendance and Education Welfare Services
5/86 Education Support Grants
6/86 Local Education Authority Training Grants: financial year 1987/88

GREEN PAPERS

Parental Influence at School (1984) Cmnd 9242

WHITE PAPERS

DES *Teaching Quality* (1983) Cmnd 8836
DES *Better Schools* (1985) Cmnd 9469
DT1 *Intellectual Property and Innovation* Cmnd 9712

REPORTS

Crowther Report 1959: *The Education of Pupils Between 5 and 18*
Newsom Report 1963: *Half our Future – The Provision of Education for 13 to 16-year-old Pupils*
Robbins Report 1963: *Future Development of Higher Education*
Plowden Report 1967: *Children and their Primary Schools*
James Report 1972: *Enquiry into Teacher Education*
Bullock Report 1975: *A Language for Life*
Taylor Report 1977: *A New Partnership for our Schools*
Warnock Report 1978: *Education of Handicapped Children and Young People*
Cockcroft Report 1982: *Mathematics Counts*
Swann Report 1985: *Education for All, Report of the Committee of Inquiry into Education of Children from Ethnic Minority Groups*
Audit Commission Report (1986): *Towards Better Management of Secondary Education*

Note: The DES publishes a monthly list (collated annually) of all its official publications. In addition, the DES library provides a series of bibliographies and reading lists on specific issues, e.g. drugs, alcohol, tobacco; teacher appraisal; sex education. A cumulative list of titles is also available. Write to: The Library, Elizabeth House, York Road, London, SE1 7PH (01-934 9139).

BOOKS

The range of books on educational topics is vast. Some have been included under the 'further reading' sections in the preceding chapters and more are referred to below. It is necessary to select with a degree of care, having considered in the first instance what it is that you hope to get from the book, and perhaps following the recommendations of tutors, fellow governors or book reviewers. It is also important to remember that few education books are meant to be read in their entirety, but more as tools of the trade to dip into as required. As a general guide, you need to consider the following: how up-to-date is it?; the contents page, with reference to your needs; the preface and introductory comments, i.e. what is the purpose of the book and for whom is it aimed?; whether further references or a bibliography are included; the extent of the index; ease of use; quality of explanation; and extent of technical language/jargon (is there a glossary?).

GOVERNORS' BOOKS

Bacon, A. W. (1978) *Public Accountability and the Schooling System*, Harper and Row, London.
An informative account of new approaches to school government. Includes chapters on headteachers and governors, teacher participation, parent power – all centred on the concept of accountability.

Baron, G. and Howell, D. (1974) *The Government and Management of Schools*, Athlone Press, London.
A scholarly book based on a survey of provision and activities of governing bodies towards the end of the 1960s. Also includes an historical perspective.

Brooksbank, K. and Revell, J. (1981) *School Governors*, Council and Education Press, London.
Well-structured, formal account of governors' role, interspersed with extracts from relevant official documents.

Burgess, T. and Sofer, A. (1986) (2nd edn.) *The School Governor's Handbook and Training Guide*, Kogan Page, London.
Useful textbook providing basic information for new and experienced governors. Small print tends to hide its many qualities. Latter part of book aimed at trainers.

Golby, M. (ed.) (1985) *Caught in the Act: Teachers and Governors after 1980*, School of Education, University of Exeter.

Thought-provoking study/report on the role of governors following the 1980 Education Act.

Kogan, M. (ed.), Johnson, D., Packwood, T., and Whitaker, T. (1984) *School Governing Bodies*, Heinemann Educational Books, London.

A study about the role of governors, based on research and incorporating detailed analysis. Relatively easy to read and well referenced.

Sallis, J. (1977) *School Managers and Governors: Taylor and After*, Ward Lock Educational, London.

Somewhat dated, but nonetheless easy to read and generally informative.

Wragg, E. C. and Partington, J. A. (1980) *A Handbook for School Governors*, Methuen, London.

Stimulating and enjoyable. Lively and worth reading from cover to cover.

GENERAL INTEREST

Adams, N. (1984) (2nd edn.) *Law and Teachers Today*, Hutchinson, London.

Do not be misled by the title. Governors will find this a comprehensive and easy-to-read book on education law. Part 2 is especially relevant.

The Auld Report (1976) *The William Tyndale Junior and Infant School*, Report by Mr Robin Auld, QC, into the teaching, organization and management of the William Tyndale Schools, ILEA, London.

Graphic account of what went wrong when parental expectations of schools were let down.

Barrell, G. and Partington, J. A. (1985) (6th edn.) *Teachers and the Law*, Methuen, London.

Good overall reference to the law on education. Many topics of direct reference to governors – especially Part 2 on the conduct of schools.

Brooksbank, K., Revell, J., Ackstine, E. and Bailey, K. (1985) (6th edn.) *County and Voluntary Schools*, Councils and Education Press, London.

Authoratative, well-documented work, of interest to governors of all schools.

Elliott, J. Bridges, D., Ebbutt, D., Gibson, R. and Nias, J. (1981) *School Accountability: the SSRC Cambridge Accountability Project*, Grant McIntyre, London.

A collection of papers, each of which addresses the central theme of accountability. Useful bibliography.

Galloway, D. (1985) *Schools and Persistent Absentees*, Pergamon Press, Oxford.

A study of conditions leading towards persistent absenteeism from school, and a consideration of available sanctions, implications and possible solutions.

Itzin, C. (1985) *How to Choose a School*, Methuen, London.
Readable guide for parents and governors offering advice. Written by a parent and based on a survey of 40 London schools (both state and private).

Kogan, M. (1971) *The Politics of Education*, Penguin, Harmondsworth.
Kogan in conversation with two former Secretaries of State for Education – Boyle and Crosland. Full of interesting insights.

Kogan, M. and van der Eyken, W. (1973) *County Hall: The Role of the Chief Education Officer*, Penguin, Harmondsworth.
Highly atmospheric account of the work of CEOs provided once again by means of an 'in conversation' approach.

Kogan, M. (1978) *The Politics of Educational Change*, Fontana, London.
Very easy to read. Full of thought-provoking ideas.

Nice, D. (ed.) (1986) *Education and the Law*, Councils and Education Press, London.
See especially Chapter 4, 'Governors'.

O'Connor, M. (1986) *A Parent's Guide to Education*, Fontana, London.
Informative, readable and comprehensive guide to all aspects of education and the education system. Good references.

Rowntree, D. (1981) *A Dictionary of Education*, Harper & Row, London.
Handy reference book explaining educational terms and jargon.

Education Year Book, Longman, London.
This is an annual publication containing a wealth of useful information.

ORGANIZATIONS AND ASSOCIATIONS

Each of the agencies listed below provides up-to-date lists of their publications on request.

Advisory Centre for Education (ACE), 18 Victoria Park Square, London E2 9PB.
   ACE publishes masses of detailed information, some directed at parents and some specifically for governors. A selection of titles includes:
Rogers, R. (1979) *Schools under Threat: a Handbook on Closures*

Sallis, J. (1982) (2nd edn.) *The Effective School Governor*
Taylor, F. (1981) (2nd edn.) *Choosing a School*
Wallis, E. (1983) (3rd edn.) *Where to Look Things Up. A–Z of sources on all major educational topics*

ACE also publishes a series of advisory sheets and special reports. Examples of the latter include: *ACE Guide to Education Law; ACE Special Education Handbook; ACE Under 5s with Special Needs; ACE School Prospectus Planning Kit.*

The ACE Bulletin is published bi-monthly and is available by subscription direct from ACE or it can be consulted in major libraries. It includes regular features for governors and a useful digest, i.e. abstracts listing recent publications with brief descriptions.

Architects and Building Group Publications, Department of Education and Science, Room 7/38 Elizabeth House, York Road, London. SE1 7PH (tel. 01-934 9000).

Often regarded as the unsung branch at DES and yet one which publishes important documents, many of which are available free of charge. Detailed list on application. Publications include: design notes; building bulletins; broadsheets; reports.

Examples of titles include: *The Renewal of Primary Schools; Planning for the 1980s; Falling School Rolls and Premises-related Costs; Playing Fields and Hard Surface Areas.*

Assessment of Performance Unit (APU), Room 211, Department of Education and Science, Elizabeth House, York Road, London SE1 7PH.

Conducts research on curriculum and related issues and publishes a variety of papers, leaflets and discussion documents, many of which are available free of charge. List available on request.

Association of County Councils (ACC), Eaton House, 66 Eaton Square, London SW1W 9BH (tel. 01-235 1200)

Authoritative organization representing the county councils. Occasional publications include:

The Way Ahead – Education (1986) Reviews present and future trends of central and local government relationships.

Education on Even Terms (1986) A discussion document on moving to a new pattern for the school year of four terms of more equal length.

Educational Publishers' Council, 19 Bedford Square, London WC1B 3HJ.

Publishes a variety of highly informative and authoritative books detailing trends in LEA spending on school textbooks. Copies available from the council – send SAE.

Inner London Education Authority (ILEA), 22 Croftdown Road, London NW5 1EA (tel. 01-485 3739).

Publishes a series of governors' guidelines, examples of which include: *Budgets, Finance and the Allocation of Resources; Getting to Know your School; Special Education Needs; Parent Governors*.

Inner London Education Authority (ILEA), Learning Resources Branch, Highbury, Station Road, London N1 1SB (tel. 01-226 9143).

Three booklets which provide checklists under the series title *Keeping the School under Review: Primary School; Secondary School;* and *Special School*. Developed by working parties of ILEA Inspectorate and reissued in 1982. Also: *Improving Secondary Schools* (1984) – a major and detailed report directed by D. H. Hargreaves.

National Association of Governors and Managers (NAGM), Hon. Secretary, Mrs B. Bullivant, 81 Rustlings Road, Sheffield S11 7AB (tel. 0742 662467).

Authoritative national interest group representing all those involved in the work of governing bodies. Operates branches up and down the country, publishes papers (e.g. *Guidelines for Governors*), holds an annual national conference and regional training programmes. Also provides a consultancy service and is increasing its research activities. Contributes to the national debate supporting the role of governors. For details of publications, membership and so on, write to the honorary secretary.

Open University (OU), PO Box 70, Milton Keynes MK7 6AA (tel. 0908 74066).

The OU runs several education courses which are of interest to governors. Easy access to these is through TV and radio programmes, but individual units can be purchased. Full details on application. Courses are revised continuously in order to bring them up to date, although the rate of renewal has slowed in recent years following expenditure cuts. Courses available at the time of writing include:

E200	Contemporary Issues
E204	Purpose and Planning in the Curriculum
E241	Special Needs in Education
E354	Ethnic Minorities and Community Education

JOURNALS AND PAPERS

There are a number of popular and easily obtainable journals and papers dealing with educational issues, all of which are used by the professionals such as education officers and teachers. All are obtainable in any good library:

Education   Weekly specialist journal, available by subscription from: Longman Group, The Pinnacles, Fourth Avenue, Harlow, Essex (tel. 0279 29655). Ideal for keeping up-to-date. Regular features include book reviews, parliamentary questions and topics of the moment.
Times Educational Supplement   Weekly paper consulted widely by all involved in education. Topical, authoritative, packed with detailed information. Easily obtainable from any large newsagent; otherwise, most public libraries carry a copy.
Education Guardian   Special supplement featuring education appears in each Tuesday edition of the *Guardian*.
The Teacher   The weekly newspaper of the National Union of Teachers. Found in staffrooms of most schools and in some libraries. Available also on subscription (see address section).

INDEXES/ABSTRACTS/BIBLIOGRAPHIES/ REFERENCE BOOKS

There are several sources of reference which governors will find useful from time to time when conducting research into a particular topic; they are usually kept in the reference section of all good libraries. Examples include:
British Education Index   Provides abstracts from a wide selection of educational journals, giving the reader a brief extract of what an article or paper contains. The journal containing a required article may be kept in the library (most keep back-copies in bound form) or it can be ordered for you.
British Humanities Index   Provides a wealth of material on just about everything you can think of, including education. Based on specialist journals as well as the 'quality' newspapers, it is good for background and topical research.
Social Trends   Published annually reporting, usually through statistics on a wide variety of social habits; good for background information.
British Books in Print   Generally available in major libraries and most bookshops. Used to trace books, providing you know the details, i.e. author, publisher, date, edition etc. Can also be used to trace particular topic headings. In some libraries the information will be stored on microfiche.
British National Bibliography   Published weekly by the British Library and arranged in author, title and subject order.

TRAINING PACKAGES

There is a growing number of training courses or packages for use on individual or group bases. Courses are prepared by LEAs, other educational institutions and interested bodies. Among the published programmes or aids which may be purchased are:

ACE: Sallis, J. (1982a) *Working Together: Training Exercises for Governors, Heads and Teachers in Primary Schools*
Sallis, J. (1982b) *Working Together: Training Exercises for Governors, Heads and Teachers in Secondary Schools*. Both obtainable direct from ACE (address as above).

ILEA Learning Resources Branch, 275 Kennington Lane, London SE1 5QZ (tel. 01-633 5971).

A series produced in conjunction with the Equal Opportunities Commission (EOC) and NAGM, consisting of four video programmes under the overall title *Equal Opportunities and the School Governor*.

NAGM: *A Training Package* Includes 'model' agendas, simulation exercise and notes for course organizers. Obtainable from the honorary secretary (see above).

Open University (1981) *Governing Schools. A Community Education Course* (P970) (address as above).

A substantial course and resource pack. A wealth of material supported by audio and video cassettes which complete the package. Fairly pricey for the individual purchaser.

SEO/NAHT: *Page One: A Training Package Assisting Governor Education*. Innovative, collaborative co-publication by the Society of Education Officers and the National Association of Headteachers. Contains a number of well-planned training exercises focusing on typical problems experienced by school governors. Obtainable from General Secretary, SEO, 21–27 Lamb's Conduit Street, London WC1N 3NJ, or General Secretary, NAHT, Holly House, 6 Paddockhall Road, Haywards Heath, West Sussex RH16 1RG.

ADDRESSES

A selection of useful addresses of organizations which can supply different perspectives on education as well as a variety of complementary information.

GENERAL LIST

British Association for Commerical and Industrial Education (BACIE), 16 Park Crescent, London W1N 4AP.

Business Education and Technician Council (BTEC), Central House, Upper Woburn Place, London WCH1 0HH.
Careers and Occupational Information Centre, Moorfoot, Sheffield S1 4PQ.
Careers Research Advisory Centre (CRAC) Ibbson Press (Cambridge) Ltd, Bateman Street, Cambridge CB2 1LZ.
Central Bureau for Educational Visits and Exchanges, Seymour Mews House, Seymour Mews, London W1H 9PE.
Chartered Institute of Public Finance and Accountancy (CIPFA), 3 Robert Street, London WC2N 6BH.
City and Guilds of London Institute, 76 Portland Place, London W1N 4AA.
Commission for Racial Equality, Elliott House, 10–12 Allington Street, London SW1E 5EH.
Confederation of British Industry (CBI), Centre Point, 103 New Oxford Street, London WC1.
Council of Local Education Authorities (CLEA), Eaton House, 66a Eaton Square, London SW1 9BH.
Department of Education and Science (DES), Elizabeth House, York Road, London SE1 7PH.
Education for Industrial Society, Robert Hyde House, 48 Bryanston Square, London W1H 7LN.
Educational Publishers' Council, The Publishers' Association, 19 Bedford Square, London WC1B 3HJ.
Equal Opportunities Commission, Overseas House, Quay Street, Manchester M3 3HN.
HMSO, 49 High Holborn, London WC1V 6HB (for local branches see telephone directory).
Institute of Personnel Management (IPM), Camp Road, Wimbledon, London SW19 4UW.
Local Authorities Conditions of Service Advisory Board (LACSAB), 41 Belgrave Square, London SW1X 8NZ.
Local Government Training Board (LGTB), Arndale House, The Arndale Centre, Luton LU1 2TS.
Manpower Services Commission, Moorfoot, Sheffield S1 4PQ.
National Association for Multi-Racial Education, PO Box 9, Walsall, West Midlands, WS1 3SF.
National Association for Pastoral Care in Education (NAPCE), Department of Education, University of Warwick, Coventry CV4 7AL.
National Confederation of Parent–Teacher Associations, 43 Stonebridge Road, Northfleet, Gravesend, Kent.
National Council for Civil Liberties, 21 Tabard Street, London SE1 4LA.

National Union of Teachers, Hamilton House, Mabledon Place, London WC1H 9BD.
Pre-School Playgroups Association, Alford House, Averling Street, London SE11 5DH.
Royal Society of Arts (RSA) 6–8 John Adam Street, Adelphi, London WC2N 6EZ.
Secondary Examinations Council, Newcombe House, 45 Notting Hill Gate, London W11 3JB.
Trade Union Congress (TUS), Congress House, 23 Great Russell Street, London WC1B 3LS.
Welsh Education Office, New Crown Building, Cathays Park, Cardiff CF1 3NQ.

CURRICULUM, EXAMINATIONS AND TESTS

This section lists addresses for information about GCSE and 'A' levels (regulations, syllabuses etc).
Associated Examining Board (AEB), Wellington House, Station Road, Aldershot, Hants GU11 1BQ.
Cambridge University Local Examinations Syndicate, 1 Hills Road, Cambridge CB1 2EU.
Midland Examining Group, 1 Hills Road, Cambridge CB1 2EU.
Joint Matriculation Board (JMB), Manchester M15 6EU.
Oxford and Cambridge Schools Examination Board, Elsefield Way Oxford OX2 8EP, and Brook House, 10 Trumpington Street, Cambridge CB2 1QB.
Southern Examining Group, 23/29 Marsh Street, Bristol BS1 4BP.
Southern Universities Joint Board, Cotham Road, Bristol BS6 6DD.
University of London Examinations Board, Stewart House, 32 Russell Square, London WC1B 5DP.
University of Oxford Delegacy of Local Examinations, Ewert Place, Banbury Road, Oxford OX2 7BZ.
Welsh Joint Education Committee, 245 Western Avenue, Cardiff CF5 2YX.

STANDARDIZED TESTING AGENCIES

Moray House College of Education, Holyrood Road, Edinburgh EH8 8AQ.
National Foundation for Educational Research (NFER), The Mere, Upton Park, Slough, Berks SL1 2DQ.

GLOSSARY OF EDUCATIONAL TERMS

The following list represents a selection of terms commonly used by those involved in education. They may be encountered during reading or at governors' meetings. Where a detailed explanation has already been provided in the text, such terms are excluded here.

abacus a calculating frame

accountability the justification of actions, policies and levels of performance to others

activity learning learning by doing

admissions policy procedures used to determine entry to the school drawn up by governors/LEA and published in the school prospectus

adviser local authority appointed officer who may be either a generalist, e.g. in primary or secondary education, or a subject specialist, e.g. music, science

aegrotat award of degree or diploma to a student too ill to take final examinations

appraisal technique applied to evaluate or assess performance

assembly official gathering of pupils at the beginning of the school day for the purpose of collective worship

assignment an exercise or task set for completion by pupils

assisted places scheme central government financial assistance in the form of help for parents in respect of tuition fees for children attending private schools

attendance order imposed by magistrates on parents who have defaulted in their obligation to ensure that their children attend school on a regular basis

audiovisual aid any nonbook material used as a teaching aid

Glossary of Educational Terms

autism an obscure mental condition preventing communication with others and often resulting in failure to benefit from new experiences

autonomy freedom to act

banding a system of organizing pupils at secondary school across the ability range to ensure a good cross-section

Black Papers a series of publications by right-wing academics attacking modern education methods

block timetabling a timetabling technique whereby several classes are taught the same subject at the same time, making it easier to transfer pupils between classes according to progress

Bloom's taxonomy a classification of learning objectives

bureaucracy formal organization, based on hierarchy, rules and procedures and commonly referred to as 'red tape'

campus site occupied by school or college buildings

care order court order placing a child whose parents cannot, for some reason, properly look after him, into the care of the local authority

carrel section partitioned in a building, e.g. in a library for private study

catchment area designated area from which a school draws its pupils

Ceefax BBC's teletext service

'chalk and talk' common expression referring to unimaginative teaching techniques which allow for little pupil participation

child-centred learning/methods where the focus is on the individual child's own interests rather than on subject matter

compensatory education a programme of education where special allowances are made to overcome disadvantages associated with the child's background (focus of the Plowden Report, 1967)

continuous assessement periodic evaluation of course work which incorporates feedback to the pupil in respect of his progress; the marks being gained lead to an overall course mark or grade

core curriculum the central subjects, common to everyday life and studied by all pupils, irrespective of elected options

counselling advising pupils on educational, career or personal problems

creative writing free written expression, especially in primary schools

criterion-referenced tests tests set against a pre-determined standard rather than pupil performance

Cuisenaire rods a method for teaching mathematics to infants based on the use of wooden rods of different lengths and colours

curriculum vitae (CV) an education and career résumé

delegation where a certain person or group is allowed to exercise authority and powers on behalf of another person or group

Dewey decimal system the most commonly used library classification system

diagnostic testing a system of identifying an individual's strengths and weaknesses

discovery learning/methods where children learn for themselves rather then by being told by the teacher

double period two sessions following on from one another on the timetable to allow pupils more time

dyslexia word blindness

empirical methods the collection of data based on experiments and verifiable facts

environmental studies interdisciplinary studies embracing geography, history, sociology and so on

ethic moral value, set of principles

ethos spirit, tone, sense of values, beliefs of people

evaluation judging the effectiveness of a learning experience by using some criteria of a general nature

extended day a scheme whereby pupils may stay on beyond the normal school hours to engage in further study or recreational pursuits of some kind

external degree a degree awarded to a student who has not formally attended a course at the university making the award, but who has studied independently, e.g. by correspondence or by attending another institution

extra-curricular activities those activities undertaken by pupils outwith the normal timetable, e.g. clubs and societies

faculty organizational term used in large secondary schools and colleges to indicate a collection of departments, e.g. a humanities faculty could include English, history and geography departments

failure rate the percentage of pupils who fail to pass an examination or satisfy course requirements

feedback knowledge of results

field studies/work learning undertaken outwith the school in support of some sort of studies or research activities, e.g. an industrial visit, work experience, nature studies, environmental studies

flashcards visual aids used as prompts, usually with young children to help with letter or number recognition, for example

flip chart a very large pad of sheets of paper on an easel-type support used as a visual aid to draw diagrams or summarize main points

form group of pupils allocated to a class comprising approximately thirty-five pupils in a secondary school

form entry the number of classes within a secondary school, e.g. four-form entry, six-form entry

form teacher teacher with specific responsibility for a particular form or class of pupils

free period a blank area on a pupil's timetable when he is expected to organize his own learning via private study

graded tests those taken when pupils reach a certain stage of proficiency rather than on a final examination basis

'the Great Debate' the call for improved standards and the introduction of a core curriculum following an initial speech by Prime Minister James Callaghan in 1976

hardware equipment, e.g. computers, video recorders

house system a method of dividing pupils into groups for sporting and other competitive activities in order to provide a sense of belonging and identity

humanities non-science/non-technical subjects of the curriculum, e.g. literature, history

ideology a set of ideas or patterns of beliefs

implementation translating into action and putting into effect new policies

indoctrination teaching of a particular set of principles in such a way as to prevent independent critical analysis

induction period brief time allocated to familiarize a new member of staff with the organization and procedures of the school

Industrial Society an important independent advisory body which organizes short training courses in all aspects of management and industrial relations

initial teaching alphabet (ITA) an alphabet of 44 letters invented by Sir James Pitman to provide an alternative approach to reading and writing

innovation introduction of change and new ideas

integrated day where there is no set timetable for subjects, where children work on projects at their own pace

intelligence quotient (IQ) the score allocated for performance on an intelligence test

invigilator a person appointed to supervise examinations

learning the acquisition of long-lasting knowledge, skills or attitudes

learning curve a graphic representation over time of performance or progress of an individual in the acquisition of a skill

learning plateau a flat period on the learning curve indicating a level of achievement before the next stage

lesson plan a teacher's systematic preparation of a lesson, indicating aims, objectives, time allocation, visual aids, questions and evaluation techniques

link course a school–college shared programme designed to introduce pupils to further education

literacy ability to read and write

maturation the process of physical and psychological development

microfiche a sheet of microfilm containing greatly reduced individual images (illegible to the unaided eye) arranged on a grid pattern, e.g. used in conjunction with a reader to consult indexes in a library

mock examinations trial examinations arranged before the real thing

modern mathematics curriculum content with emphasis on understanding concepts across a wide range of topics rather than on memorizing formulae

module unit of study within a course

multicultural education provision made to meet the needs of children from ethnic minority groups

multiple choice question a form of objective testing where the pupil is asked to choose from a selection of possible answers

norm a standard or average value or performance or customary behaviour

normal curve of distribution a bell-shaped curve where the bulk is represented by the 'hump' in the middle and the least common (i.e. above and below the norm) are represented at the extreme ends of the curve, where it levels out

norm-referenced tests tests set against pupil's performance measured against the performance of others rather than pre-determined criteria

numeracy proficiency with numbers

objective test a test where a pupil can only score marks according to a pre-determined marking scheme

Oracle The teletext service provided by ITV

oral test where a pupil is assessed on the quality of face-to-face discussion

overhead projector (OHP) a system of projecting enlarged images on a wall or white board as an alternative to using the traditional chalkboard

open plan school designed with the minimum of internal partitions and walls in order to allow free movement of pupils and teachers, as their work requires

pastoral care the system used by secondary schools to provide for the care and welfare of pupils

peace studies directed at considering conflict and war

pedagogy the principles and methods of teaching

peripatetic teacher one employed to travel across several schools – usually a subject specialist, e.g music

plagiarism taking and using of another's thoughts, writings or ideas as one's own

Prestel British Telecom's viewdata system

probationary year applies to the first year served by a newly qualified teacher, during which their abilities are assessed

profiling an open system of recording a pupil's personal achievements used to supplement formal examination results

Glossary of Educational Terms

project a specific task or topic undertaken by a pupil or group, designed to develop a range of skills and abilities and where the teacher provides guidance rather than instruction

pupil–teacher ratio (PTR) number of pupils per teacher

reading age age determined by reading ability rather than chronological age, e.g. a five-year-old with a reading age of seven

reception class the first class at an infants school

referral reference to an expert for advice, e.g. educational psychologist or education welfare officer

remedial work special arrangement to provide extra help for children with learning difficulties in specific areas

reprographics duplicating, photocopying and printing facilities

'rising fives' is used to describe children admitted to school a term earlier than is required by law

role play the acting out of situations

rote learning memorizing word for word without fully understanding the meaning

sabbatical a period of leave for academic study

Schonnel test reading and mathematical tests used mainly with slow-learning primary school children

screening a selection process

secondment teacher assigned on a temporary basis away from normal duties

seminar a small class or group for discussion purposes

setting placing pupils in different classes for different subjects according to ability

sibling a brother or sister

simulation a mock-up or imitation of a real-life situation

sin-bin special unit set aside for disruptive pupils

social and life skills abilities needed to communicate effectively, cope with day-to-day living and develop meaningful relationships

software originally computer programmes, now a generic term covering support material for all technological equipment

split-site school a school which operates on more than one site

standardized test a test which has been tried out and evaluated and for which there are established norms

streaming allocation of pupils within a year to a particular class on the basis of their ability across the subject range

supply teacher a teacher employed by an LEA on a day-to-day basis to fill an absence or temporary vacancy

syllabus a programme of work on a given subject

teaching practice period spent in a school by a student teacher gaining practical 'on the job' experience during training

team teaching co-operative teaching system in which several teachers work together with the same group of pupils

teletext an information-providing service, broadcasting hundreds of pages of text on a specially adapted TV set

'three Rs' reading, (w)riting and (a)rithmatic

tutorial individual tuition

upper school a secondary school catering for children after middle school

verbal reasoning test a test where the emphasis is placed on the ability to understand written and spoken language

vertical grouping organization in primary schools of pupils of different ages into the same class for some or part of the time

visual display unit (VDU) television monitor used to display text or other data

vocational education work-related studies aimed at a particular job or career

voluntary duties duties which teachers undertake beyond their contractual obligation, e.g. meals supervision

voucher system a system where parents are able to use their voucher (e.g. cheque) on a school of their choice in respect of their child's education

work experience a period during which a pupil is placed with an employer to obtain job familiarization and practical experience

ABBREVIATIONS AND ACRONYMS

The following is a list of abbreviations and acronyms commonly used in education, some of which appear within this text.

ACAS	Advisory Conciliation and Arbitration Service
ACC	Association of County Councils
ACE	Advisory Centre for Education
ACP	Associate of the College of Preceptors
ACS	Alternative Curriculum Strategy
ACSET	Advisory Committee on the Supply and Education of Teachers
AEB	Associated Examining Board
AEC	Association of Education Committees
AEO	Assistant Education Officer
AFE	Advanced Further Education
AMA	Association of Metropolitan Authorities
APS	Assisted Places Scheme
APU	Assessment of Performance Unit
AUR	Alternative Use of Resources
BA	Bachelor of Arts
BACIE	British Association for Commercial and Industrial Education
BEd	Bachelor of Education
BIM	British Institute of Management
BMus	Bachelor of Music
BSc	Bachelor of Science
BSI	British Standards Institution

BSU	Basic Skills Unit
BT	British Telecom
BTEC	Business and Technician Education Council
BTh	Bachelor of Theology
CACE	Central Advisory Council for Education
CADCAM	Computer aided design and manufacturing in the mechanical and electrical engineering fields
CADMAT	Computer aided design, manufacture and test in the field of electronics
CAE	Computer Aided Engineering
CAFD	Council for Academic Freedom and Democracy
CAL	Computer-aided (assisted) Learning
CASE	Confederation for the Advancement of State Education
CASSOE	Campaign Against Sexism and Sexual Oppression in Education
CATE	Council for the Accreditation of Teacher Education
CBI	Confederation of British Industries
CCETSW	Central Council for Education and Training in Social Work
CDT	Craft, Design, Technology
CEDAR	Computers in Education as a Resource
CEE	Certificate of Extended Education
CEG	Computer Education Group
CEI	Council of Engineering Institutions
CELP	College Employers Links Project
CEO	Chief Education Officer
CERI	Centre for Educational Research and Innovation
Cert. Ed	Certificate in Education
CET	Council for Educational Technology
CFE	College of Further Education
CGLI	City and Guilds of London Institute
CHE	College of Higher Education
CIPFA	Chartered Institute of Public Finance and Accountancy
CISSY	Campaign to Impede Sex Stereotyping in the Young
CLEA	Council of Local Education Authorities
CNAA	Council for National Academic Awards
COI	Central Office of Information
COIC	Careers and Occupational Information Centre
COSTA	Conference of Subject Teaching Associations
CPAG	Child Poverty Action Group
CPU	Central Processor Unit (re computers)

CQSW	Certificate of Qualification in Social Work
CRAC	Careers Research and Advisory Centre
CRE	Commission for Racial Equality
CSE	Certificate of Secondary Education
CV	Curriculum vitae
DASE	Diploma in Advanced Studies in Education
DATEC	Design and Art Committee of BTEC
DE	Department of Employment
DES	Department of Education and Science
DHSS	Department of Health and Social Security
DI	Divisional Inspector
Dip. AD	Diploma in Art and Design
Dip. HE	Diploma in Higher Education
Dip. SM	Diploma in Safety Management
DISC	Drop-in Skills Centre
DOE	Department of the Environment
DTI	Department of Trade and Industry
ELT	English Language Teaching
EOC	Equal Opportunities Commission
EPA	Educational Priority Area
ERIC	Educational Resources Information Centres
ESF	European Social Fund
ESG	Education Support Grant
ESN	Educationally Subnormal
ESPRIT	European Strategic Programme of Research on Information Technology
ESRC	Economic and Social Research Council
EWO	Educational Welfare Officer
FACT	Federation Against Copyright Theft
FAST	Federation Against Software Theft
FE	Further Education
FEU	Further Education Curriculum and Development Unit
FPA	Family Planning Association
FTE	Full-time Equivalent
GCE	General Certificate of Education
GCSE	General Certificate of Secondary Education
GREA	Grant-related Expenditure Assessment
GRIST	Grant-Related In-Service Training
HAPA	Handicapped Adventure Playground Association
HASAWA	Health and Safety at Work, etc Act

HE	Higher Education
HMI	Her Majesty's Inspectorate
HMSO	Her Majesty's Stationery Office
HNC	Higher National Certificate
HND	Higher National Diploma
HORSA	Hut Operation for Raising School-Leaving Age
HSE	Health and Safety Executive
ICMA	Institute of Cost and Management Accountants
IDS	Interdisciplinary studies
IEE	Institute of Electrical Engineers
ILEA	Inner London Education Authority
ILTU	Industrial Language Training Unit
INSET	In-Service Education of Teachers
IPM	Institute of Personnel Management
IQ	Intelligence quotient
IS	Industrial Society
ISBN	International Standard Book Number
IT	Information Technology
ITA	Initial Teaching Alphabet
ITB	Industrial Training Board
JMB	Joint Matriculation Board
LA	Library Association
LACSAB	Local Authorities' Conditions of Service Advisory Board
LAMSAC	Local Authorities' Management Services and Computer Committee
LCCI	London Chamber of Commerce and Industry
LCP	Licentiate of the College of Preceptors
LEA	Local Education Authority
LGTB	Local Government Training Board
MA	Master of Arts
MEd	Master of Education
MENCAP	National Society for Mentally Handicapped Children and Adults
MEP	Microelectronics Education Programme
MEP	Member of the European Parliament
MIME	Micros in Mathematics Education
MIND	National Association for Mental Health
MSC	Manpower Services Commission
MSc	Master of Science
NAB	National Advisory Body

Abbreviations and Acronyms

NAFE	Non-Advanced Further Education
NAGM	National Association of Governors and Managers
NAHT	National Association of Head Teachers
NALGO	National and Local Government Officers Association
NASUWT	National Association of Schoolmasters and Union of Women Teachers
NATFHE	National Association of Teachers in Further and Higher Education
NCCL	National Council for Civil Liberties
NCPTA	National Confederation of Parent Teachers Associations
NFER	National Foundation for Educational Research
NSPCC	National Society for the Prevention of Cruelty to Children
NTI	National Training Initiative
NUPE	National Union of Public Employees
NUS	National Union of Students
NUT	National Union of Teachers
OECD	Organization for Economic Co-operation and Development
ONC	Ordinary National Certificate
OND	Ordinary National Diploma
OU	Open University
PAT	Professional Association of Teachers
PESC	Public Expenditure Survey Committee
PGCE	Post Graduate Certificate in Education
PHAB	Physically Handicapped and Able-Bodied
PhD	Doctor of Philosophy
PICKUP	Professional, Industrial and Commerical Updating
PNEU	Parents National Educational Union
PTA	Parent Teachers Association
PTR	Pupil–teacher ratio
QTS	Qualified teacher status
QUANGO	Quasi-Autonomous Non-Governmental Organization
RAC	Regional Advisory Council
REB	Regional Examining Board
RIBA	Royal Institute of British Architects
RNIB	Royal National Institute for the Blind
RNID	Royal National Institute for the Deaf
ROSPA	Royal Society for the Prevention of Accidents
RSA	Royal Society of Arts
RSG	Rate Support Grant
RSI	Regional Staff Inspector

RVQ	Review of Vocational Qualifications
SBCD	School Based Curriculum Development
SCDC	School Curriculum Development Service
SCE	Scottish Certificate of Education
SEC	Secondary Examinations Council
SEO	Society of Education Officers
SERC	Science and Engineering Research Council
SHA	Secondary Heads Association
SI	Statutory Instrument
SLAPONS	School Leavers Attainment Profile of Numerical Skills
SMP	School Mathematics Project
SPCK	Society for Promoting Christian Knowledge
SRC	Science Research Council
SREB	South Regional Examinations Board
SRHE	Society for Research into Higher Education
SSCR	Secondary Science Curriculum Review
SSEC	Secondary Schools Examinations Council
STOPP	Society of Teachers Opposed to Physical Punishment
TA	Transactional Analysis
TEFL	Teaching English as a Foreign Language
TES	*Times Educational Supplement*
TRIST	TVEI-Related In-Service Training project
TVEI	Technical and Vocational Education Initiative
TWI	Training Within Industry
UCCA	Universities' Central Council for Admissions
VSO	Voluntary Service Overseas
WEA	Workers' Educational Association
YOP	Youth Opportunities Programme
YTS	Youth Training Scheme

APPENDIX

GOVERNOR'S REFERENCE LIST

1. School details

Name of school _____

Address _____

_____ Post Code _____

Main tel. no. _____ Additional nos. _____

_____

Name and address of Headteacher _____

_____ Tel. no. _____

Deputy head(s) _____ Tel. no. _____

_____ Tel. no. _____

_____ Tel. no. _____

School Secretary _____

School Safety Officer _____

School Caretaker's address _____

_____ Tel. no. _____

2. Staff information

Names of staff with special responsibilities:

Name	Responsibility

3. Governing body

Chairman _____

Address _____

_____ Tel. no. _____

Vice-chairman _____

Address _____

_____ Tel. no. _____

Clerk _____ Tel. no. _____

Names of members	Tel. nos.	Parent/Teacher/LEA/Co-opted

4. Subcommittees

Title	Chairman	Membership

5. Local Education Authority

Name _____

Address _____

_____ Tel. no. _____

Chief Education Officer _____

Assistant Education Officer(s) _____

_____

Chairman of the Education Committee _____

Note: Most LEAs provide a directory of officials, their particular responsibilties, e.g. primary, secondary education advisers, education psychologist, education welfare officer, and where they may be contacted.

6. General information

Local Councillors

Name	Ward	Tel. no.

Contact in Architect's Department _____

Name of Members of Parliament for your area _____

_____

Name of Member of the European Parliament _____

7. Additional useful information

_____

INDEX

accommodation 115–16
accountability 4, 247
Acts of Parliament 30–1
Administrative Memorandum 29
admissions policy 93
advertisement 175–6
advisers 45, 153, 165
agenda 203–6, 236
aided schools 51
aide-mémoire 226
aims 53–4
   primary schools 56–9
   secondary schools 59-63
ancillary staff 80–1
appeals, 147, 149
application forms 181-3
appointment of teachers 168–70
Articles of Government 87–8, 91, 92
assessment 164–5
Assessment Performance Unit
   (APU) 27, 158, 164
Audit Commission 20, 22, 172
autonomy:
   of LEAs 23, 38–9, 100
   of teachers 155

Black Papers 158
buildings 114–15
Bullock Report, 1975 26
Burnham Committee 38, 172

Cabinet 22, 23, 27
Callaghan, James 158
capital equipment 105
capitation 100, 103–4
central government 19–23
   grants 97–9
centralization 39–40, 246, 254
change 156–9
chairman:
   education committee 40–2
   governing body 232–9
Chief Education Officer 43–4, 247
circulars:
   10/65 50
   10/70 50
classification of schools 50–1
clerk to the governing body 240–3
Cockroft Report, 1981 26
Code of Safe Working Practice 122
collective powers 88

collective responsibilities 27
committee:
  local government 43
  structure 41
community 3, 249–50
composition of governing bodies 70–2
comprehensive school 50
conduct 137
confidence-building 7–8
confidentiality 12–13
consumables 105
controlled schools 51
co-opted member:
  education committee 42
  governing body 79
core curriculum 158
corporal punishment 147–8
costs 51
councillors 42
Crosland, Anthony 30
curriculum:
  aims 159–62
  development 165
  primary 159–60
  secondary 160–2
  vitae (c.v.) 181

Data Protection Act, 1984 171, 247
debarment 93
decentralization 21, 23, 158
decision-making 219–20, 225–6
delegation 136–7
Department of Education and Science (DES) 20, 22, 26–7, 246–7, 250–1
Department of Employment (DE) 20, 22
Department of the Environment (DoE) 20, 22

detention 147
director of education *see* Chief Education Officer
Disabled Persons Employment Acts, 1944, 1958 171
disciplinary action 145
disciplinary committee 140–1
discipline 137, 142ff.
discussion 219
disqualification 80

Education Acts:
  1902 35
  1918 49, 50
  1944 36, 50
  1980 72–3
  1981 36, 64–5
  (No. 2) 1986 87, 169, 253-5
Education Bill, 1986 25
education committee 40–2
education office 44
education support grant 98–9
education welfare service 45
educational psychological services 45
effective meetings 239–40
elections of parent governors 74–5
elementary schools 49
eligibility:
  chairman 233
  governors 73–9
Employment Acts, 1980, 1982 171
Employment and Training Act, 1983 38
Employment Protection (Consolidation) Act, 1978 171
endowed schools 3
environment 113–14
equal opportunity employer 171
Equal Pay Act, 1970 171
equipment 163–4

Index

estimates:
  local government 101
  schools 104–5
examinations 164–5
ex officio governor 79
expenditure 104
expenses, governors' 252
expulsion 145–6
extra meetings 207

falling rolls 126
finance committee 101–3
fire drills 122
fittings 119–20
fund-raising 105–6
furniture 119–20
'further particulars' 175–6

General Certificate of Secondary Education (GCSE) 26, 86, 159, 164
governing bodies, powers and functions 90–3
governors:
  ancillary staff 80–1
  co-opted 79–80
  headteacher 79
  LEA 75–7
  parent 73
  pupil 80
  teacher 77–9
graffiti 89
grammar schools 3, 49
Grant-related Expenditure Assessment (GREA) 98
grants 97–9
'Great Debate' 158
Green Papers 30
group total 173–4

Hadow Report, 1926 49
headteacher:
  appointment of 190
  duties and responsibilities 51
  as governor 78–9
  leadership styles 52
  as manager 51–2
headteacher's report 220–2
Health and Safety at Work, etc. Act, 1974 38
heating 120–1
Her Majesty's Inspectorate (HMI) 22, 27–8
  reports 28
'hidden' curriculum 137
home–school links 52–3
House of Commons 22, 40
House of Lords 22

indiscipline 138–9
infant schools 55
influence 224–5
informal contacts, chairman 235
informal teaching methods 163
information 6–12
information technology (IT) 156
In-service Teacher Education (INSET) 155, 180, 251–2
inspections 27
Instrument of Government 92
integrated day 157
interview checklist 192–4
interviews 189

job:
  description 176–8
  specification 177–8

leadership styles:
  autocratic 52

bureaucratic 52
consultative 52
democratic 52
LEA governors 75–7
lighting 120–1
lobbying 31–2, 108–9
local authority 40
local education authority:
  duties 36–7
  powers 37
  support services 45
Local Government Acts, 1888, 1972 35
Local Government (Access to Information) Act, 1986 38, 44–7
Local Government and Planning Act, 1980 100
location 113
loco parentis 137

maintained schools 51
mandarins 27
Manpower Services Commission 20–2
meetings:
  glossary 212–15
  opening and closing 237, 239
  pacing 237–8
  proceedings 208–9
middle schools 59
minutes 210–12
misconduct 139–40
Model Articles and Instrument of Government 88, 91–2
Moray House 164

National Confederation of Parent–Teachers' Associations (NCPTA) 114–15
National Foundation for Education Research (NFER) 27, 158, 164
National Health Service Reorganization Act, 1973 37
Newsom Report, 1963 26
notetaking 226–7

objectives:
  primary schools 56–9
  secondary schools 59–63
'open all hours' 126–7
open plan 114
organization chart:
  primary school 56
  secondary school 60
origins:
  central government 19
  governing bodies 3
  local government 35
  schools 49

parental influence 74
parent governors 73–4
parent–teachers' association (PTA) 105
Parliament 19, 22
partnership 38–9
pastoral care 59–60
peer group pressure 137–8
per capita:
  allowance 104
  spending 39
permanent secretary 27
person profile 177–8
playing fields 113–14
Plowden Report, 1967 26
points 172–4
policy-making 20
political parties 76–7, 247
Poundswick School 89
power-sharing 85–7

premises:
  condition 114–15
  maintenance 116–17
  use of 126–9
primary schools:
  aims and objectives 49, 56–9
  curriculum 159–61
  organization chart 56
  rules 142
professionals, teachers as 78, 155, 163, 251
prospectus 54, 122, 159, 161
punishment 145–6
pupils 36
pupil–teacher ratio (PTR) 23, 38, 172, 251
purchasing agency 105

qualifications 178–9
qualified teacher status 172, 179
questions:
  at governor's meetings 223–4
  at interviews 195–8

Race Relations Act, 1976 38, 171
Rate Support Grant (RSG) 27, 97–8, 101
rates 99
references 184
Rehabilitation of Offenders Act, 1974 171
reports:
  headteacher 220–2
  working party 227–8
report-writing:
  presentation 227–8
  style 228
rules and regulations:
  meetings 202–3
  schools 141–5

safety 121–2
safety subcommittee 123–4
safety officer 124
salaries 254
scale post 171–4
school fund 106
school-leaving age 50
school meals 37
schools:
  aims and objectives 56–63
  buildings 114–15
  classification of 50–1
  curriculum 159–65
  finance 103–6, 247–9
  premises 112–15
  safety 121–2
  security 124–5
  staffing 171–4
secondary school:
  aims and objectives 59–63
  curriculum 160–3
  organization chart 60
  rules 142–5
Secretary of State 23–6
security 124–5
shortlist 184
Sex Discrimination Act, 1975 38, 171
sixth-form college 63
space, alternative use of 127–9
special agreement schools 51
special education 64–5
special needs 36, 64–5
specialist facilities 115–16
staff:
  development 78, 155
  discipline 148
staffrooms 129
standardized testing 164
standards 158, 250
Statutory Instruments 30–1

Statutory Instrument 809 79, 81
Statutory Instrument 909 20, 36, 37
subcommittee:
　governors 207
　LEA 41, 43
Superannuation Act, 1972 171
suspension 146–7

Taylor Report, 1977 29, 53–4, 147
teacher governors 77–9
teacher unions 23, 159
teaching methods 155, 163
tertiary college 63
Thatcher, Margaret 30
Trade Union Act, 1984 171
Trade Unions and Labour Relations
　Act, 1974 171
training for governors 251–2

transfers 49
transport 37
Treasury 22

ultra vires 25
uniform 37, 142, 143, 144
unit total 172

vacancies 174–6
vandalism 125–6
ventilation 121
virement 100, 105
voluntary schools 51, 109
voting 237

Warnock Report, 1978 64
White Papers 30
Widdicombe Report, 1986 42
William Tyndale School 86, 157